SCRIPTURE REFLECTIONS DAY BY DAY

Scripture
Reflections
Day by Day

JOSEPH G. DONDERS

TWENTY-THIRD PUBLICATIONS
Mystic, Connecticut 06355

Acknowledgment

The predominant Scripture translation used is The Jerusalem Bible, copyright © 1985 by Darton & Todd, Ltd. and a division of Bantam Doubleday Dell Publishing Group, Inc.

Twenty-Third Publications
185 Willow Street
P.O. Box 180
Mystic CT 06355
(203) 536-2611
800-321-0411

ISBN 0-89622-494-5
Library of Congress Catalog Card Number 91-65954

Subject Index

[vi]

[*ix*]

Introduction

The aim of the book

The intention of this book is simple—to help you bring out your life in Jesus Christ. We believe his life to be in us. But even people who have no doubt about that can face a problem.

We have many examples of this difficulty in our daily lives. All kinds of technical and electronic tools surround us. We rarely use all their potential. Take a computer. How many of us even know all our computer can do? I know people who had been working with their computer for years before they knew that it could bring forth sound, let alone music. Or take the software you use—research shows that most people use only a fraction of a program's possibilities.

According to the same research, this is also true for VCRs—the great majority of owners don't even know how to program them. They only use them for the simplest operations, such as playing a video-tape.

Something similar is true of our Christian life. The spirit of Jesus is hidden in us. We live it, but we have not yet touched all its power. We probably never fully will as long as we are on earth. Yet, we should try each day to live his spirit better and better.

These reflections seek to help us do this.

This book presents over 360 topics drawn from our daily lives and connects them to Holy Scripture, to the life of Jesus Christ, and to those who lived his spirit. These reflections suggest how the ordinary and extraordinary events and things in our lives correspond to his life and the lives of the saints.

The reflections take into account recent developments in our understanding of sacred Scripture, and frequently refer to the way the American bishops and Pope John Paul II interpret modern life and society.

How to use this book

The topics you find in the extensive Subject Index are like buttons you press. When you "press" them you make contact with a relevant scriptural text. For example, if you press the "last breakfast" button, you are connected to that place in the gospel where Jesus has breakfast with his disciples (John 21:1-19).

You can also turn this process around. In the Scriptural Index, you can look up the Bible text you are interested in, press that button, and make contact with a theme in your daily life. To give an example, if you are interested in Luke 1:46-56, where Mary sings her Magnificat when meeting Elizabeth, you will find, when you press that button, some references to your daily life, like recognizing and responding to your own "gut feelings."

In this way we hope to help you make a conscious connection between the life of Jesus and his disciples in Holy Scripture and your own life.

Note: As you approach each day's reflection in this book, you should, for maximum benefit, first read the assigned verses for the day from your Bible. Even if you are very familiar with the Bible and can recognize what a passage is about from the few key words of Scripture at the beginning of each reflection, you are advised to first read the entire passage in the Bible in a prayerful manner. There is particular value in this reading done in faith, and it will also make the reflection more effective.

After you read the reflection for the day, spend a few moments continuing the reflection on your own. Then conclude your reading and reflection with prayer of your own.

A multi-purpose book

The simplest way to use the book is to proceed as the book itself is organized, day by day. You just take the day you start using the book, and that's that. Another way is to use it as suggested above, by looking up themes or Scripture texts.

The book is intended to be as practical as possible, so some extras are provided in the text. A reflection is foreseen for every Sunday of the three liturgical cycles. This might be handy for priests, ministers, or others who are looking for an idea for their Sunday ministry.

Just look up the gospel text of the Sunday in question in the Scriptural Index and you will find a reflection. There are some rare cases when one of the two other texts of the Sunday was used, and not the gospel text. So if you don't find a reflection through the gospel reading, look up either the first or second reading of that Sunday and you will find your reflection.

The book also provides reflections for all weekdays during Lent, the fifty days between Easter and Pentecost, and Advent. Just take the readings of any of those days and you will always find a reflection, most often on the gospel, but sometimes on the first reading. Besides those reflections for Sundays and weekdays, there are about 100 other reflections on scriptural texts.

Two mini-courses

To enhance the usefulness of the book, two mini-courses are added on topics that will be of great interest to those who use a book like this. There is a series of nine reflections on *How to Pray*, and a set of seven on *What to Do in a Bible Group*. You can find those mini-courses in the Subject Index under "Prayer" and "Bible Group," respectively.

Enjoy these reflections. Let them empower you to discover some measure of the depth and height of the spirit of Jesus in yourself.

May the Lord be with you!

Washington, D.C.
On the Feast of the Martyrs of Uganda

Pilgrim

"...all nations will stream...to the house of God." Isaiah 2:1-5

We start from a beginning, as if nothing had happened before. We start the cycle all over again.

"There is nothing new under the sun." "History repeats itself.""The more things change, the more they remain the same." These are sayings so old and so human you can find them in the oldest and most sacred scriptures. But their age does not make them true.

They never sounded true to the prophets among us. Isaiah describes in a vision how he sees the whole of humanity on a journey. He sees people coming from all sides of the globe, on their way to a mountain top. They are on their way to a sanctuary, to God, and on their way to each other.

Pierre Teilhard de Chardin, a Jesuit scientist who lived and died in this century, saw the same development. He describes how long ago the human family began to spread out from their ancestral home in Africa. They fanned out on a safari that brought them farther and farther from each other. But since this migration takes place on a globe, we unavoidably will meet each other one day. Isaiah foresees all kinds of things happening during our journey, things that initially seemed impossible. We started our journey armed to the teeth to defend ourselves against the dangers of the road and against each other. Yet, one day those arms would be done away with, swords would be made into plowshares and sickles, and peace would reign.

We are on a journey. We are all pilgrims. We are not marching in an endless, closed circle. We are journeying in a direction. Though we are starting a new year, and hope—please God—to start another one next year, and so on for years and years to come, we are not caught in a vicious circle. We may be turning around and around, but we are not turning in a circle. We are turning in a spiral, climbing higher and higher toward our final destination.

Retribution

"...who warned you to flee from the coming retribution?"
Matthew 3:1-12

We find John the Baptizer at the beginning of each gospel. He is no easy prophet. He is a prophet of doom. He sees the axe already lying at the root of the trees. He writes off the world-as-is. We will not be able to escape the retribution that is coming.

That word "retribution" is often translated another way. "Anger" is the word we use. We will not be able to escape that anger. Anger is something in a person. That is why we often interpret John as saying we will not be able to escape God's anger. God is angry with the way we are dealing with ourselves and our world. So we should do something to appease God's anger.

How could that be true? How would we be able to influence God in that way? John cannot have meant this. John the Baptizer must have meant something else when he prophesied that the world was on the point of falling apart.

The axe is not lying at the roots of our trees because God is so angry. Death threatens our trees because those trees can no longer tolerate the way we have been treating them. They are dying because acid rain is destroying them, not because God is sending over revenging angels. The trees are not the only things that are sick because we are poisoning them. Think of dying lakes, polluted air, oil slicks, and eroded land.

Our human society is not threatened by God, it is threatened by us. If a society succumbs because of its injustice, it is not because God is punishing it. It is the consequence of the way that society has mishandled its affairs.

When the people around John the Baptizer ask him what they should do, he does not ask them to pray, to go into the desert with him, or to bring sacrifices. Change your lifestyle, he says. There is no other way to escape the threatening retribution.

Interior Change

"...blessed is anyone who does not find me a cause of falling."
Matthew 11:2-11

John the Baptizer does not understand what is happening. He is in prison, while Jesus is walking around free as a bird, even attending parties like the one at Cana. John had been announcing how Jesus would start bending the crooked world straight. He had been speaking about an axe at the root of the trees; he had been announcing a fire that would burn all pollution away. He had been dreaming about a manifestation of God's power. He was waiting for the first rumors about the great takeover. He heard nothing of the kind. He sent some friends to Jesus to ask him what he was up to.

They returned with Jesus' answer. "Blind ones see, lame ones are walking, lepers are healed, the dead arise, and the good news is spreading."

The good news is that in all those wounded women and men a new life force is at work, healing them. In Jesus' presence something happens to them. Touched by him, they heal from within.

John expected that God would take over by force. It is the way we often speak when discussing the troubles of our world. If only the government would use its might more efficiently, the police had more power, the death penalty were more harshly applied, and so on.

We forget that real change can come only from within. A change of heart cannot be forced from outside. It simply does not work. The whole of human history with all its concentration camps, wars, and even mass graves is proof of that fact. A real rebirth can only come from within our hearts, from within our own lives and families. Every development that does not come from within is doomed to fail. New life can be born only from within us, as happened to those in Jesus' presence. That change was taking place, Jesus told John's messengers. Humanity is getting healed. Jesus adds, "Happy the one who does not lose faith in me."

Emmanuel

"In the beginning was the Word: the Word was with God and the Word was God....the Word became flesh, he lived among us."
                                                               John 1:1-18

This beginning of the gospel of John sounds difficult and abstract. It is like a play of words, beautiful words. Those who study the text and compare it with other texts are convinced that the text is an old hymn, a hymn celebrating the coming of Jesus among us.

For those who composed the text, this celebration had nothing to do with a specific date like December 25th. They commemorated Jesus' birth in a different way. They celebrated the coming of Jesus in the every day of our human lives.

The Word of God had become a human being, one of us. An old promise had been fulfilled. An ancient word had become a deed. Emmanuel means *God-with-us*. It is a question of solidarity. It is encouraging news to us living in this world. The goodness of that news can be felt when we compare it with our own human experiences of solidarity—the moments when a friend remains with us in times of sickness, depression, or distress, the times that you yourself decided to be with someone during a troublesome time.

We can discuss the lot of the poor endlessly. It is only when we share their lives that they will be able to say: "Now we know that you are with us!" Words become fact. Now we can speak from our own experience.

In Jesus, God speaks in terms of our own human experience. He is one of us in our joys, trials, struggles, moments of discouragement, and hopes.

Emmanuel, *God-with-us*, can be personalized by each one of us. Emmanuel is *God-with-me, God-with-you* in all the circumstances of our lives, a real presence that shows the passionate way God loves you, the others, and me. Together we form God's offspring, a reality so much greater than just ourselves.

[8]

Child in Us

"And suddenly the star halted...over the place where the child was."
Matthew 2:1-12

Today is one of the last days of Christmas time. Tomorrow we celebrate how the Magi from the East saw a new star in their skies and, following it, found a newly-born child in a cot in Bethlehem. A new human and divine beginning.

Describing the final peace in our world, the prophet Isaiah wrote that it would be led by a child (Isaiah 11:6). Jesus himself said: "Truly I tell you: whoever does not accept the kingdom of God like a child will never enter it" (Mark 10:15).

Many of us live with a sense of loss. We seem to remember something from days long gone. We look for something we can't discover, long for what we cannot find. We carry in us the memory of an ideal, of a lived enchantment, of a Garden of Eden, almost but not totally forgotten. We seem to be longing not for a non-existent and impossible ideal, but a nearly forgotten memory of a once-lived experience.

The serene completeness of our early childhood lodged in our heart and memory remains as a dream. The Indian Jesuit Anthony de Mello wrote: "Liberate the playful child in yourself."

We all carry in ourselves a charming, loving, naughty, and cheerful child that—silenced in many ways—was almost lost. To find and free that child in you is the key to a more fulfilling life. As adults we often forget the innate knowledge we had as children, the awareness that creation is a friendly place to be, that plants, animals, and people belong together, and that we are connected by thousands of threads, nourished and kept by the same sea, sky, earth, air, and sun.

By freeing the playful child in us, we will once again rediscover the threads that connect us to creation, to God, and to each other, and we will come again to echo the human-divine mystery we were at the beginning of our lives.

It is at the cradle in Nazareth that the Magi from the East found their deepest self. We do, too.

Staying Power

*"I saw the Spirit come down on him like a dove from heaven and rest
on him."*   John 1:29-34

Reading papers and magazines, you notice some themes that turn up
again and again. They belong to the matter of our human story. They
inspire ballads and songs. They are broadcast over radio and television. They are the mainstay of country music.

One of those themes is the fragility of human love, lovers jilted by
former lovers, children abandoned by their parents, friendships begun
in glory fading away.

These complaints are so frequent that one wonders in the end
whether there is any human love that really lasts, a question often
asked in these songs, as well. So many things started full of promise
end in utter disappointment. The enchantment is great, but how long
will it last? Is it going to be the same with Jesus?

John the Evangelist answers this question by using the Greek verb
menein, meaning "to remain" or "to stay," more than forty times in his
writings. From the beginning he stresses that what appears in Jesus is
something definite, something lasting. It is that staying power that
made John the Baptizer recognize Jesus, as he said, using the word
"remain" twice: "I saw the Spirit come down from heaven as a dove
and *remain* on him. I would not have known him, except that the one
who sent me to baptize with water told me, 'The man on whom you
see the Spirit come down and *remain* is he who will baptize with the
Holy Spirit'" (John 1:32-33).

Though human love may fade away, God's Spirit and love never
leave Jesus, just as he in his turn promised that he will never leave us,
whatever happens: "And surely I am with you always, to the very end
of time" (Matthew 28:20).

[10]

Settling In

"...leaving Nazareth he went and settled in Capernaum, beside the lake, on the borders of Zebulun and Naphtali."   Matthew 4:12-17

Once he began his mission, Jesus had to decide where to live, a decision all of us have to make at least once and probably more often during our lifetimes. It is a difficult decision. You have to take so many factors into account—your family, your work, but also your ideas about what to do with your life.

Jesus was facing the same kind of issue. With what he had to do, where was he going to have his home and his headquarters? Nazareth, Bethlehem, Jerusalem...there were many possibilities.

He chose Capernaum. At first sight this was a strange choice, because Capernaum had a bad reputation. It was a harbor town of sorts, situated in a region known for its cutthroats and pagans. Capernaum was the least Judaic town in the least Judaic province. It was also its most cosmopolitan.

Going to Capernaum did not mean that he wanted to lie low, or to hide. John was arrested by the same King Herod who ruled over Galilee. By deciding on Capernaum, Jesus settled in the eye of the storm.

He rented, bought, or borrowed a house in a region about which the prophet Isaiah had proclaimed: "O land of Zabulun and Naphtali, Galilee of the Gentiles, the people living in darkness have seen a great light; on those who lived in a land as dark as death a light has dawned" (Isaiah 8:23–9:1).

According to Isaiah, Jesus came to liberate God's people, "to break the yoke that burdened them, the rod laid over their shoulders...for his title will be Wonderful Counsellor, Mighty Hero, Eternal Father, Prince of Peace!" (Isaiah 9:4, 6b). He settled in Capernaum in view of his task and intention to establish God's kingdom in this world.

This is an indication we should take that Kingdom into account when we have to decide where to settle!

Beatitudes

"How blessed are the poor in spirit, the kingdom of Heaven is theirs."
Matthew 5:1-12a

The eight beatitudes in the gospel of Matthew begin with "Blessed are the poor in spirit for theirs is the kingdom of heaven," and they end with "Blessed are those who are persecuted because of righteousness, for theirs is the kingdom of heaven." Those two beatitudes differ from the other six. The first and the last one promise the kingdom of heaven in the present. The six others promise things in the future:

Blessed are those who mourn, for they *will* be comforted. Blessed are the meek, for they *will* inherit the earth. Blessed are those who hunger and and thirst for righteousness, for they *will* be filled. Blessed are the merciful, for they *will* be shown mercy. Blessed are the pure in heart, for they *will* see God. Blessed are the peacemakers, for they *will* be called sons and daughters of God.

The poor in spirit belong to the kingdom of heaven now, and so do the ones who are persecuted because of righteousness. Why should that be?

The poor in spirit are those who know that, notwithstanding all our achievements, successes, and advances, the kingdom of God is not yet realized in this world. They sense that, though we might be quite happy about the way we have organized our society, there are too many left out who suffer, who starve, and who are abused. The poor in spirit are the ones who are intent on changing things as they are, in view of a greater justice for all. That is why they are the ones so often persecuted, vilified, ridiculed, and sometimes murdered because of their thirst for righteousness. The poor in spirit belong to the Kingdom of God, because they are living in this tension. They want to change the world so that the six other beatitudes may be fulfilled, so this world will be freed of weeping, arrogance, homelessness, injustice, darkness, and war.

Light for the World

"You are the light for the world....your light must shine in people's sight...."
Matthew 5:13-16

Jesus tells us: "You are the light for the world." It sounds pretentious when we say it of ourselves. According to many contemporaries, it even sounds pretentious when it comes from Jesus' lips, calling himself the light of the world. They forget that he called them the light of the world, too.

That does not seem to be the only misunderstanding when using that analogy of light to describe his and our role. Light is enormous, light is a great help. Without light we would be in the dark. Yet, we should not exaggerate. Light does much, but it does not bring anything. When I switch on the light in a dark room full of people and furniture, that light does not cause or create those people and those tables and chairs. Light shows what is there already.

In a similar way, Jesus is a light in our world. It is in the light of his life that we see who we are and what we are capable of being. This is a role others play, too. It is what a lover, a friend, or an artist do. They reveal in us physical, psychological, and spiritual dimensions we would never have known if they had not helped to light them up in our person.

None of them, however, does it the way Jesus did. Nobody showed better what human love is capable of. Nobody showed better how to relate to the source of our being, or to each other. It is in his light that we discover our own depth, width, length, and worth. Who would we be without him?

Law and Love

"Do not imagine that I have come to abolish the Law or the Prophets. I have come not to abolish but to complete them."   *Matthew 5:17-37*

It is a story we know. We hear it too often: someone in difficulty because the ones he was treated by stuck strictly to regulations: a medicine not administered, a door not opened.

Jesus warns us against the law. He is not against the law as such. He had not come to abolish the the law. He wanted to be faithful to the prophets, and he was. He had a lively sense that laws and regulations oblige us to render each other the essential duties and rights we owe each other. But he looked further than that. His ideal stretched much further than just realizing what we legally owe each other.

We have to love each other with God's love. "Be perfect, as your heavenly Father is perfect" (Matthew 5:48). That is quite a mission. It is a task high as a mountain, reaching into heaven. The discipline of the law obliges us to realize that ideal little by little. Without the rigor of the law it would be difficult, if not impossible, to love with God's love. To obey the ten commandments is a life condition. It is sacred, but it is also something that we must go beyond, something that has to be surpassed again and again.

In his sermon on the mount Jesus insists that we should go beyond what the law prescribes. We should not murder physically; that is what the law says. We should not assassinate someone's character, either; that is what God's love in us forbids. We should not drag our neighbor to court—though the law provides that possibility—but settle our matters in a friendly way.

The moment someone tells us: "I am only going to do for you what I am legally obliged to do," we know that we are in for trouble. Among us, it should not be like that.

Enemy

"But I say this to you: love your enemies and pray for those who per-secute you."
Matthew 5:38-48

Jesus' love is inclusive. So is his logic. He does not exclude anyone. He knows that he has enemies. How he knows that! He feels that others have broken with him, judging him unjustly and treating him accord-ingly. He refuses to break with them. He advises us: "Do not resist those who wrong you! Love your enemies and pray for your persecu-tors." According to Jesus, even if they betray us, we, fueled with his love, simply can't do the same.

From the earliest days there have been Christians who radically lived his love and logic. Did you ever hear the story of Maximilian? It was March 12 in the year 295. Conscripted as a soldier, he refused to serve. He was brought into the court of Dion, the Proconsul. Valerian Quintian, the imperial commissioner, was present. The first to speak was the attorney, Pomeianus: "As Maximilian is liable for military ser-vice, I request that his height be measured." When the proconsul asked his name, Maximilian answered: "Why do you want to know my name? I am not allowed to be a soldier, I am a Christian." He was measured: five feet and ten inches. Dion then said: "Put the military badge on him." Maximilian protested: "I refuse, I cannot serve." "Be a soldier, otherwise you must die." "I will not be a soldier. You can cut my head off, but I will not be a soldier of this world. I already bear the sign of Christ my God." The dialogue went on until Dion said, "Strike his name off." When this was done he said to Maximilian, "Since you have insubordinately refused to serve in the army, you shall suffer the penalty of the law...you are condemned to die by the sword." Maxi-milian said, "God be praised." He was twenty-one years, three months, and eighteen days old. He was not the only one to stand firm in the radical love of Jesus. The impact of his story is still felt as a kind of promise to be fulfilled.

Ownership

"No one can be the slave of two masters: he will either hate the first and love the second, or be attached to the first and despise the second. You cannot be the slave both of God and of Money."

Matthew 6: 24-34a

"You cannot serve both God and money," Jesus says, leaving us with quite a problem. How then should we have money and possessions?

In the same way Jesus did. In view of the service of everyone. That is what his "poverty" is about. It does not mean that he did not need his food and drink, his rest and sleep, his clothing and sandals, his partygoing and picnics, but in the final instance it was in the service of all.

He never owned anything the way the rich man in Luke's gospel did (Luke 12:16–22). When God gives that landowner the bountiful gift of a rich harvest, he builds barns to store that harvest all for himself, saying, "You have plenty of good things laid by, enough for many years to come: take life easy; eat, drink, and enjoy yourself."

This does not pertain only to money or ownership. It is true also of friendship, relations, information, skills, talents, technical know-how, our spiritual power, charisms, and gifts. Jesus suggests that we should be like nature around us, the plants and the flowers.

We should be as a beautiful flower, gifted with color and fragrance that gives all it has to the world around, enriching our lives, pleasing our senses. We should *be* and *live* with all we have in view of all, like a flower in the sun, like the sun itself!

Any property we own is, as we are ourselves, God's gift. Nothing is really ours alone. Pope John Paul II says it very simply in his encyclical *On Social Concern*: "The goods of the world are meant for all."

Of course, the right to private property is valid. We obviously need to own things. But, writes the pope, this private property is under a social mortgage. It has to be referred and related to the "whole" of the human and creational "body."

[16]

Temptation

"Human beings live not on bread alone...." Matthew 4:1-11

Immediately after his baptism by John and the revelation of how the Holy Spirit relates to him, Jesus takes refuge in the desert, or—as some translations say—in the wilderness. It is in that lonely and unorganized space that he wants to discern how to respond to his call, just as we do when we go on retreat to be alone with God.

It is in the desert that Jesus meets God and God's opponent. He fasts all that time. There can't have been too much food in that place in any case. At the end of that fast he is hungry. His opponent, the devil, thinks he will be thinking about something to eat—bread.

The devil is mistaken, for even after those forty days Jesus is hungering for something else. "A human being does not live on bread alone." He is hungering for something we forget about when we think that the economy is the bottom line, that only money count in this world.

Some years ago, at the beginning of the new changes that are sweeping through Russia, a Russian film producer from Georgia, T. Abuladze, made a film that became a major cultural event. The title of the film was *Repentance*.

At the end of the film an older woman asks the heroine of the film, "Tell me, does this street lead to a church?" "No, this street does not lead to a church," she replies, knowing what she was speaking about, for that street reminded her of the tragic events of her childhood and the church that had been blown up long ago. The last words of the film are those of the astonished old woman: "What is this street for then, if it does not lead to a church?"

Indeed, if the street we walk does not lead to God, what is the use of walking that street? What is the use of walking any path that does not lead us back to the home we all come from, the home of our heavenly ancestry?

Body

"There in their presence he was transfigured: his face shone like the sun...." Matthew 17:1-9

He had taken Peter, James, and John with him to the mountain top. It can't have been a high mountain, because there are no high mountains in the region. On top he turned to them, and suddenly, before their eyes, Jesus began to shine. All the fatigue slipped from his face, his whole tired body began to shine as pure light until he was light all over, dazzling like the sun, glorious like heaven.

Jesus himself related this transfiguration to his resurrection when he warned them not to tell anyone about what they saw before he rose from the dead.

When Jesus died on the cross and his whole body ached with pain and misery, he cried for his Father in heaven. No answer seemed to come at that moment.

The answer came some days later. The answer was his resurrection, when once more, but now forever and ever, his body shone before them.

Yes, the body is important, and so are all the elements that form and nourish it: the water and the sky, the earth and its minerals, the light and its brightness!

After our death our bodies will be buried like Jesus', or they might be cremated, but in the end, God will beckon our bodies and in the twinkling of an eye, those bodies that were scattered over all the elements will be set down before God in a glorious resurrection. Together with Jesus we will shine as he did on that high mountain. All our fatigue, the weariness of growing old, all our ills and complaints will be over. We will shine as he did on that mountain before his death, and as he would do—and is doing—forever and ever once his task in this world was over. We will shine with him. Nature and the whole of creation will rise and shine with us. Let us therefore respect and honor our own bodies and the bodies of others; let us honor the elements that form them, shape them, and hold them together.

Gathering the Nations

"The Samaritan woman said to him, 'You are a Jew. How is it that you ask me, a Samaritan, for something to drink?'"   John 4:5-42

Driving a car almost always means driving behind another car. If those other cars have bumper stickers you cannot help but notice them, especially when you get stuck in traffic. Sometimes the stickers are funny, sometimes they are obscene. There are pious ones and up-setting ones. A rather popular one reads: "Born to Shop." That must be a joke, or is it?

Why are we born? Why are you born? Why are we sent into this world? The answer from the older catechisms is to serve God and to be happy in the life hereafter.

That answer remains rather vague. What does serving God mean?

Jesus has his answer. He is in this world to do God's will, and God's will is to bring God's work, God's creation, to completion. That is a beautiful way of saying what doing God's will means, a saying that applies not only to Jesus, but also to us.

And if that sounds too vague, Jesus specifies what he intends to do to bring God's work to completion. He comes to gather God's family together.

He does that, for instance, when he talks to the Samaritan woman, who is herself amazed that a Jew speaks to her. How is this possible, she asks him, for Jews do not associate with Samaritans. It is in view of that "gathering together" that Jesus travels all over his world as far and wide as his feet can carry him. It is the reason that he organizes the enormous picnics for thousands of guests with plenty of bread and fish for everyone and in at least one instance even much first-class wine. He obviously enjoyed occasions when large crowds of people ate and drank together. He saw them as a foretaste of the banquet he often dreamed of, where all of humankind would be celebrating.

Sin

"'Neither he nor his parents sinned,' Jesus answered; 'he was born blind so that the works of God might be revealed in him.'" John 9:1-41

Failures are not always just disasters. Take the story of the man born blind. Even Jesus thought this a disaster, otherwise he would not have healed him. At the same time, the man's blindness proved to be a blessing, as Jesus noted when he said, "Neither he nor his parents sinned, but this happened so that the work of God might be displayed in his life." At first hearing this is a hard statement, but that does not make it less true. Many questions were asked that otherwise would not have been asked, deep and important questions about the relation between sin and sickness, about law and punishment, about signs and being a prophet. Jesus clarified these haunting questions. He not only made that blind man see; he made all those who listened to him begin to "see."

Disasters often work like that. Think of the atomic disaster in Chernobyl in Russia, when a nuclear power station caught fire and melted through. That disaster with the deaths of so many made the whole world reflect on the use of unbridled atomic energy. It made an atomic war less likely. It made the production and stockpiling of tens of thousands of atomic weapons all over the world seem like an obsolete and life-endangering enterprise. A disaster like the one at Chernobyl helps us to see that even the thought of atomic warfare should be abandoned. Similarly, any war unmasks the horror of the use of violence against humanity and nature.

The same is true in our more personal lives. How often does a sudden death bring a divided family together? We should not hope for difficulties and disasters, yet when we are struck by them, we might see them as opportunities.

Weeping

"Jesus wept." John 11:1-45

Jesus must have been a lovely person. Mothers had no hesitation in bringing their children to him, and "he put his arms around them." Obviously the children had no difficulties with him either. Only his male disciples protested and wanted to chase children and mothers away. Jesus was neither "masculine" nor "feminine"; he was a fully integrated human person.

Some people have difficulty believing that Jesus ever laughed. When an artist in the 1960s drew a picture of a laughing Jesus, he caused some consternation, though Jesus once said that all those blessed will laugh (Luke 6:21). He not only laughed, he also wept.

Jesus was on his way to visit his friends Lazarus and his two sisters Martha and Mary when he heard that Lazarus had died.

Martha went to meet him, saying, "If you had been here, my brother would not have died." Then Mary came to greet him, and she also said, with tears in her eyes, "Lord, if you had been here, my brother would not have died."

When Jesus saw her weeping and the Jews who had come along with her also weeping, he was deeply moved in spirit and troubled in spirit. "Where have you laid him?" he asked. "Lord, come and see," they replied. Jesus wept. Then the Jews said: "See how much he loved him." But some of them said: "Could not he who opened the eyes of the blind man have kept this man from dying?"

Jesus is described here not only as a person with deep emotions who is not ashamed to show them publicly, he also reveals himself as one who is influenced by the emotional reprimands of Martha, Mary, and the others.

His feelings of friendship and love not only make him raise Lazarus from his tomb, giving him back to his sisters—that is only a beginning—they would also lead him to his death on the cross for them and for us.

[21]

Connectedness

"From the sixth hour there was darkness over all the land until the
ninth hour."   *Matthew 26:14-75, 27:1-66*

When Jesus entered Jerusalem on the back of a donkey he was surrounded by singing people carrying branches and flowers to honor
him. When his opponents told the crowd to stop celebrating his entry
in Jerusalem in such a provocative and exuberant way, he said that if
they were silenced the very stones in the street would start to shout.
He implied that the whole of nature—organic and inorganic, humans,
animals, plants, and minerals—was involved in what he did.

The whole of creation was engaged then and when he died on the
cross. The sun faded, the sky got dark, the earth shook, and the cur-
tain in the temple tore apart. The darkness that came over the land at
that moment has always been seen as a sign that the whole of nature
mourned at the moment of his death.

When all is created in God's Son Jesus—as John tells us in the introduction to his gospel—then touching him means touching the whole
of creation. Whatever you do to him is done to all.

No wonder that the sun eclipsed, that the moon did not shine, the
earth shook, and darkness fell over plants, animals, and humanity
alike at the moment of his suffering and death. We are all together in
this. Did Paul not say that the whole of creation is groaning to be liber-
ated and free? We are all interconnected in Jesus. Together we form
God's offspring.

What was done to Jesus was done to the whole of creation. You can
turn this around. Jesus did that himself, when he said that anything
done to the least is done to him.

Passionist Father Thomas Berry does not hesitate to use this image
radically. Thinking of the violence done to forests, animals, oceans,
the sky, and even the stratosphere, he writes: "The most appropriate
image of Christ is Mother Earth crucified."

Kindness

*"After the Sabbath, and towards dawn on the first day of the week,
Mary of Magdala and the other Mary went to visit the sepulchre."*
Matthew 28:1-10

We often overlook the ordinary things in the life of Jesus and those
who accompanied him. They were hungry and thirsty, just as we are
hungry and thirsty. They depended on ordinary, everyday human
goodness and kindness, just as we do. He had to go to bed and get up
in the morning. That ordinariness can be found even at the most important moment of his life.

Take what happened on Easter morning. Some women, Mary of
Magdala, Mary the mother of James and Joseph, Salome, and some
others came to the tomb to bury him properly. They had bought some
oils, herbs, and spices. They went to the tomb to wash and clean him,
to anoint him. Simple acts of friendly kindness. All they could do.
They knew that he had been buried in a hurry. He had been taken
down from the cross late in the afternoon, and there had been no time
to do anything but put him in the tomb. He had to be taken care of.
They could not just leave him like that.

It was simple human kindness and friendship that made them take
this initiative. It was the kindness and friendship they had learned
from him. Even before they knew about the resurrection, his life had
begun in them, a life that manifested itself not only in all kinds of extraordinary things, but in the way their ordinary lives had changed.
Their fears had passed. In him they found new meaning and an immense joy.

Forgiveness

"If you forgive anyone's sins, they are forgiven...." John 20:19-31

All of us have had the experience. You have betrayed someone. You talked about him, and your gossip went around and reached him. It was no light matter. It was something of importance. A total breach of confidence, a real betrayal.

It can happen in other ways. At the moment that someone really needed your word of encouragement, you did not speak it, though you knew. When someone really needed to be helped, you did not extend your hand. You refused. You closed your heart.

That is what Jesus' disciples did during the last days of his life. They fell asleep when he asked for support with their prayers. They ran away at the moment of his arrest. Someone like Peter even said he never had heard of him.

They must have done this because they thought all was lost, that they would never see him again, that it had been one of those periods in their lives that pass over and are forgotten.

That was not so. They had heard from the women that he was no longer in his tomb, that he was risen and about. No wonder he had not appeared to them, but only to those women! The men were discussing this, sitting together in the relative safety of a closed upper room, when he suddenly appeared and stood in their midst and said: "Shalom, peace!" That one word was sufficient. They understood immediately that though they had broken with him, he had not broken with them. Their betrayal had not undone Jesus' relationship to them. Jesus' self-confidence was so great that their treachery did not hinder his love. Hadn't he told them that nothing would be able to undo his love, that he always would remain with them, whatever might happen (Matthew 28:20)? Then he breathed over them, saying: "As the Father sent me, so I send you." With that same breath he gave us his love, self-confidence, and power to forgive.

Recognizing Jesus

"...how they had recognized him at the breaking of bread."
Luke 24:13-35

If Jesus appeared again, how would you recognize him? It is an intriguing question that remains of interest. When Father Joseph F. Girzone wrote a book about it, he called it *Joshua*. At first no publisher believed in his book. They thought it would not sell. He had to publish it with his own money. Who would read a book about Jesus returning as a woodworker to an American township? They must have laughed at the idea.

Their question was answered. Thousands and thousands of people read the book. You can meet people who have read it a dozen times over. The book became a bestseller. A big publishing house acquired the publishing rights, and copies in the hundreds of thousands have been sold.

How do the people in the book recognize Jesus? It is in fact an old story. The first time the story is told it involves Cleopas and his companion from Emmaus walking with Jesus. Who is that companion? Luke, who tells the story, does not give a name. Was it Cleopas's wife? We don't know.

We do know that the two are upset. They go to Jerusalem expecting to see a victorious Jesus. Instead, they come home with the story of his death. They have heard a rumor about his resurrection, but obviously that is not what they had been hoping for.

Then Jesus "comes up" and walks with them. They talk and they argue. Jesus explains to them "everything in scripture that refers to him, starting from Moses and all the prophets." They don't recognize him. They have no clue! His words do not reveal him.

They arrive in Emmaus. It is late. They persuade him to stay. They sit down at table. "He took bread, said the blessing, and broke it." Then they recognize him and he disappears, leaving them with their bread in their hands. He leaves them with a clue about how to recognize him, and how to make themselves recognizable as his disciples, breaking in their turn the bread he left them.

Named

"...one by one he calls his own sheep and leads them out."

John 10:1-10

He is a shepherd who knows the names of all his sheep. I once met a
shepherd who knew the names of his sheep. He did not have so many,
but they all had names. When he called a name, one would look up,
and he would say, "You see, they know me, they know their names."

Knowing the name of someone can be important. We all have been
in a situation where we know we should remember the name of someone we meet, and we don't. Some people are quite brazen about
that—they just use a name that comes to mind, so they can be correct-
ed and thereby learn the name they forgot. When you are not so daring you have to ask for the name, and you can see the disappointment
on the face of the other. You forgot this person's name—how could
you?

It must also have happened to you that someone prominent in your
eyes, someone whom you don't meet too often, nevertheless—to your
great surprise—remembers your name.

To be called by your name by a friend always gives you a warm
feeling. Your uttered name touches something in you like nothing
else.

Jesus says of himself that he knows us by name. In the Hebrew
Scriptures we are told how God inscribed the name of his people on
the palm of God's hand. Jesus reveals to us the personal love of God
for each one of us. God knows you by name. God knows me by name.
It is a love that resembles the love the Father has for Jesus, and Jesus
for the Father. It is a love that not only relates us to God, but also to
each other. It makes us belong to the same family, or to use the image
of Jesus, it makes us members of the same flock.

Homestead

"I am going to prepare a place for you, and after I have gone and pre-
pared you a place, I shall return to take you to myself, so that you may
be with me where I am."   *John 14:1-12*

He was an old man, a very old man. He had not only outlived all his
friends and family and almost all his contemporaries, but every one of
his teeth. He told me he was tired and was afraid that something had
gone wrong in the heavenly administration. He feared he had been
forgotten. He wanted to go home.

There is a beautiful Scottish tale about a monastery of pious monks
somewhere on the border between Scotland and England. In the monastery nobody ever died; the monks just got older and older. They
could not even take in new ones because all the places in the chapel
were occupied and not a single place ever fell vacant. The monks did
not like it, but no one knew what to do.

Then one day the old abbot had a dream. In that dream he saw the
angels descend day and night between heaven and earth exactly on
the spot where the monastery was built. The monastery was almost
part of heaven, a kind of bridgehead. When he woke up, he understood this was the reason no one ever died.

He told his story after morning prayers in the chapel. The monks
came together, and that very day they began to evacuate the place
where they had been living for so long; they rebuilt their monastery a
couple of miles from the old one. And they started their final journey
to their heavenly home, one by one, the oldest first. For long enough
they had been asking the question Philip asked: "Lord, show us the
Father; we ask no more!"

Jesus told Philip that being in his presence meant being in the presence of Almighty God. He added that we have a heavenly homestead,
that he himself was gladly going there, and that he would take care to
prepare for us a place. A place that will be ready once our turn comes
to go home, having done our part here on earth.

Maturity

"I shall ask the Father, and he will give you another Paraclete to be with you for ever." John 14: 15-21

Before he left his disciples, Jesus made it clear that he was not going to leave them alone. He said that explicitly: "I will not leave you alone!" (John 14:18). He promised to send them—and us—God's Spirit.

He even explained that it was a good thing for them that he was leaving them, otherwise they would never become aware of the Spirit of God in themselves. They would just gaze at him, as they had been doing practically all the time. They would never come to themselves.

All this has to do with development and growth. A baby is totally dependent on its parents. The more the child grows, the more independent it becomes. First the child has to be brought to school; one day the child will go alone for the first time. The child who expects its parents to tell it what to do grows into a teenager who starts to decide on its own. If that should not happen, the parents have got something to worry about. They will have to say: "Make up your own mind. You know what we think and how we would decide; you know the principles and norms we would take into account. Now it is up to you."

During his last supper Jesus spoke in a similar way to the disciples, and, by inference, to us. He left us. Thank God! We are supposed to come to ourselves. We know who he is, we know his principles and norms, he told us everything we need to know, he equipped us with what is necessary to find our way.

He even assured his disciples that—once on their way—they would discover things he was not able to explain to them. Realities they could only discover for themselves by their own experience.

This does not mean that they would break their relations with him. On the contrary, those relationships would become even more intimate.

All that is true not only of them; it is true of us.

World

"I am not praying for the world, but for those you have given me...."
John 17:1-11a

It is surprising to hear Jesus say, "I am not praying for the world" (John 17:9). I did not understand it until one day I met someone who expressed the same kind of feeling. I had asked her why she always dressed in black. She looked at me with her beautiful eyes and said, "How else could I dress in this world?" Then she asked me, "So you noticed, did you?"

Suddenly I understood that I should not have asked her that question. It had been stupid and unnecessary. It was obvious what she meant by dressing in the color that in her culture expressed mourning and sadness. Her dress was an obvious sign; she was grieving for the state of this world. She herself was an obvious sign; she was unable to pray for the world, as the world is at the moment. At the same time she was expressing her hope for an alternative world. She was walking around in the eye-catching black to bear witness to that alternative world.

When Jesus says that he had no prayer for this world, he must have been thinking about the way the world around him was organized. He must have been thinking about its structures of racism, competition, exploitation, violence, discrimination, greed, and neglect. He must have been thinking about the poor and the wretched, the lepers and the orphans, the so often spiritually impoverished rich, and the economically poor. He could not pray for that world. He could only dream of an alternative world, the realization of God's Kingdom among us. He said that he was willing to give his life for that alternative world (John 6:51). He did.

Jesus also mentioned whom he was praying for. He was praying for those in the world who followed him, who were dreaming his dream, who were willing to put their treasure, time, and talent on the line in view of God's Kingdom.

We all should hope and live to be in his prayers!

Dynamics

"Peace be with you. As the Father sent me, so am I sending you."
John 20:19-23

It was during a seminar at the School of Philosophy at a Catholic university. The topic was "Social Change and Humanization." Participants from all over the world, Russians, Chinese, Japanese, and Nigerians represented various academic specializations and skills. One of the questions under discussion was: "What are the dynamics that seem to energize the recent changes all over the world?" Before that question was answered, there was another issue. "What is the nature of all those changes?" A professor from Moscow said it had something to do with empowerment. People who up to recently did not feel that they counted for much in human history now feel that they do. But how and why did that happen? Nobody knew the answer, although they all agreed that it had something to do with the human spirit. The actual crisis is something spiritual, they said.

At that point a Chinese participant started to speak. He said spirituality always has something to do with how you relate to what goes beyond the human being, to the transcendent. He had always been interested in that relationship, and—though not a Christian—had read the Christian Scriptures because of this interest. He had been struck, he said, by the way humanity's relation to God was formulated in the baptismal formula in the gospels. The baptismal formula tells us that we come from the same parental source (Father), are created together in God's offspring (Son), and are energized by the same Spirit. He looked at us—almost all baptized Christians—and he added: "If you really believe that, you are the root of all human dynamics!"

He was right. It is that divine dynamic that is at the root of what happened from the very beginning at Pentecost to the women and men in the streets of Jerusalem.

Dancing Our Life

"...so that everyone who believes in him...may have eternal life."
                                                              John 3:16-18

The late president of Kenya, Jomo Kenyatta, liked to invite the ambassadors to his country to the celebration of the national feast days of his country. They would sit for hours watching people dance their traditional dances. One of the ambassadors once complained to the president of this use of their time. The president replied that the core of African culture is the celebration of life, and that you can't do that better than by dancing.

You don't have to be African to like dancing. Whenever an ethnic group celebrates a folklorist festival, you can be sure there will be dancing.

Dancing is so much part of our human nature, we might ask ourselves if it is inborn. Haven't you seen small children dance around their very serious looking mothers on their way to kindergarten?

The Bible says: "God created the human being in God's own image; male and female God created them." If it is so natural to us to dance, is it in God's nature to dance? Has it to do with our promised eternal life?

From ancient times Christian mystics and theologians have been trying to understand the life in God's Holy Trinity. How do those three relate to each other? A difficult question. All kinds of technical Greek terms were used to answer it. One of the terms used was *perichoresis*. Maybe you recognize something in that word. Some common English words find their root in it: choir or chorus, choral, carol, carolling (which originally meant to dance in a circle).

Ancient mystics described God's inner life as a dance, *perichoresis*, a circle dance. They thought (and felt) that the persons in the Blessed Trinity are celebrating their divine life, dancing together! It is a dance to which all of us are invited. The dancing around us is a sign of our final vocation. We should take our dancing more seriously. Once Jesus complained, "We piped for you and you would not dance" (Luke 7:32).

Eucharist

"Whoever eats my flesh and drinks my blood lives in me and I live in that person."　　　　　　　　　　　　　*John 6:51-58*

What happened at that last supper is not difficult to understand. It was some hours before his arrest. They had been partaking of the meal during which Jews remember their Exodus from Egypt. The meal was over. He wanted to express how much he loved them, and how much he liked them to be with him.

He is in a situation you know from own personal experience. It is the evening of a departure. You are not going to see each other for some time. You would like to express your feelings and your love, but how do you do it? Every gesture falls short.

Some bread and wine remain on the table. They are looking at him. Though they do not know what is at stake, they have some idea. They know that something drastic is going to happen. He takes the bread and says: "This is my body that will be broken for you; this is my blood that will be shed for you." The bread is passed around. So is the wine. They eat and drink themselves into the same body, the same spirit. He adds: "Do this when you want to commemorate me."

That is what we do, commemorate him, when we celebrate the Eucharist. Or do we?

Was that commemoration of him the only thing he asked of them that evening? Did he come to be worshiped by us? Is that the mission he left to you and me? Did he shed his blood because of that?

When Jesus takes the bread and the wine he is thinking, as he himself says, about what is going to happen to him, about what he is willing to do. He is giving himself in view of the healing of this wounded world, reconnecting creation to its creator. He is not only hungering and thirsting for the Kingdom of God, he is putting his person and life on the line for that reign. Commemorating him is not only breaking his bread and sharing his wine; it means partaking of his life and his mission.

Trust

"So do not be afraid...." Matthew 10: 26-33

Etty Hillesum was a young Jewish woman arrested and killed in one of the Nazi extermination camps. Years after her death her diaries were published under the title *An Interrupted Life*. It is an almost unbelievable story.

She discovered what Jesus assured us when he said, "Do not be afraid of those who kill the body, but who cannot kill the soul." She had not only read these words. She understood them.

On New Year's Eve, 1941, she discovered the possibility of listening to her inner self. She learned "a greater awareness and hence easier access to my inner sources." Soon she understood what she was doing was "listening in" on God in her innermost being.

She discovered in the deepest center of her soul, her still point, the presence of God: "Somewhere there is something inside me that will never desert me again."

She found that God had a dwelling place in her. Having located this "home" in herself, she is at home everywhere. "I have no nostalgia left. I feel at home. I have learned so much about it here. We are at home. Under the sky, in every place on earth, if only we carry everything with us. I often felt, and I still feel, like a ship with a precious cargo—the moorings have been slipped and now the ship is free to take its load to any place on earth. We must be our own country."

Realizing this, nothing can happen to her. There is, indeed, no need to be afraid of those who cannot steal your soul! Nothing can happen to us that can undo the divine presence. We are always in God's hands.

September 7, 1943, she sat in the freight train that brought her to her death. She threw a postcard out of that train. It was found by a farmer. She wrote: "Opening my Bible at random, I read 'the Lord is my dwelling place.'" She had opened Scripture at the place that explained her trust in God: "Do not be afraid!"

January 30 _____

Baptism

*"...you must see yourselves as being dead to sin but alive for God in
Christ Jesus."* *Romans 6:3-4, 8-11*

Paul was right when he wrote: "You have been taught that when we
were baptized in Christ Jesus we were baptized in his death; in other
words, when we were baptized we went into the tomb with him and
joined him in death, so that as Christ was raised from the dead by the
Father's glory, we too might live a new life" (Romans 6:3-4). That instruction has been taught to me many a time.

But the truth of that lesson never startled me more than in the heart
of Africa, the continent in which Jesus found refuge almost immediately after his birth, when his life was threatened by the political powers of his time.

Once, during a baptism-by-immersion ceremony I attended, I overheard one of the candidates for baptism ask the baptizer to keep him
under water for quite some time, "so that the old will really die," he
said. He was kept under water for some time, so that when he came
out he really gasped for breath, for life, for the new life of the one who
showed us by his life, death, and resurrection what our human life is
about: life to the full, risen life, a life in justice leading to a peace only
God's Spirit can give us. The life given to us in Jesus. Alleluia!

Later the baptizer told me that most of the baptismal candidates
asked to be baptized like that. If they did not, he did it nevertheless,
he added with a smile. The old had to die. They really wanted the experience of going through death and a tomb. They wanted the new
life to get rid of the sins and the evil that blocked their lives, spoiled
their relationships, and made them turn in an ever smaller circle. They
wanted a new life, a new name, a new relationship to God, and a new
human community, a community larger than the one they had belonged to. They wanted "to be dead to sin but alive for God in Christ"
(Romans 6:11). They wanted to live the life of Jesus.

Burden

"Come to me, all you who labor and are overburdened, and I will give you rest. Shoulder my yoke and learn from me, for I am gentle and humble in heart, and you will find rest for your souls. Yes, my yoke is easy and my burden light."   Matthew 11:25-30

We observe so many people carrying heavy loads. They go through life pulling a very heavy cart. They don't travel light. They remember everything that ever happened to them. They remember the harm and damage done to them better than the joy and affirmation they met.

They don't like to eat beans and rice, because it reminds them of their food during their unprosperous youth at home. They won't relate to a certain group of persons, because some from that group harmed them long, long ago. They don't shake hands with a brother or a sister because of something that happened ages before, though they might have forgotten the details. They are saddled with a load so heavy that in the end they succumb. But, before they succumb, they have been a terrible burden to themselves, not to speak of those around them. They never forget, they never forgive.

All of us know people like that. All of us have something of it in our own systems.

It is here that Jesus hopes to come in. He would like to take that load away from us. He would like us to exchange it for another yoke. He tells us what that yoke is about when he describes himself as gentle and humble, as someone who forgives and forgets. He does not say that his yoke is easy, but he suggests that it will be lighter in the long run than the one we are carrying. Taking his yoke upon ourselves will mean the end of much tension and depression, discouragement and negativity.

With your burden lighter, you will travel lighter and breathe easier.

Family

"...Jesus left the house and sat by the lake side...." Matthew 13:1-23

It sounds perfectly normal. It is something all of us like to do now and then. Just leave all behind, go into nature, and sit quietly at a lakeside.

There is more to this text, however, than just a hike to the lake. We know from the gospels that Jesus had certain difficulties at home. His family and the villagers of Nazareth were afraid that he was out of his mind, and they had tried to get him home. His disciples did not understand him very well either. When he left the house, he broke away from them. They wanted to catch and encircle him. He did not like to be fenced in.

While he is sitting there a crowd of people gathers around him. The crowd is so large that he can't address them. So he gets into a boat and addresses them a bit offshore in the lake.

He found a new family, a larger circle, the family of God.

Matthew uses that theme of "leaving his house" six times. He not only notes that Jesus leaves his house, but also mentions every time that he went home again. "Then, leaving the crowds, he went to the house" (Matthew 13:36). He returns in a different way than he left. He left his family alone, and he returns to them in the company of a crowd.

Jesus is someone who constantly leaves a home to start a larger household. He refuses to be restricted to a group, however charismatic it might be. He leaves the closeness of Nazareth and settles in Capernaum. He leaves Capernaum to move on. Every house seems too small for him, all limits too restrictive. He will not rest before all of us will be relating to each other in a Kingdom of God that is like one great *kin-dom*. He remained faithful to his roots, but he grew out into a tree in which all of us will find a home.

Gentle Powers

"The laborers said, 'Do you want us to go and weed it out?' But he said: 'No…let them both grow till harvest.'"   Matthew 13:24-43

We have the awful tendency to wage war, not only to protect ourselves against political enemies, but also in view of all kinds of other causes. We declare war on crime, drunken drivers, cancer, abortion, and on drugs. In many cases this is not only a figure of speech. It is a reality. In Washington, D.C.—a city with about 850,000 inhabitants—about 2000 people were killed in drug wars from 1989 to 1991. People shot each other or were shot by the police.

War has something to do with old apocalyptic ideas. Heaven should open and destroy everything that hinders us.

Jesus' companions thought in those terms. When a town in Samaria does not wish to receive them, James and John ask him, "Lord, do you want to call down fire from heaven to destroy them?" Jesus rebukes them. That is not his approach. He does not believe in that type of force. He prefers another power: the fantastic power of a seed, the penetrating power of yeast. He prefers energies that change things from within.

We think that change can only come from outside, that you can force it upon people as you can force it upon things. Jesus asks us to trust the soft powers in ourselves, in others, and in the world.

The Kingdom of God begins with an inner potential that is given to everybody, something that will grow. If stimulated correctly and gently it will overgrow the weeds and all evil.

Jesus is a friend of all of us. You can notice that even in the examples he uses. He is inclusive. He speaks about a man who goes out to sow, and about a woman who is kneading the yeast through the dough.

Jesus has the bold gentleness attributed to God in the Book of Wisdom—a gentle confidence in our inborn goodness and possibilities. Let us trust those gentle powers in ourselves and in others. Let us stir them, before we burn.

Storytelling

"The kingdom of Heaven is like a householder...." Matthew 13:44-52

"Those who tell the stories rule the world," wrote an Indian Navajo author as an introduction to a collection of old American stories. You know that from your own family. You know how some stories can be told, and how others are banned. Just listen to the stories we tell each other at home, at work. Listen to the stories children tell their parents and parents tell their children. Listen to the preachers and their sermons.

Is it not true to say that the world around us does not change more than it does because we are listening only to certain types of stories? Who is listening to the stories of the poor and the neglected, of the abused and wretched? And even when those stories are told in a documentary about the hunger in Africa or war in the Middle East, aren't we inclined to switch off our television or radio, because we don't like to hear those tales of endless woe, those stories that come from the underside of our society?

Jesus was an accomplished storyteller. He told marvelous parables about the Kingdom of God. It is like a fish hiding in us in the deep water that should be fished out. The Kingdom is like a pearl, like a treasure, hidden in the earth. They have to be found. It is like a householder who brings forth the new and the old!

Hiding in the old, the newness of the Kingdom has to be brought out. You can't bring it forth when you are repeating the same old things. You fail to discover it when you are listening only to the traditional melody.

The greatest challenge to the world and the church of today are the new stories that come to us from Africa and Latin America, from Asia and Australia, from minority groups and the marginalized people among us. Are you willing to listen to them? Are you willing to be like that householder who brings out from the storeroom things both new and old?

Personal

"Nothing...can ever come between us and the love of God...."
Romans 8:35, 37–39

A friend of mine told me how he attended a talk given by Dom Helder
Camara, then the Bishop of Recife in Brazil. He was full of this experience, and told me his impression. The hall was full, standing room
only. Camara's English was poor and almost incomprehensible. He
got totally confused in the papers he had with him. At the end of a
talk that fascinated everyone in spite of his stammering and stutter-
ing, he put both his arms up, as in surrender, and he said, radiating an
immense joy: "God loves you, God loves every one of us. I am sure of
that! Jesus died for every one of us!"

At that moment something happened. My friend said it was as if
Helder Camara's enthusiasm suddenly ignited everybody in the hall.
People stood up. Strangers embraced each other. Others began to ap-
plaud. Someone started to sing. Others took up the melody. Many
wept like small children.

Bishop Helder Camara's personal witness to his belief electrified all
those present, who suddenly realized what it means to be personally
loved by God.

This is the kind of experience we find in Paul's letter to the Romans, when he writes: "I am certain of this: neither death nor life, no
angel, no president, nothing that exists, nothing still to come, not any
power, or height or depth, not any created thing, can ever become between us and the love of God made visible in Christ Jesus our Lord"
(Romans 8:39).

It is not often that we are experientially aware of God's love. We
don't listen to God's plea to pay attention to God's love: "Thus says
the Lord: O, come to the water all you who are thirsty, though you
have no money, come! Listen, listen to me and you will have good
things to eat, and rich food to enjoy (Isaiah 55:1-3). In this text God is
like a street vendor trying to sell his wares: wine, bread, honey, substance, life! Hurry!

Fear

"Courage! Do not be afraid!" Matthew 14:22-33

We all know the story of the storm on the lake, how the disciples were deathly afraid. Jesus had left them to be by himself. They were trying to get to the other side of the lake. They wanted to go home, but hit a head wind that became stronger and stronger, finally turning into a storm. They were afraid, but when they suddenly saw someone walking towards them over the water, they were terrified. They cried out in fear.

Fear is a killer. Fear is a murderer, not only because fear can lead us to murder others—and there are plenty of examples of that in our recent human history—but also because fear can kill us. It can make us deadly sick.

Those disciples in the boat were not only afraid of the wind and the water; they were terrified to see him. They must often have had mixed feelings about that man, Jesus, who was changing their lives so radically.

Are you always happy to be one of his disciples? Did you ever have the feeling that you would like to be left alone? That he is asking too much of you? That the cross you are supposed to bear is too heavy?

His disciples had left him behind. They were trying to go home to the situation they knew so well at the other side of the lake. But then, suddenly, he appears on the lake walking over the water.

"It is a ghost," they said, and cried out in fear. But at once Jesus called out to them: "Courage! It is I! Don't be afraid." Peter wanted to cut his fears and doubts once and for all, and he shouted: "Tell me to come to you, and I will come!" He got out of the boat but he did not make it. He started to sink, shouting: "Lord, save me!"

That is what Jesus does, adding: "Man of little faith, why did you doubt?" He suggests that Peter had it in him to believe. And Peter did, when he said with the others and all of us: "Truly, you are the Son of God!" Why should we, why should you, be afraid?

Mary's Son

"Why should I be honored with a visit from the mother of my Lord?"
Luke 1:39-56

When Mary meets Elizabeth she sings a song. It is the song of someone who has already been rescued from the limits of her time, society,
and religion, someone who is on her way to the final exodus out of all
oppression and injustice. "My soul proclaims the greatness of the
Lord, and my spirit exults in God my savior; because God has looked
down on the lowly handmaid." It is possible that Luke puts this song
in her mouth. If so, Luke must have had a good reason to do so. To let
anyone sing a song like that indicates that you think her heart was
bursting with it.

Mary not only shows knowledge of the problems of her time and
society, she also knows what has to happen to remedy the situation:
"God has shown the power of his arm, routed the proud of heart,
pulled down princes from their thrones, and exalted the lowly. The
hungry God has filled with good things, the rich sent away empty.
God has come to the help of Israel the servant, mindful of mercy."

In other words, God listens to the oppressed and the oppressors
had better take that into account. Mary's song is like a battle hymn. It
is a wave of compassion. It is a song that gives hope to everyone. It is
not against anyone, but it is for the poor and oppressed.

It must have been quite something for Jesus to have a mother like
Mary! Just imagine your mother singing you to sleep with a song like
Mary's Magnificat!

Mary's hymn remained a woman's tune. The women in Manila
sang it in front of ex-president Marcos's palace. The women in Argen-
tina, who came together every week to protest the disappearance of
their husbands and sons, sang it. Mother Teresa and her sisters were
singing it when they opened a hospice for AIDS patients in Washington, D.C. All those women are ahead of their time. So is Mary, taken
up into heaven, ahead of all of us!

[41]

Peter's Faith

"It was not flesh and blood that revealed this to you but my Father in Heaven."   *Matthew 16:13-20*

When Jesus asks his disciples: "Who do people say the Son of Man is?" he is not asking them a rhetorical question. It is a real question. He wants an answer. First they all try to dodge the issue. Jesus repeats his question. It is Simon who gives the answer: "You are the Christ, the Son of the living God!"

Jesus replies: "Simon, the son of Jonah, you are a happy man, because it was not flesh and blood that revealed this to you, but my Father in heaven." And he gives him a new name: "I now say to you, you are Peter and on this rock I will build my church."

Peter not only discovered the real identity of Jesus that day. Jesus helped him to discover his own identity, too. Simon the fisherman discovers that he has something in him that makes him Peter. That something is the reality of God in him.

Peter is not the only one who carries God's presence, but he is the first one who discovers it through Jesus. Millions of others would follow him in that discovery. Yet, he is the first one to understand and to feel what all this will lead to. He remains a first among equals.

The others in the early Christian community never let him forget that. They respected him as the leader, but they were the ones who sent him on his mission (Acts 8:14). They called him to give account of himself and his way of handling issues, when they thought that necessary (Acts 11:1-18).

Peter's conviction is shared by others. It is shared by you and me. It is that faith that taps in to the same divine presence in all of us.

All of us sharing that belief are built on the persuasion that made Jesus call Simon "Rock." "Everyone who hears these words of mine and puts them into practice is like a wise man, who built his house on the rock" (Matthew 7:24-25).

Self-Sacrifice

"Jesus began to make it clear...that he was destined to suffer."
Matthew 16:21-27

When Florence Nightingale decided to dedicate her life to the wounded on the battlefield, risking her life and good reputation, her family and friends told her that she should think of herself. Flemish missionary Damian de Veuster, who gave his life for the lepers in Molokai, (whose statue stands in the gallery of national heroes in the Capitol in Washington, D.C.), was told the same thing.

When Jesus informs his disciples that he is going to Jerusalem to put his life on the line, his disciples use the same argument to dissuade him. "Heaven preserve you, " they say. "This must not happen to you!" On another occasion his family had even come to fetch him and bring him home. They thought that he was a danger to himself and to them.

They do not understand how the giving of yourself for others can make any sense. They do not see how putting your life at the service of others in that radical way makes you discover your real self.

When the executioners of the Christian martyr Dietrich Bonhoeffer came to fetch him from his cell in an extermination camp, he turned to his fellow prisoners and said, "This is the end, and for me the beginning of my life."

When Jesus tells them that he is going to give his life for the life of this world, Peter is the first to protest. He does not do it only because he is concerned about Jesus. He is concerned about himself. He knows he should be like Jesus but he is not. That is why he tries to convince Jesus that he is wrong. Jesus, who called him "Rock" only a few lines earlier, now gives him another name, "Satan," a name that means opponent.

Here, too, Peter is the first among equals. Did you ever forsake Jesus when confronted with the integrity, honesty, justice, and love of Jesus in the concreteness of your life?

February 9

Two or Three

"For where two or three meet in my name, I shall be there with them."
Matthew 18:15-20

It happened regularly, and yet I was surprised every time. I was accustomed to prayer. I prayed a lot with my family at home. In those days we went to church every day of the week. I prayed by myself, and later on with the community of missionaries I belonged to. We were sitting in the chapel for hours and hours a day, meditating, examining our consciences, celebrating the Eucharist, and even preparing for death!

Yet, I was surprised once I got to Africa. Practically every time I was invited to a family, celebrated one or another occasion together, visited a sick person, or was invited to a cup of tea, my hosts would ask me to pray together with them. I often forgot. I was not accustomed to it. I would already be at the door, shaking hands and saying "God bless you," when my friends would say: "Aren't we going to pray together?" And that is what we did, sometimes with only two or three, sometimes in a family.

I read a report of one of the students evaluating his pastoral experience on one of the West Indian Islands. He mentions the same kind of experience. It was in the middle of the night when he was awakened by someone who was obviously disturbed. She had had a terrible nightmare and had gone to the rectory to knock on the door for help. He did not know what to do. Should he give her something to eat, to drink? She saw his consternation, and she said: "I don't need anything. I only came to pray together with you for a moment. I am alone at home." He did, and while the two were praying her anxiety disappeared. In Jesus' presence her anxiety cleared. He promised: "When two or three are meeting in my name, I will be there with them" (Matthew 18:20).

Living and Dead

"The life and death of each of us has its influence on others...."
Romans 14:7-9

The Irish author James Joyce wrote a story about that influence. It is called "The Dead," and is in his book *Dubliners*. Gretta and her husband Gabriel return to their hotel after a New Year's party. They begin to undress. He approaches her. She hesitates. He asks her what she is thinking of. She answers that she is thinking of a song, "The Lass of Aughrim." She disengages herself, sits down on the bed, and begins to weep. She then tells him that she is thinking of Michael Furey, a boy who sang that song, a boy she loved and who died. He was sick when she was sent to a boarding school in Dublin. The evening before her departure she heard some gravel thrown against her window. She ran outside and found him there in the back of the garden, standing in the cold rain, deadly sick. "I implored him to go home at once and told him he would get his death in the rain. But he said he did not want to live....He was standing at the end of the wall where there was a tree."

A week later she heard in the convent that he had died and was buried in Oughterard, where his people came from. The man who died for her sake remained a part of her life!

The dead and the living belong together, Paul wrote. Jesus had said it before, when he explained that we all belong together as the leaves and branches of the one tree of which he is the trunk.

In the end of Joyce's story it is snowing..."snow falling faintly through the universe and faintly falling, like the descent of their last end, upon all the living and the dead."

First and Last

"Thus the last will be first, and the first, last." Matthew 20:1-16a

We have thousands of ways of dividing ourselves against each other into first ones and last ones. The one who is driving an eight-cylinder car expects the one in a two- or four-cylinder car to give way to him. The one with more money is sure to be treated first in an emergency. The non-smoker feels superior to the smoker, and, until recently, right-handed people felt superior to left-handed ones. The able-bodied people look down on the so-called disabled people; those who went through therapy look down on those who did not, and the other way around.

There is no end to the categories we find to be first ones looking down on last ones: money, muscles, race, skin, age, smell, gender, abode, origin, street, piety, religion, health, name, ordination, and so on. The list is endless and the difficulties that these prejudices cause are enormous.

When Jesus tells us that the last ones will be the first ones and the first ones the last, he does not want to change people of position. He does not want to put those who are presently standing in front of the row in the back. That would only be a reversal and a perpetuating of the differences. He wants to abolish those differences. The first ones and the last ones are equal—regardless of age, race, gender, religion. In his vision we are equal as sisters and brothers, who are friends.

Righteousness

"My boy, you go and work in the vineyard today." Matthew 21:28-32

In the story about the two sons, Jesus blames the leaders of the people for not doing the will of God. He does this indirectly, by asking them which of the two sons did the will of the father, the one who said "no" but who did go to the vineyard, or the one who said "yes" but who did not go to do the work he was asked to do.

In Matthew's gospel text, Jesus gives the work that the two sons are asked to do a name, *dikaiosune*. It is the work John the Baptizer did.

Dikaiosune is one of the key words in Matthew's gospel. He uses it seven times when reporting the words of Jesus. Jesus uses it when he gives us the eight beatitudes: "Blessed are those who hunger and thirst for *dikaiosune*, for they shall be satisfied" (Matthew 5:6). We usually translate the word as "righteousness." The word means "worked out, or realized, justice."

It is the "working out" of God's justice in this world, a justice that is based on God's love for everyone. Having God's Spirit in us, we carry God's love in us, a love that should not only be a question of "yes" or "no," but a love that has to express itself in deeds. Whether we say "yes" to it as the first son did, or "no" as the second, we should in fact be working for that righteousness in our own lives and in our world.

We can do that in several ways. In the gospel of Matthew, Jesus asks us to pray, to fast, and to give alms.

We should do that, but we are not going to solve the problems of the world's inequity that way. More should be done. For over a hundred years popes have insisted in their social teaching that the order of the world has to be restructured. Pope John Paul II stresses the need for this work for righteousness in his encyclicals. A lot of work still has to be done in the vineyard of the Lord. We are all called: "My child, you go and work in the vineyard today!"

Sour Grapes

"Let me sing to my friend, the song of his love...." Isaiah 5:1-7

It not only sounds like a song, it is a song, a country ballad:

> Let me sing to my friend,
> the song of his love for his vineyard.
> · My friend had vineyard on a fertile hillside.
> He dug the soil, cleared it of stones.
> he planted choice vines in it.
> In the middle he built a tower,
> he dug a press there too.
> He expected it to yield grapes,
> but sour grapes were all that it gave.

According to the experts, this song, "The Song of the Vineyard," was a popular lyric in Isaiah's time, purportedly sung at wedding feasts. It is the song of a jilted lover. Isaiah places the song in another context. He makes God sing it, speaking of the world and humanity.

Isaiah does not mince words when he applies and adapts this love song in this way. He writes that the owner expected *mishpat* (Hebrew for justice), and he found *mispah*, a bloodbath. He looked for *zedakah*, righteousness, but he found *ze'akah*, cries of terror. Isaiah is writing poetry, rhyming poetry, but what he describes is far from poetic.

Jesus adopts rhyme when he in his turn tells his stories about vineyards and vines—collectivities and individuals that render only sour grapes, notwithstanding all the love and care he gave them. Singing his song, he hopes to win us over.

Refusal

"'Come to my wedding.' But they were not interested."
Matthew 22:1-14

The banquet is prepared. Everything is in order. The roast is sliced, the salad bar ready, the vegetables steaming, but the guests do not come. The guests have other things to do.

Those hesitations count especially in this case. It is God who did the inviting. Accepting such an invitation is a serious issue.

To be invited by God and Jesus Christ? You never know how it will end. Or maybe you do know, and do not want it.

Many of us live on that kind of edge. We are attracted by God, we know we are invited by Jesus' love, and yet we don't dare accept. We hesitate. We refuse.

And yet we can't deny that that invitation has come to us. We can almost hear the music in the hall and smell the roast on the fire. The American Quaker Thomas Kelly described this intuition in a striking way:

> And we are unhappy, uneasy, strained, oppressed, and fearful we shall be shallow. For over the margins of life comes a whisper, a faint call, a premonition of richer living which we know we are passing by. Strained by the very mad pace of our daily outer burdens, we are further strained by an inward uneasiness, because we have hints that there is a way of life vastly richer and deeper than all this hurried existence, a life of unhurried serenity and peace and power. If only we could slip over into that Center! If only we could find the Silence which is the source of sound! (*A Testament of Devotion*, Harper & Row, 1941, p. 115)

All of us are more religious and more mystical than we appear to be. We have seen more than we want to admit even to ourselves—bits of light, rays of goodness, fragment of songs, patches of heaven. But most times we act as if we never heard or saw a thing.

Mission

"We...constantly remember before God our Father how you have shown your faith in action...."   *Thessalonians 1:1-5b*

It is with patent joy and pride that Paul writes to the Thessalonians: "We know, sisters and brothers, that God loves you and that you have been chosen, because when we brought the Good News to you, it came to you not only as words, but as power and as the Holy Spirit and as utter conviction" (1 Thessalonians 1:5). There was a time when practically everyone was engaged in the spreading of this good news. Mission was a popular issue. Even if we ourselves did not feel the call to go out to the mission field we supported our missionaries. We collected all kinds of valuable things. Probably we were the first ones that profited from recycling metals and paper in view of helping our missionaries. The number of American missionaries working overseas is diminishing every year, notwithstanding the happy fact that the number of lay missionaries is growing. Statistics seem to show that the bulk of the financial support for their work comes from senior Christians. It is as if Paul's enthusiasm has disappeared among us.

Yet, humanity needs the good news that God loves all of us more than ever before. We live in a world where people are living ever nearer to each other, a nearness that causes ever more problems.

We need to hear that we all come from the same divine source, that we all have the same Father, that we are all created together in God's Son, and that we are all carried by the same divine and holy Spirit.

It is in those terms in the gospel of Matthew that Jesus expresses the mission he left us, asking us to take care that everyone is baptized and initiated: "Go, therefore, to all nations and make them my disciples; baptize them in the name of the Father, and of the Son, and of the holy Spirit."

We have to live that mission. The future of this world and the one to come depends on it.

As Yourself

"You must love your neighbor as yourself." Matthew 22:34-40

They asked him: "What is the most important commandment?" He answered: "You must love the Lord your God with all your heart, with all your soul, and with all your mind. This is the greatest and first commandment. The second is like it: You must love your neighbor as yourself."

Love your neighbor as yourself! Did you ever ask yourself why we should do that? We often ask ourselves how we should do it, but do we ask why?

It is because we are in this creation all together. In your essence you are the dwelling place of God. So is your neighbor. You might not feel God's presence, but that does not mean that God is absent. Your neighbor might not feel God's presence, but again that does not mean that she or he is not carried by God's love. We belong together—God, you, and I. When we are one like this, we can see God and Christ in everyone. You might even go further and say that we ourselves are in the heart of everyone. What we do for another is done to ourselves. When another is hurt, we are hurt. We can repeat in our lives the words of Jesus: "Anything done to any of my sisters and brothers is done to me!" Our heart is not as large as the one in our chest; it is as large as Jesus' heart, as God's heart!

Sociologists, psychologists, and philosophers have been expressing worries about the ever-growing self-consciousness and consequent individualization of the younger generation. If you stick to Jesus' words, that growing self-awareness can only be a blessing, not only for those persons who are so highly conscious of themselves, but also for all humanity. The more you love yourself, the more you see who you are, the more Jesus' directive "Love the other as you love yourself" will be a blessing for all humanity!

New Order

"The greatest among you must be your servant." Matthew 23:1-12

A "New Order" is something we are all looking forward to. Politicians know this. They often display those very words on their banners. So do the millions and millions of people who have been demonstrating recently—and all through the history of democracy—through the streets and squares of the world.

It is a word we often see used when things have changed, or when improvements are promised—a gas station that has a sign reading "Under New Management," or even a detergent that promises new cleansing power.

This phrase is often abused. Some years ago, the words "New Order" appeared in the program of a convention of the Association of Mission Studies in Rome. Some older European participants wanted them scrapped. The words reminded them of the Hitler Nazi regime. He, too, had spoken about a new order of things, in which one ethnic group was going to rule the whole world. The discussion was long and sometimes fierce. In the end it was pointed out that even Jesus uses the term, speaking about "the world that is to be" *(paliggenesia)* (Matthew 19:28).

It is an order where no one can be called father or master or teacher, a world where we will be sisters and brothers who are friends, without discrimination, a world in which we are servants to each other in our daily relationships. It is a world where no one puts herself or himself above—or below—another, where each person is a gift, God's gift, to the others.

End of Time

"Stay awake, because you do not know either the day or the hour."
Matthew 25:1-13

We are approaching the year 2000. That number 2000 is a very full, very complete number. We not only end a century, we end a period of thousand years.

It is a number that makes people afraid. They fear that it might mean the end of this world. We seem to live in a dangerous and thrilling time. Prophets and pseudo-prophets are rereading the Hebrew Scriptures, especially a prophetic book like Daniel, or the Book of Revelation in the Christian Scriptures.

It is not the first time that this has happened. We have a report of the Mass that Pope Sylvester II celebrated in the old Saint Peter's Basilica in Rome at midnight December 31 of the year 999. The basilica was full. Some people had given everything they had to the poor just before Mass began. They were sitting in sackcloth and ashes in the church. Some of them did not even dare to look up at the moment of consecration. They were lying flat on the earth with their arms outstretched as on a cross. At the moment that the bells started to ring at midnight, some of those present died of pure fear. But when the tolling of the bells was over, and the earth did not open, and no fire came down from heaven, it was as if everyone woke up from a nightmare. Weeping and laughing, the crowd stared to embrace each other, man and woman, friend and foe, master and servant, and the bells of all the churches in Rome started ringing.

Jesus asks us to be prepared. We should be as ready as the five sensible bridesmaids at the moment of the bridegroom's arrival.

We have to do some long-range planning for the coming of Jesus at the end of our own days, and even for his return at the apocalyptic end of human history. It is as important to do some short-range planning for the coming of Jesus in the "now" and "here" of our daily life.

Gain

"The person who had received five talents promptly went and traded with them and made five more." Matthew 25:14-30

Several times Jesus expresses his amazement about what people do to enrich themselves. He calls them children of the darkness, because they misjudge what their lives are about, but he admires their dedication.

He does not admire what they do. He makes it clear that it is very difficult, if not impossible, to combine a mere interest in money with an interest in the Kingdom of God.

We do not need Jesus to know this. Human history itself witnesses to that difficulty. Hundreds of years ago Bartolomé de Las Casas wrote what became a classic about the greed of the Spanish conquerors of Latin America. In it he says: "I am not saying that they are out to murder, but I do say that they want to get rich. They want to swim in gold by the labor of and the sweat of the wretched natives, which they use as if they were tools, with the unavoidable result that they all die in exhaustion and misery."

The people de Las Casas wrote about were not bad. They were not necessarily aggressive. Maybe they did not even want to kill. But they wanted to get rich. Their greed blinded them to any Kingdom of God value.

This kind of attitude is at work all around us. Shops are kept open even at the most impossible hours. Appointment books are overbooked. The deadliest deals are made. Wars are waged. Health, honor, integrity, and leisure are sacrificed to make more money. No wonder Jesus was amazed.

Jesus says: If only the children of the light would be as eager to establish the Kingdom of God as the children of the darkness are eager to get rich.

Royal

"...he will take his seat on his throne of glory...." Matthew 25:31-46

The time of kings and queens is over. It even becomes difficult to speak about the Kingdom of God in a republic like the United States of America.

There are two ways to look at the disappearance of queens and kings. They disappeared because we no longer tolerate that others not elected are put over us in any way. Or, you might say that they vanished because all of us proved to be of royal stock and dignity.

The Old Testament uses the word "king" more than 2500 times! It expects much of a king. Psalm 72 is one of the texts that outlines those expectations:

God, endow the king with your own justice,
his royal person with your righteousness,
that he may rule your people rightly
and deal justly with the oppressed ones (1-2).
For he will rescue the needy who appeal for help,
the distressed who have no protector.
He will have pity on the poor and the needy,
and deliver the needy from death.
He will redeem them from oppression and violence
and their blood will be precious in his eyes (12-14).

When, at the end of Matthew's gospel, Jesus appears on the clouds at the end of time, he appears sitting on a throne as a king. In that description all of us will be standing before him. He will ask us some questions about our lives. You know the questions. Did you feed the hungry, did you help the oppressed, did you have pity on the poor and the needy? He will ask us whether we did what a king or queen is supposed to do according to Psalm 72!

Jesus Christ is king, but all of us are called to be royal as he was, is, and shall be!

[55]

Ashes

"...the day of salvation is here...." 2 Corinthians 5:20-6:2

In 1964 Thomas Merton, the famous American Trappist monk, got permission to leave his monastery at Gethsemane in Kentucky to live alone in a hermitage, not far from his abbey. He had had a bit of trouble getting permission from his superiors to do so, but finally the permission was granted. He was delighted. An old dream was going to be realized.

It meant that he had to move. Moving is an ordeal. It is an experience most of us know and few of us like. It can also be a favorable time, a time of liberation, a time of loosening all kinds of old bonds. Such a moment makes you realize how many things you have collected over the years, things that make your moving almost impossible.

Merton describes in his diary how he prepared for the life of solitude he had been seeking for so long. He went through his room to clean up. He emptied closets and files. He went through his papers and things. He was amazed at what he found, things he had kept because he once thought them indispensable.

He filled wastepaper basket after wastepaper basket. Lots of things could be left behind. So many things could be burned. Though it was sometimes difficult to decide whether to throw certain items out, every new load that left his room was really like a liberation to him. It was a relief for him to see everything turned into ashes. He could start anew, afresh, and more simply. He realized as never before how one's life can become cluttered under a pile of things that are not really necessary.

It was like a housecleaning day. When he left for his hermitage he was free. In the ashes he left his past behind and could start anew.

Fasting

"Choose life, then, so that you and your descendants may live...."
                                        Deuteronomy 30:15-20

In 1981 a university chaplain, Father Thomas Ryan, published a book that he called *Fasting Rediscovered: A Guide to Health and Wholeness for Your Body-Spirit.* He included a whole set of testimonies from people who had rediscovered fasting. "I fast to pull the loose ends together in my life." "I used to do a lot of things that were at cross-purposes with my own health and well-being." "Fasting introduced me to a more genuinely life-supporting way to live."

All kinds of people are fasting again. Athletes, boxers, musicians, dancers, astronauts, medical professionals, students, teachers, designers, writers, secretaries, bus drivers, store managers, homemakers, people from all backgrounds and in all professions are doing it.

We are surrounded by people who stopped smoking, restrained their drinking, or became vegetarians, people who overcame their addiction to caffeine, sugar, chocolate, alcohol, nicotine, and drugs.

They shop in health shops, drink soya milk, eat lean food, watch their weight and calories. As Father Ryan noted, most times it has something to do with what one might call body-ecology. For almost all of these people fasting is a conscious option for a healthier life and a clearer mind. Even for those whose religious faith can't motivate them to do it, fasting seems worth doing.

Others don't fast only for their own sake. They do it also for the sake of others, for the sake of the earth, and for God's sake! They restrict their over-consumption so that they can support others who haven't enough to consume and to live with. They do it opting for life—their own life and the lives of others.

Sharing

"Is not this the sort of fasting that pleases me to break unjust fetters...to let the oppressed go free...."   *Isaiah 58:1-9*

About the year 128, a journalist named Aristides was called to the imperial court of the emperor Hadrian. The emperor wanted some information about Christians. Aristides told his amazed audience: "When someone is poor among them who has need of help, they fast for two or three days, and they have the custom of sending the hungry person the food they prepared for themselves."

An old Christian custom recommended by Saint Augustine when he wrote about fasting and mortification: "Don't believe that fasting suffices. Fasting punishes you, but it does not restore your brother! Your fasting will be fruitful if you provide for the needs of another. How many poor people could be nourished by the meal you did not take today?" He echoed Isaiah who, in the name of God, once said: "Is not this the sort of fasting that pleases me...to share your bread with the hungry" (Isaiah 58:6–7).

This is an idea that Christians have never lost. In 1961, in order to promote a Family Fast Day, the British bishops stated: "What we save thereby can be offered for the hungry and the starving. Such a sacrifice would be very much in the spirit of Lent, for it would touch both palate and purse."

The bishops of the United States made the same kind of suggestion, not restricting it to Lent, but suggesting it for every single Friday of the year. They did that when they wrote a letter to all of us on the need to reconsider our economic structures, recommendations that rarely seem to be followed. If we did, we would not only be reorganizing our own lives and priorities, but even society itself. The needs of others would find a new place in our "new agenda." And all of us would be happier because of it.

Healing

"It is not those who are well who need a doctor, but those who are sick."   Luke 5:27-32

Luke was a doctor seeing the world from a physician's point of view. He even looks at Jesus from a medical viewpoint. In fact, he makes Jesus into a doctor. In Luke's gospel, when Jesus introduces himself in the synagogue of his hometown, Nazareth, he tells them: "No doubt you will quote me the saying: 'Physician, heal yourself'" (Luke 4:23). Jesus here called himself a doctor. It was not the only time in the gospel of Luke that he did this. He also did it when he was accused of eating and drinking with sinners. He answered his accusers: "It is not the healthy that need a doctor, but the sick" (Luke 5:31).

According to Luke, Jesus came to heal a world and a humanity that was sick and needed a doctor. You don't need to be a health expert or a doctor to note that the world around us is sick. Acid rain is killing trees; fish and waterfowl are dying in polluted rivers and lakes. Sometimes you can hardly breath without doing damage to your lungs, and you even have to be careful when you take a shower, because the water you use might be full of chemicals. We all need a doctor; we all need to be healed, not only us, but also the plants, animals, rivers, seas, forests, and deserts.

Something has to be done; you always have to take some steps to regain your health. Jesus suggests repentance. A doctor will not use that word when he recommends a diet or discontinuing one or another habit in order to restore your health. What he recommends, however, often comes to the same thing: You have to change your life to make up for what went wrong in the past.

The healing we need does not ask only for a personal and individual transformation. It asks for a structural revision of our society and of the world, a change we have to be interested in if we want to be touched by the healing power of that physician Jesus!

Heroism

"...I was sick and you visited me...." Matthew 25:31-46

Reinhold Niebuhr was one of the most influential theologians of this century. When he was 59 he suffered a slight stroke that left him partially paralyzed on his left side. It cut his energy back to a fraction of what it had been. His wife Ursula adjusted her workload as a professor in order to care for him.

Niebuhr wrote afterwards that he made a discovery. "I learned to know the goodness of men and women who went out of their way to help an invalid. Among the persons who impressed me with their helpfulness were my doctors, nurses, and therapists, my colleagues and friends. I soon learned that some of these people who entered my life professionally, or who served me non-professionally with visits and walks, showed me an almost charismatic gift of love. And, of course, my chief source of spiritual strength was my wife. She was my nurse, secretary, editor, counselor, and friendly critic through all those years of illness and occasional depression."

We often forget the heroism of the ordinary people around us. We often overlook our own visits to the sick, the attention others show us, and the love we show others.

Craig Shergold, a boy from Great Britain, developed a brain tumor. His doctors could do nothing for him. One of them told the boy not to lose courage and to be a winner, to be the greatest picture postcard collector in the world. So the news spread that terminally-ill Craig was collecting picture postcards. He received 33 million of them! There were times that the Royal Mail unloaded 60 postal bags a day at his door. Then a rich man was asked to send him a postcard. He called Craig's doctor and arranged for an operation. John's tumor was brought under control. Wasn't that wonderful? "Anything you did for one of my brothers or sisters here, however insignificant, you did for me" (Matthew 25: 40).

Cleansing

"And forgive us our debts, as we have forgiven those who are in debt to us."   *Matthew 6:7-15*

A parish youth group met for a retreat on a winter evening in Melbourne, Australia. They had to decide how to organize their day. There was some discussion about how to start. Soon ideas began to fall into place. The first thing they decided to do was that each one would write down anything from the past that might hinder the group from having a fruitful retreat. They did this, and then, one by one, burned those papers to ashes. There was silence during this whole solemn exercise.

It was Christmas time in Dublin, Ireland, at another youth retreat. In the middle of the conference room was a large Christmas tree. The tree was without decoration. Under the tree was a high pile of yellow and purple pieces of ribbon. The participants were asked to remember any person they had not forgiven, and to put a ribbon on the tree if they could forgive them now. By evening time the tree was full of ribbons.

It is not only the things that clutter up our kitchen shelves, our cupboards and wardrobes, our table drawers, lofts, basements, and garages that hinder us from moving and breathing freely. There are the less tangible, but often more trying spiritual and moral burdens we carry with us.

Unforgiven offenses, guilt feelings from the past, wrong choices, betrayed loves—they should be burned into ashes, too.

That is difficult. It asks for a lot of discipline. It is all too easy to remain caught in the past, to use the past as an excuse not to do anything at all. It is much easier to continue accusing and complaining.

Forgiving others is difficult; to forgive yourself is sometimes even more difficult. Yet, it is a step we have to take before we can proceed much further.

Signs

"This is an evil generation; it is asking for a sign." Luke 11:29-32

Jesus told them that they had to change their ways. He said: "This is a wicked generation; it is asking for a sign!" They did not believe him. They asked him to give them a sign that he was right about their situation. Jesus was upset about that. Why would they need a sign? Was it not obvious that things would fall apart if they did not change their ways?

Not only prophets, but even concerned scientists in our day often have the same difficulty as Jesus. Economists tell us that the world will run out of resources if we continue to exploit the earth as we are currently doing. Biologists speak about the disastrous effects of our waste of energy, of the destruction of the rain forests, of the pollution of the atmosphere, of the dumping of radioactive waste, of using materials like plastic that are not biodegradable. Physicians insist that that we eat too much fatty stuff, that many drink too much, that we should drive our cars less and use our feet and bodies more. Sociologists warn that families are falling apart, that children are not well educated, and that there are too many homeless people in our streets.

Too few listen. Those who do not listen often say that they want clearer signs, more proof, clearer evidence, while all around us forests die, fishes rot, air and water are polluted, and human beings suffer.

We do not need more signs. We need changes. Of course, it would be impossible to change everything in one go and at the same time. But we all can begin and enter the process. Today you might change one of your consumer habits. Take a mug or cup with you to work instead of using paper or Styrofoam cups.

Asking and Receiving

"Everyone who asks receives; everyone who searches finds; everyone who knocks will have the door opened." Matthew 7:7-12

You know the story. You've heard it so often. He did not look well. That is what everybody who cared for him told him. He himself had some vague worries about his health. He sometimes had those strange pains. He felt so deadly tired even before the day was half over. His friends told him to go to a doctor to find out. He did not want to do that. He might have to change his lifestyle and he did not want that. In a way he acted like a child who did not want to know the truth. His fear stifled him, made him deny everything. It would pass, he told himself; he had had something like that before. He delayed and delayed. He did not dare to ask any question. He did not want to find out.

We often accuse ostriches of this kind of practice. They are supposed to stick their heads in the desert sand when danger approaches, so that they will not see the danger. That is only a legend that is not even fair to those birds. Ostriches are wiser. They organize themselves better than that.

Jesus, too, asks us to question and to search what went wrong, or what our situation is.

That is not easy. When you start to question yourself about some event or situation, you might gain some awareness of things you never knew before. The one who asks always receives. If you have no questions, you will not be answered. And in the end you risk mistaking a stone for bread, a snake for fish, and your sickness for health.

Taking Life

"You have heard how it was said to our ancestors, You shall not kill...."
                                                            Matthew 5:20-26

He was a theologian speaking in an African students' community. The subject was: "You must not kill." During the talk the topic of abortion came up. The discussion afterwards was mainly on that issue. All went well until one student asked a question the speaker could not answer: "Why is it that the church leadership pays so much attention to voluntary abortion and not to spontaneous abortions that are due to the fact that in slum areas so many pregnant women abort spontaneously because of their poverty, their misery, their sickness, and their hunger?" When the answer did not come, the student who asked the question gave the answer himself: "It is, I think, because in that case you would have to do something about the economic order, and you are not willing to do that, are you?"

The remark may not have been a fair one, but it definitely pointed at something: There is a whole infrastructure of unhealthy and even sinful circumstances that are killing human life.

Other theologians and bishops do address this issue when they speak about the "seamless garment." Human life is woven in one piece, just like the garment Jesus was wearing when he was stripped to be put on the cross. The seamless garment of human life should not be rent into pieces. It should not be divided against itself.

If we want to do justice to Jesus' words, we have to tackle the circumstances that make this world a killer of so many people.

Love Your Enemies

"You must therefore set no bounds to your life, just as your heavenly Father sets none to his."   Matthew 5:43-48

We had been listening to her for over an hour. She spoke about hoping against hope. She explained how the whole world would learn to live in harmony. She was very optimistic.

A pastor, known for his gloomy outlook on life, stood up to respond. He did not agree. He said it was all too optimistic. He explained that he grew up without any religion at all. After the Second World War he had volunteered to work among the millions of refugees in Europe. He described how during that work he was so unnerved by the hatred he found in this world that he had started to search for some hope somewhere.

After searching for a while he decided to become a Christian. Christianity, he said, was the only religion that gave an answer to a world where people are almost unavoidably each other's enemies. Jesus not only told us that we should love our enemies, he also showed us in his life that this is a human possibility.

And that, he concluded, is the only answer to the problems of our times. To be at peace is not only a state of mind. We are often surrounded by unavoidable conflicts. We will have conflicts at home, at school, at work, and during leisure time, not to speak of the conflicts we are involved in because we belong to a larger community like our country and even our church.

The bottom line, the only way to keep us all together, is Jesus' advice: "Love your enemies and pray for those who persecute you!"

Ecology

"Be compassionate just as your Father is compassionate."

Luke 6:36-38

Yesterday as I passed a bush I caught myself picking off a tip of one of its branches. I don't know why I did that. I walked away with a twig, something I often catch myself doing.

An old Indian saint said once that you should never just pick a leaf or a branch from a plant when you are passing it. He must have noticed that many of us do that almost automatically. We should have respect for those plants. We should have compassion and empathy for all forms of life around us. This is not something new, discovered in our "environmental" days!

Old biblical rules asked pity for the animals that work for you. It is even one of the reasons given for the seventh day of rest: "So that your ox, your donkey, or any of your cattle may rest as you do" (Exodus 23:12).

Even the earth was respected and not overtaxed. The land should lie fallow in the seventh year to recuperate and come to itself. People should respect their workers, and give a rest even to their slaves. They should not overwork themselves, either.

These biblical suggestions give a new meaning to the remainder of the gospel text of today: "Give, and there will be gifts for you: a full measure pressed down, shaken together, and running over, will be poured into your lap."

These suggestions are needed to survive in a world where we are depleting the soil and causing massive erosion. It is estimated that forty-seven billion tons of soil are lost every year because we do not care for trees and plants as we should. Our love should extend to the piece of land we might own, even if it is a small plot around our house. Take care to protect it against pollution and destruction as well as you can. Plant a tree in it to help the oxygenation of your environment.

Being the Greatest

"The greatest among you must be your servant." Matthew 23:1-12

Ordinary examples of everyday sanctity and asceticism almost always seem overlooked. Even a visionary such as Thomas Merton, the Trappist monk, is guilty of that. "Merton writes about the marginal man, the monk, the displaced person, the prisoner, those who live in the presence of death and go beyond it to become 'witnesses to life.' Why does he leave the other experts off his list—the old, the desperately ill?" (M. Barrett, "A Kind of Dying," *The New Yorker*, October 12, 1987).

Professor Elizabeth Ann Dreyer, a specialist in these matters at the Washington Theological Union, took up this challenge. She pointed out that not only the sick and dying called to lay down their lives often show signs of heroic sanctity, but that the loved ones of the sick and elderly are invited to their own brand of asceticism and—to speak in the terms of the gospel—servitude.

She wrote: "How to deal with the fatigue and burnout of hospital visits? How do we manage to keep up the daily round of responsibilities that do not abate when someone in the family is ill or dying?...The weight of such experiences can crush us or be seen as a call to lay down our lives in love..." (*Weavings*, December 1988). Anyone who humbles herself or himself will be exalted.

This humbling does not mean, however, that we should not be realistic about what we are doing to support others in their need. Our whole world is filled with strands of love and care that keep us together and alive.

Just check once for yourself at the end of the day what you have done to help and serve others. You might have done more, all right, but that does not mean that you did not do anything. It only indicates that you might do even more.

Raising Children

"Anyone who wants to be great among you must be your servant...."
                                                      Matthew 20:17-28

At a parish meeting without much of a focus, where those present talked about anything, the conversation soon turned to the topic of this world and its sad state. Something should be done. All kinds of action programs were thought of. Then a homemaker, a mother of young children, said something that put everything in a new perspective. "I think that the best contribution to the betterment of the world that I can make is the careful raising of my children." While she said that, she put her hand on the head of her cute youngest.

"Child rearing is almost always an invitation to asceticism," wrote Elizabeth Dreyer. "In our society the raising of children is perhaps the ascetic opportunity par excellence."

Again, that is not something we spontaneously think of when speaking about mortification. Too often we imagine people like Father Damian, the hero of Molokai, Mother Teresa of Calcutta, or great saints from the past when using those words.

"A full night's sleep, time to oneself, the freedom to come and go as one pleases—all this must be given up in a way that is quite different from a monk who chooses to rise once or twice during the night to recite his prayers....Huge chunks of life are laid down at the behest of infants."

As Jesus' saying goes: "As you did to the least of my sisters and brothers you did to me."

Besides, Jesus himself seems to have lived for thirty years in the circle of his family in the modest conditions of Nazareth, preparing himself, his family, and the people around for God's Kingdom.

Aid

"There was a rich man who used to dress in purple and fine linen and feast magnificently every day." Luke 16:19-31

The poor of the world are lying at the gates of the rich. "This is a situation that is particularly embarrassing for Christians. The 1.5 billion followers of him who had no place to lay his head now control two-thirds of the Earth's resources and, on average, are three times better off than their non-Christian neighbors," wrote Father Sean McDonagh, an Irish missionary priest in the Philippines (*To Care for the Earth*, 1987).

The distance between the poor and rich has been growing ever since colonial times. The gap has never been so large.

Jesus tells the story about the rich man eating and drinking to his stomach's content, dressed in silk and purple, with poor, hungry, and sick Lazarus at his door. It is only when they both die that the rich man discovers that the gulf between the two has become so wide they cannot help each other any more.

Fortunately there are signs that things are changing. Christians in the "developed" world are becoming more and more aware of this gulf separating rich from poor. They are becoming better informed about the poverty "at home," too.

We are becoming more aware of the legacy of a history of colonialism and exploitation. A new challenge is felt. Many people feel helpless when thinking of the consequences. How to be faithful to Jesus' words? It is difficult to do that just on one's own. It is obvious that it is a task we can only tackle together. That is why aid organizations and networks like Bread for the World and Catholic Relief Services are growing, a development that should be promoted and joined by all of good will.

Fruitfulness

"...the kingdom of God...will be given to a people who will produce its fruit."   Matthew 21:33-43, 45-46

It is still a bit early in the year, but in a few weeks' time a great silent activity will begin in garden and field. Buds will swell and unfold. Some of them will blossom, turning into fruits. Again the fields will be full with wheat, rye, barley, corn, and oats. The branches of the trees will hang loaded with a bounty of apples, pears, and plums.

The whole of nature will be groaning, giving birth to new life. In the vision of a sane, safe world, with the reign of God in our midst, mother earth produces its fruits, its boundless and endless life.

We are taken up in that life-giving process. We belong to that groaning nature. We should be participating in this life-giving process, not only individually, but also communally in the nations we belong to. Do we bring forth those fruits?

In the United States alone the money earned by the export of arms from 1968 to 1982 escalated from $1 billion to $21 billion. Fifty percent of the world's one million scientists are involved with the military in one way or another. There are two-and-one-half times as many military personnel as health workers.

It is a pity that so much effort and money is spent on war and preparation for war. It is an even greater pity that the livelihood of so many depends on the production and servicing of arms. Their effort and money, too, would be such an asset in improving our common lot in this world.

How do we change this? How can we be fruitful in view of the Kingdom of God, that reign of justice and peace? Peace and justice start at home; they begin in your heart. Let us begin there!

Prodigal Son

"He ran to the boy, clasped him in his arms, and kissed him."
Luke 15:1-3, 11-32

In 1988, people in Washington, D.C., voted on the mandatory introduction of returnable bottles. As long as people do not get anything back for their empties, they throw them away. When they are paid something for them, they are returned more often than not.

The new law was voted down. The big bottlers had been campaigning against it. It would have cost them too much money, they said. So bottles are still thrown away.

So much is thrown away in our society: paper, plastics, clothing, food, and all kinds of unnecessary packing material.

Like the lost and prodigal son, those who have the money to buy squander the resources of the earth.

Many people in First World countries have developed a lifestyle and consumption pattern way beyond what mother earth can support. They can only be maintained by exploiting the vast majority of the world's resources and population.

You might object that this has nothing to with a Bible reflection. If you think that way, it might be helpful to reflect on what Arthur Simon said as the Executive Director of Bread for the World: "The urgent need is not for churches as churches to enter the political fray (although they must take a moral stand), but for Christians as citizens to exercise their renewed consciences and contact decision makers."

It is no use trying to put the blame for the sorry state of the world on others. It is no good to think that we are so much better than the others, like the older brother did when the prodigal son returned to his father. We are a mixed bag, all of us. We all have to change our ways if we want to avoid sitting at the end of our days on top of a polluted world. We all need to say, "Father, I have sinned!" We all need the arms of our creator, Abba, Father, around us again.

It is in those arms that we should find our new ways!

Prophet

"In truth I tell you, no prophet is ever accepted in his own country."
Luke 4:24-30

When Jesus faced his family, acquaintances, and villagers in the Nazareth synagogue, he told them: "No prophet is ever accepted in his own country." If what Jesus says is true, then no country is able to be saved on its own. Whole countries would never find the help they need. The prophets who would be able to help them would have to come from elsewhere.

Jesus illustrates his point by telling the story of a woman and a man (he is always "inclusive") who did not find a solution to their problems with their compatriots, but had to go for help to someone alien to them. Zarephath, a Sidonian woman, and Naaman, a Syrian army commander, did not belong to the Jewish people. They needed to be rescued, Zarephath from a drought and Naaman from his leprosy. They needed a prophet and a healer. They could not find one among their own. They had to look outside their own circle. They could not help themselves in isolation.

Nowadays there is not a single human group that would be able to assure a solution to the problems of humanity. There is not even a single human group of religious believers that would be able to do that.

Many religious leaders in the world know this. That is why Pope John Paul II called religious leaders of all convictions together in Assisi a few years ago. That is why the Catholic and Protestant churches in Europe called together a special Ecumenical Assembly in 1989 in Basel, Switzerland, to discuss the issue of the healing of our planet, and the assurance of justice and peace.

One of the difficulties those leaders have is the same one Jesus had in Nazareth. The people who listened to him were too provincial, too bigoted to understand his universal vision. They did not want to hear of it. They even preferred to kill him.

Reconciliation

"Were you not bound, then, to have pity...?" Matthew 18:21-35

Sometimes we speak about nature as if it is a person. We have that kind of instinctive feeling deep in ourselves that, if we force nature too much, it will take revenge. You hear that feeling expressed when a dam breaks, when a bridge collapses, when a new sickness breaks out, when an over-busy person suffers a heart attack, or when all the trees in an area suddenly start to die.

The older religions are full of rites to appease nature, to be reconciled with her. That is what the old shaman did, putting people back in the rhythm of nature they had lost contact with.

It is a reconciliation we urgently need.

It is a need that up to now was hardly ever mentioned in any of the church's documents on reconciliation and penance.

Only one bishop spoke about it at the Special Synod on Penance in 1983. He came from Japan, the country with a very bitter atomic experience. Bishop Stephen Fumio Hamao said: "Work for peace will be effective if all become aware of their deep connection with nature, especially with all living beings. We must not only dominate nature, but also seek harmony with it, and admire in it the beauty, the wisdom, and love of its Creator. Thus men and women will be freed from their frenzy for possessions and domination and will become partisans of peace."

The Lord, our God, created this world as a beautiful garden for us, just as a lover gives flowers to a loved one. The whole of creation is God's gift to be enjoyed by all of us. On several occasions Jesus said: "Look at the flowers, the birds, the sky, the trees, the water, and the sunset!" Appreciate God's gifts from your heart, and make up for the damage done to it. Reconcile yourself with sister water.

Law's Purpose

"...not one dot, not one little stroke, is to disappear from the law until all its purpose is achieved."   *Matthew 5:17-19*

Children often have difficulty with the things they are supposed to do, like washing their hands before meals, brushing their teeth afterwards. It is very difficult to convince them that you don't ask them to do those things just to annoy them, but because they are good for them.

When those children grow older they sometimes have the same difficulty with the Ten Commandments, not realizing what Moses said of them in his time: "Observe them, that you may have life."

It would be difficult to imagine a society that would be able to survive without a set of fundamental principles as expressed in the Ten Commandments. Most—if not all—of them are about the organization of human society. Without them life really would be brutish and short, as we all know from periods in our history when they were overlooked.

No wonder Moses added: "Tell them to your children and to your children's children." No wonder Jesus said that he did not even think of abolishing them: "Do not imagine that I came to abolish the Law or the Prophets."

It would be the end of human society, and that would be the end of human life. The Ten Commandments protect human life and human society. The same is true of so many of our human laws that are derived from them.

Think of the laws that oblige us to keep to one side of the street, that restrict us to a maximum speed, that forbid us to drive while intoxicated. They not only make driving safer, they make driving possible.

God's laws are our lifeline. They deserve our esteem and appreciation.

Gathering In

"...anyone who does not gather in with me throws away."
Luke 11:14-23

Jesus describes his work among us more than once as a bringing to-gether, a gathering. He speaks in terms of a common table, a common home with many rooms, fish that are brought together, a harvest that is brought in, a party to be started.

He uses the same images when he describes the mission he left to his disciples. They were the ones sent out to bring the guests together. They were going to be the fishers of men and women, the harvesters who would bring the crops and the fruits together.

We too are called to participate in that bringing together.

Missionaries are those among us who went out to other societies to tell them about God's desire to gather all human nations together in one body, under the influence of one Spirit. They are the ones who re-minded us of all that binds humanity together, and also of our cultu-ral, social, and religious differences. They help us to understand how we may complement each other in the different ways we develop and approach our common world.

Today, this task shows dimensions that were never seen before. The whole world is coming together through communication and travel, while at the same time religious, political, racial, and economic conflicts are tearing us apart.

The need for this togetherness is more strongly felt than ever before. We are unable to save ourselves, either individually or com-munally, without it. Jesus' words, "He who does not gather with me scatters," are more significant than ever before. They are not only sig-nificant in a vague and abstract way. It is true of each of us. If we are not willing to gather together, we are scattered, harming our common human fabric.

Interdependency

"You must love your neighbor as yourself." Mark 12:28-34

He was a very old African warrior, a Masai. In his youth he had killed a lion with his bare hands to show his bravery in order to be accepted as an adult. He had also defended his family and homestead in fierce and bloody battles against others whom he considered hardly human.

Then a foreign missionary came into his village. All he ever did was tell the stories of the gospel. Everyone loves stories, the missionary reasoned, and his listeners were quite capable of drawing their own conclusions.

He was right.

When he told the story of the Good Samaritan one evening, the Masai elder spoke up. "If I understand you well, you want to tell us that God made the other people, too?" While he said this, he pointed to some faraway hills, behind which those "others" were living. "It is you who say so," the missionary answered. "If they are God's people, we respect them," the warrior said. "Loving God means loving God's offspring."

Did not Paul write that we should love each other because we are all members of the same body, members of the same divine family? Does not the introduction to the gospel of John say that we are all created in the Son, God's offspring? That we belong together is no longer only a spiritual feeling, but almost a physical reality.

"When I call England, when I get my fax messages from Japan, I really feel part of the world in a way that I certainly didn't ten or twenty years ago," a student in the United States said recently in *The Washington Post*.

Our interdependence is becoming global. We know about the most distant places, we suffer with everyone who suffers. We are becoming more and more the one people of the world. No wonder Jesus stressed that we should love our neighbor as ourselves.

Prayer, Fasting, and Doing Good

"...anyone who humbles himself will be raised up." Luke 18:9-14

In the time of Jesus Jews fasted twice a week—on Monday and Thursday. Whoever wished to fast did so on those two days, though there was no general command for it.

The hypocritical Pharisee who prayed in the temple, "I thank you, God...I fast twice a week," did fast those two days. He thanked God for that. He even did some other, extra things like paying a prescribed temple tax. The people around him might have thought him a good person (the priests who received the extra temple tax were definitely of that opinion). Yet something had gone wrong. The man in question fasted to please God. But why would God be pleased by anyone who is fasting? Didn't that person fast only as a kind of spiritual self-indulgence, so that he would be able to brag about it to himself, and in a way now even to God?

The early Christians did not fast that way, but in another context. Some spiritual authors call it the Big Three: (1) prayer, (2) fasting, and (3) doing good to others. They practiced the Big Three especially when they had to discern the Holy Spirit, when they wanted to find out where God wanted to lead them.

To give you one example from the Acts of the Apostles: before Paul and Barnabas set off on a special mission to bring the good news of Jesus Christ to others, the prophets, teachers, and the whole community fasted and prayed. And "after they had fasted and prayed, they imposed hands on them and sent them off" (Acts 13: 2-3; 14:23).

Fasting should not be done in view of self-righteousness, righteousness in the eyes of others, or even righteousness in the eyes of God. Fasting should be done to clear your body and mind, to take away what stands between you and God in your innermost self.

Journey in Faith

"The man believed what Jesus had said and went on his way home."
John 4:43-54

The official's son was sick. He went to Jesus and asked him to heal his son. Jesus gave him his promise: "Your son will live." He believed Jesus, petitioned Jesus no longer, and started the long journey home. As John writes in his gospel: "The man believed what Jesus had said and started on his way."

For part of the journey he traveled in pure faith and confidence. He had no further proof that anything had happened at home. There was no sign of healing, no news. It was during that time that the healing process of his son began, because while still on his way they came to tell him that his boy was alive.

All of us are on a journey; we are on our way. We have the promise of Jesus, and of the prophets before him, that the whole of humankind will be healed, that there will be wholesomeness, peace, and harmony. It is under the protection of that confidence that we should continue our journey home. It is in that light that we find the courage to give life to children in this world and that we can educate them, sharing our hope with them.

There often seem to be good reasons to give up on the good outcome of our journey. Yet, we believe that Jesus is walking with us toward that goal.

We are not traveling alone with Jesus. We should help each other to continue our journey, not giving up, not asking for special signs, doing whatever we can to help others along the way, and being assured of the final human and divine outcome.

Initiative

"Get up, pick up your sleeping mat and walk around!"
John 5:1-3, 5-16

Jesus must have been participating in the life around him during the thirty years when we hardly hear anything about him. In the evenings he must have sat down with his family, friends, and acquaintances, and talked about the world in which they lived. That talk was not very much different from the talk we are accustomed to hear in our evening hours, though it was in another time, in another country, in another set of difficulties. There must have been complaints about the political, economic, and religious leadership, laments about prices and exploitation, horror stories about injustice, discrimination, and oppression.

We can find all those themes in the things Jesus would say once he appeared on the public scene.

Jesus did what the other talkers and lamenters did not do. He not only complained, he not only asked why others did not do something; he left Nazareth, his sleepy hometown, and took an active part in bringing about change.

He did not wait for others. He took the initiative. He picked himself up and walked.

He asked others to do the same. Don't sit there and just lament. Don't wonder all the time why others, why the leadership is not doing things. Take the initiative. Start yourself. It is what Jesus suggested to the man who complained that he had no one to put him into the pool to be healed when the water was disturbed. "Jesus answered: 'Stand up, take your bed and walk.' The man recovered instantly; he took up his bed, and began to walk."

It might be good to listen once carefully to our own complaints about ourselves, others, working conditions, or whatever—there is indeed no end to our grievances—and decide to take the initiative toward remedying some of them.

Gardener

"My Father still goes on working, and I am at work, too."

John 5:17-30

Jesus not only says that his Father is working, he compares the work God does to that of a farmer or a gardener. Our world started as a garden. It is that garden of God that made human life possible.

Even nowadays the tropical forests are among the richest life systems in the world. They contain millions of plants, animals, insects, and birds. They produce the masses of the oxygen all living beings need.

Tropical forests are intimately bound up with the quality of our air and water: they preserve soil, they moderate climate, they affect water distribution, they break down carbon dioxide. The rain forests are God's most abundant nurseries, supplying the raw material for the plants that feed and heal us.

Even a common medicine like aspirin was originally the product of a tree. Experts agree that there is probably a plant for every human disease.

Yet this life system is being destroyed during our lifetime. An area of the size of England, Scotland, and Wales is being destroyed each year. Obviously this is leading to complete extinction of those life systems. In some countries the day of reckoning has already arrived. God's garden entrusted to us is often in very poor hands indeed.

Alarming thoughts. Thoughts that might lead us to try to do something about it, yet thoughts that may also help us in another way. It may help us to be good gardeners ourselves. It may help us to instill in our family a deep respect for anything that is alive, and for the earth itself, a respect so well developed by some of the best gardeners and farmers in this country, like the Amish people in Pennsylvania and Ohio—a respect that is the reason for their success.

Co-Responsibility

"How can you believe since you look at each other for glory?"
John 5:31-47

It struck the priest for the first time years ago while hearing confessions. The woman on the other side of the screen said: "I confess my responsibility for the drug war in the streets of my city." He was not only struck, he did not understand. Confession had almost always been about individual personal sins and about interpersonal behavior. Much less thought, if any, was given to group behavior. Later on the priest understood the shift. He understood better and better how much of the evil in the world is due to group behavior.

This is not a new idea as far as the Bible is concerned. It is an experience that is brought out so well in the words of Jesus: "How can you believe, since you look to one another for approval?" We approve of things because all of us do them. We look at each other to see that others are doing it, so we can go ahead.

This is true in less important things. We speed on the interstate because everyone is doing it, even though we know that the police do not accept our reasoning. We are dishonest in small things at work because everyone is, and we take it for granted. We are often too lazy to reflect upon what we are doing, just following what others do, who in their turn do what they do because they see us doing it. "How can you believe, since you look to one another for approval," and Jesus adds, "and not to the approval that comes from God?"

We have to come to ourselves; we have to enter into the inner sanctuary of our own conscience. It is true that it is difficult to remain on one's own even in this. We really are all in this together. That is the reason that more and more Christians are beginning to share their faith experiences, forming groups or communities that are standing up in this world with a new sense of responsibility, seeking the approval of God together.

Outlaw

"They wanted to arrest him then...." John 7:1-2, 10, 25-30

It is not impossible that what happened to Jesus could happen today. In fact, it is a story that repeats itself all the time.

Oscar Romero was a bishop who championed the rights of the poor who was shot to death while celebrating the Eucharist. Reverend Martin Luther King, Jr., pleaded for equal rights and he was assassinated.

Any bishop, any priest, any believer who takes the side of justice and peace as Jesus did will be treated as Jesus was. Didn't he say that his followers would be persecuted as he himself was? They wrote him off; they will write off his followers.

Indeed, how can we escape from that wrath of the enemies of God's Kingdom, if we are really and actively faithful to what Pope Paul VI asked us to do:

> For the church it is a question not only of preaching the gospel...but also of affecting and as it were upsetting, through the power of the Gospel, humankind's criteria of judgment, determining values, points of interest, lines of thought, sources of inspiration, and models of life, which are in contrast with the Word of God and the plan of salvation. (*Evangelii Nuntiandi*, 19)

As followers of Jesus, we are engaged in the process he introduced in this world, a non-violent struggle against all that is sinful and evil. Those engaged in that struggle will have to carry the cross that goes with it, a cross that is to be their glory and pride. Oscar Romero and Martin Luther King are not the only ones. There are many others, such as the Maryknoll sisters, the Jesuit fathers and their helpers who were murdered in Central America, but also the people in our own neighborhood, and maybe we ourselves, suffering for the sake of justice.

Let us, too, reach out our hands to Jesus and be ready to walk in his ways together with all those of good will.

The Jesus Prayer

"He is indeed the prophet....he is the Christ." John 7:40-52

It is a temptation to think that piety, virtue, and care are for weaklings. This is a serious error in judgment. It is simply not true. There is a quality in a genuinely virtuous person that fascinates, invites, attracts, and challenges.

Jesus was not a weak and unattractive human being for being virtuous and pious. He brought all his human powers and capacities to fulfillment as the Spirit prompted him. He was fully alive, an admired and loved human being because he was loving, just, courageous, and unpretentious. His spiritual vibrations were immediately felt by all. He changed everyone at the first contact; some loved him intensely, others hated him fiercely.

That is why those poor guards sent to arrest him came back without him. According to the gospel of John they reported to their commanding officer: "There has never been anybody who has spoken like him!" They were completely taken with him.

Our own spiritual leaders sometimes have the same effect. When then Vice President Mondale said good-bye to John Paul II at the airport, he said: "You have unleashed the best and most generous sentiments within us, and given us courage to go forward."

There is an old way to get into contact with the good vibrations that go out from Jesus. It is called the Jesus prayer. It is simple. Just sit down in a relaxed way, get control of your breathing, and say the name "Jesus" slowly while breathing in and breathing out.

It is a gentle way of picking up his wavelength and starting to resonate with him. It is a very effective way of tuning in to his spirit. It is a practice that has changed the life of millions.

One Table

"You do not know me, nor do you know my Father." John 8:12-20

In a university cafeteria in a far-off country a student came from the serving counter with his food tray. People were sitting at every table. There were still a few empty places at them, but he hesitated to take one. But he could not just stand there, so he decided to sit at one of the tables. When he did, he was told that he was not welcome. They told him the places at the table were only for saved Christians, and since he—coming from a non-Christian country—was no Christian, he could not sit with them. When he asked them for their reason, they told him that he did not accept Jesus as his personal Savior as they did.

An exaggerated story? Oh, no. It happens regularly all over the world. And it does not happen only among Christians; other bigoted religionists might do it, too. This attitude, however, would not be acceptable to Jesus. He would repeat what he once said long ago: "You do not know me, nor do you know my Father; if you did know me, you would know my Father as well." Our Father in heaven invites us all to his table.

That is why Jesus reached out beyond himself to all that exists. If we are true to ourselves we should do the same, since we are of his spirit. We should reach out to God, the source of all our being, to all other human beings, and even to the rest of creation. Look around you, wherever you happen to be just now, and embrace in spirit humans, animals, plants, and everything around you, and you are dancing with God!

Universe

"He who sent me is with me, and has not left me to myself."
                                                    John 8:21-30

God is not only the Father of humanity, but of all creation. Jesus did not come to save only the human community. He came to save the world. Paul expressed this best when he wrote: "Through him God chose to reconcile the whole universe to himself, making peace through the shedding of his blood upon the cross—to reconcile all things, whether on earth or in heaven, through him alone" (Colossians 1:20).

We should extend God's embrace not only to the whole of humanity, relating to all human beings as sisters and brothers; we should extend it to the whole of creation. As long as we think that the world is here to be used by human beings, doomed to pass away in the future, pollution and the extinction of animal and plant life do not matter.

No wonder the whole of creation is eagerly waiting for the moment that we will be revealed as the daughters and sons of the Father who created all of us and put us as shepherds and guardians over the rest of creation. It is then that we will do what pleases the Father as Jesus did. It is then that we will be able to pray as he did: "God has not left me to myself, for I always do what pleases him."

A meditation like this one should not remain a mere pious thought. A lot of information is available on what is detrimental to our environment. You can find out how and whether you are contributing to the ozone breakdown, the pollution of the air, and the destruction of your environment.

Let us ask our almighty Father to live the life we were created for, a life that depends on the air we breathe, the things we eat, the water we drink, and the earth we walk on. Let us respect those relations now that they are threatened by our waste and abuse of them.

Truth

"You will learn the truth and the truth will set you free."
John 8:31-42

We are inclined to say what Pilate said to Jesus, when Jesus used the word "truth" as he stood in front of that Roman governor. Pilate cynically asked: "What is truth?"

Jesus did not speak about truth in an abstract way, as Pilate did. His words and deeds explained that truth about us. We find it expressed in our prayers. Listen to this part from the preface in the Mass for Justice in the Roman Missal:

> Father, you have given all peoples one common origin, and your will is to gather them as one family in yourself. Fill the hearts of all with the fire of your love, and the desire to ensure justice for all their brothers and sisters. By sharing the good things you give us, may we secure justice and equality for every human being, an end to all division, and a human society built on love and peace. Amen.

The truth is that we have one common origin. We belong together. The truth is that we form one family.

In 1987 John Paul II wrote an encyclical letter, *On Social Concerns*. He stresses several times in that letter that we belong together and that the goods of creation are not meant for only a few, but meant for all. He explains that it is a shame that we speak with the greatest ease about the First World, the Second World, the Third World, and even about the Fourth World.

The use of those names indicates that we do not live in the truth. They indicate that things are not going well, that our unity is compromised. We live a lie.

Because of this lack of unity we have to arm ourselves against each other. The rich have to protect themselves against the poor. And the poor have to protect themselves against the ever-growing greed of the rich. Only the truth about ourselves can save us.

Holy Shroud

"...in fact my glory is conferred by the Father...." John 8:51-59

The holy shroud in Italy is believed by many to be the linen in which Jesus was buried. For that reason it is considered very sacred.

Splinters of the wood of the cross on which Jesus died are venerated in crosses and reliquaries all over the world. They are considered sanctified by Jesus' touch.

The holy places in Bethlehem and Nazareth, in Jerusalem, and at the Sea of Galilee are visited by thousands of pilgrims because Jesus sanctified those places with his presence.

We restrict our devotion to these special relics and localities. That is a pity, because this whole world is a sanctuary in a way, because Jesus walked with us. He walked on the same earth we are walking on; he breathed the same air we are breathing. The molecules and atoms he was using when eating his food and quenching his thirst are still with us—they are all around us. He sanctified the whole of creation because of his presence.

He would never have been able to exist if there had not been the trees and plants that made human life possible. The whole of the earth was in a way his holy vestment and shroud!

In him all things are united. In him all things come together. John wrote in the beginning of his gospel that all things are created in him, who said of himself (and of us): "My glory is conferred by the Father, by the one of whom you say, 'He is our God.'" This union makes us live in fellowship with the whole of creation, the heavenly and earthly host.

All this is reason for us Christians to love and cherish the earth and to find the divine therein, to develop a respect based on the living unity of all in Christ.

You Are Gods

"Is it not written in your Law: I said you are Gods?" John 10:31-42

Not so long ago, a married couple was visiting one of the husband's friends, who happened to be an important clergyman.

The clergyman never spoke to her. He only addressed the husband; he spoke not a single direct word to her. Anything he wanted to tell her was directed to the husband. She considered his behavior rude and offensive. By not speaking to her, the clergyman showed her that she was a mere nothing in his eyes.

It is the same story you hear from people who are disabled and sitting in a wheelchair, helped by a friend or parent. It happens that the person who is helping them is addressed, not they.

Jesus says all those who are addressed by God should be called gods! "It is those to whom God's words came who are called gods" (John 10:35). We should appreciate ourselves as daughters and sons of God, because we are all addressed by him. "Holy Scripture used the word 'gods' of those to whom the word of God was directed" (John 10:34).

How could anyone look down upon people whom the Bible considers are daughters and sons of God? How could anyone not think them worthy to be addressed by us, if God considers them worthy of being so addressed?

That is easy to say but not easy to do. Just like all the words of Jesus, they are often not difficult to understand, but hard to do.

At the moment a wave of new immigrants is trying to find a place for themselves in North America. Many of them are Hispanic Catholics who sometimes complain that they are not well received in some of our settled Catholic communities, that people look down on them. It is as if they are not taken seriously as people as much willed and loved by God as the others who are having difficulties receiving them. Jesus uses the word "gods" for all those God addressed; we are God's own daughters and sons, all of us!

Annunciation

"Rejoice, you who enjoy God's favor." Luke 1:26-38

The angel came as a great surprise, and as no surprise at all. Mary had always been waiting for an intervention by God. She had been expecting someone like that all her praying life. She was aware with a keen perception of the sinfulness of the world around her, and how badly it needed a new life to be born in it, as we hear later when she sings her Magnificat. She sang about the gap between the rulers and the ruled, the rich and the poor, all kinds of other sinful human relations and the final power of death.

Yet, the angel came as a surprise. She felt "deeply disturbed." That Jesus (a name that means "savior") was going to be born was not surprising. That he was going to be born from her must have been. But calling her son Jesus was no problem. It was an answer to her prayers, and the prayers of all the just who ever lived on this earth.

In a way we are still in Mary's situation. The work of Jesus is not yet finished. We are still divided against each other. We should still be on the lookout for a further birth of Jesus into this world!

Mary definitely would like us to follow her example more closely. Meister Eckhart said it in the way only a mystic can put it: "What would the birth of Jesus mean to me, if I wouldn't myself give birth to him."

Holy Mary, Mother of God, pray for us sinners, now and at the hour of our death!

Scent and Perfume

"...the house was filled with the scent of the ointment." John 12:1-11

Mary must have loved Jesus very much. Love often makes lovers intuit each other's feelings. When Mary anoints Jesus' feet, Jesus sees this as a gesture having something to do with his death. Mary comes to embalm him before he dies. She comes to tell him that she loves him, that she knows that he is going to give himself up to death for the life of the world, but that she does not believe in the finality of his death.

Her gesture makes her different from all the others. They could have known what he was going to do. They, too, could have known that he was not only going to risk his life, but that he was even going to give it. He had told them often enough. They do not believe. They avert their gaze. They do not pay attention. Mary does.

There must have been an intimate understanding between the two, while she anointed his feet and he spoke about his burial. When Judas protested, "Could not this perfume have been sold for three hundred denarii, and the money given to the poor?" Jesus said, "Leave her alone; it was the intention that she should save this perfume for the day of my burial!"

She was affirming him and he was affirming her. He, intent on giving himself up for her and for all of us, and she, sealing her willingness to be with him until the end that would be a new beginning. She was not embalming a friend who was going to remain dead; she was anointing one who was going to rise from death. She understood. Maybe she would not have been able to say it in so many words. That is why she came with her oils and scent, to express it in deeds. He understood her intent. No wonder he appeared to her first after his resurrection!

Betrayal

"As soon as Judas had taken the piece of bread he went out. It was night."   *John 13:21-33, 36-38*

The darkness of night falls over us after each betrayal. It is when we take our own piece of bread and leave others behind, thinking only about how to get more out of our situation. Did you ever leave others behind in that dark of night?

People built their lives on your promises and you never kept them. They waited for your return, and you never came back.

Were you ever left in the dark by others who betrayed you?

This kind of betrayal is not something we only do as individuals toward the persons around us. It is something we often do with others as a community.

We rarely see how all is bound together. We fail to see ourselves and others as part of the universe, as part of all that is created in Christ. We look too seldom at long-range efforts and pursuits. We are out for a quick gain. We squander energy, we cut down trees irresponsibly, we consume irreplaceable goods, we let whole species of animals and plants just die off.

We, the current dwellers of this earth, are impoverishing and betraying our offspring. We took our piece of bread, and so much more than that, and we often thought of nothing else.

Night will be falling over the whole of the earth. It will be falling over all of us if we don't change our ways.

Dying

"When evening came he was at table with the twelve."
Matthew 26:20-25

He was sitting at table, eating with those who were going to betray him. He even went so far as to wash their feet. This is Jesus' way of handling opposition, violence, and betrayal. Not only Judas would run away from his arrest and death. But in the end only John would return, brought by Jesus' mother, Mary.

Jesus took the road of non-violence, of consistent love, a road taken by the best of his followers even in our days. Listen to what one of them, Martin Luther King, Jr., said:

> To our most bitter opponents we say: "We shall match your capacity to inflict suffering by our capacity to endure suffering. We shall meet your physical force with soul force. Do to us what you will, and we shall continue to love you. Throw us in jail, and we shall still love you. Bomb our homes and threaten our children, and we shall still love you. Send your hooded perpetrators of violence into our communities at the midnight hour and beat us and leave us half dead, and we shall still love you. But be ye assured that we will wear you down by our capacity to suffer. One day we shall win our freedom, but not only for ourselves. We shall appeal to your heart and conscience that we shall win you in the process, and our victory will be a double victory."

Another great mind and heart in this country, Father John L. McKenzie, summed it up in his own poignant way. "If Jesus taught us anything it was how to die, not how to kill!" These are words worth reflecting upon in the violence and harshness of our days.

Feet Washing

"...you must wash each other's feet." John 13:1-15

He took a bowl, a jug full of water, and a towel. He went down on his hands and knees and washed their feet, not even looking up. He washed all of them, one by one, lovingly and thoroughly.

He washed the feet of all of us, believers and unbelievers, old and young, saints and sinners, pimps and women of the street, popes and bishops, rulers and ruled, rich and poor, filled and hungry, dressed and naked. He washed and washed, after having looked with eyes full of love and tenderness at the faces of those whose feet he was washing.

Mary had washed his feet. He had said that her gesture of love would never be forgotten. Now he was doing to us what she did to him.

When you lovingly wash the feet of someone else, you withdraw your attention from self and focus it on the one whose feet you wash.

That is what he did to all of them.

He never intended to stop, because he said: "Do you understand what I have done to you? You call me Master and Lord, and rightly, so I am. If I, then, the Lord and Master, have washed your feet, you should wash each other's feet" (John 13:13-15).

He gave us a model of what we should do to each other, washing each other's feet and, after that, breaking our bread, sharing it all over the world, all over humanity, until he is with us again in the Kingdom to come.

There are Christian communities that pay as much attention to the washing of the feet as to the celebration of the Eucharist. It is a pity that we don't all do that. Can you imagine the power of that loving gesture extended to all of us? Just think of the powerful in this world washing each other's feet before one of their important meetings, after having washed the feet of the orphans, widows, and the destitute in their own countries!

Foolishness of the Cross

"Put your sword back in your scabbard." John 18:1-19, 42

They killed Jesus. That killing was their last resort against him, just as it remains the means of those who are willing to use weapons against others. That same willingness is the taproot of violence in our society today.

It sounds like a terrible indictment, but our intent, or at least our consent, to use nuclear weapons or even to wage war against others makes the violence in our streets and parks, trains and buses, comprehensible and defensible.

If you have children and buy a gun, even to defend yourself, your children will think that violence is the way to live.

Standing before Pilate, Jesus told him that he could have used violence, that he could have resorted to legions and legions of angels, to the whole of the heavenly host and their precision armaments, but that he chose not to do so. He continued choosing life, even in that ultimate moment of distress.

The cycle of violence can only be broken the way he did it, by simply refusing to enter it.

The sun darkened. The curtains in the temple ripped apart. The earth shook in vehemence when it received his body. When they left him hanging on the cross, allowing some of his friends to take him off and bury him, his opponents must have thought they had made a fool of him. When he rose from the death they had inflicted upon him, he proved them wrong. He was killed, but the cycle of violence was broken. Foolishness? Foolishness in the eyes of the wise of this world, the foolishness of the cross.

Easter

*"And very early in the morning on the first day of the week they went
to the tomb when the sun had risen."*   Mark 16:1-8

Mark tells us how, very early in the morning, as soon as the Sabbath
time was over and they could leave their homes, Mary of Magdala,
Mary the mother of James, and Salome came to the tomb to bury him
properly. They had bought some oils, herbs, and spices, hoping to
wash, clean, and anoint the body. Simple acts of kindness; it was all
they could do. Jesus had been taken down from the cross in haste and,
because of the Sabbath, there had been no time to do anything but put
him in the tomb.

It was a risky mission. They had heard about the soldiers at the
graveside.

In a way they had not even taken sufficient precautions. They wondered who was going to push the stone away from the tomb entrance.
At their arrival they found the tomb open with a young man in a
white robe telling them that Jesus had risen and that they should go to
meet him.

The person in the white garment is an indication of the new life giv-
en at Easter. Aren't all those who are baptized dressed in white to indicate their new risen life? At first the women were afraid. They ran
away and did not tell anyone what they had discovered. It was all too
new for them. It came as a shock. Once they understood its meaning,
they experienced a resurgence of their faith and joy. It renewed their
lives. As Jesus broke through the walls of the tomb, they broke
through the limits of their old lives.

Jesus' risen life opened a whole new world to them. No wonder
their first reaction was one of alarm. Yet, their fear passed and turned
into joy, a joy that changed their lives. Everything changed: their
prayer, their relationships, their whole lives.

That is how it all started!

Acts of the Apostles

"The apostles continued to testify to the resurrection of the Lord."
Acts 4:33

The Acts of the Apostles describes what happened to the followers of Jesus, those who had accepted his spirit in their lives. It gives an account of the enormous joy and hope unleashed in them. "With great power the apostles continued to witness to the resurrection of the Lord" (Acts 4:33).

The four gospels describe the life of Jesus. They contain Jesus' life as his will, the last will of someone not dead but alive, and we are its executors.

The letters from Paul, Peter, James, John, and the author of the Letter to the Hebrews explain how we should live that life. Acts tells us how Christians lived it. It is a story that has not ended. It continues all through history to our day. The life of the church, the life of the communities we belong to, and our own lives are part of that story—all a continuation of what began when Jesus' spirit began to manifest itself in the lives of an ever-growing multitude of people.

What began in Acts is the story of the risen life we publicly embrace at the moment of our baptism and openly witness as being ours when we renew our baptismal vows at Easter.

Acts not only reveals how the risen life of Jesus affected the apostles; it describes what the new life did to scores of individuals, women and men, old and young, rich and poor; it describes how whole communities, sometimes hundreds and even thousands of people, were touched by the Spirit. It describes a life, a movement, that has never stopped but has reached through the centuries to our time.

What is described in Acts is, in a way, our acts. We are bound by the same last will of Jesus. We live the same risen life as the first Christians did. We do this in another time, in a different world. We have to do in our world *now* what the first Christians did *then*.

Resident Alien

"Save yourselves from this perverse generation."
                                      Acts 2:14, 22-23, 36-41

The first thing that struck the people in Jerusalem was the joy of those who experienced the life and spirit of Jesus in them. They thought that joy unrealistic, utopian, and crazy. Sometimes they even thought that the Christians' behavior was due to drugs. "They have been drinking," they said to each other. "This is not for real, they are nuts!" It was what his critics (and his own family!) had been saying of Jesus. Those first Christians were laughed at and considered naïve.

Today, when we feel embarrassed to be identified as Christians, or when we hesitate to confess ourselves as such, we ourselves can feel victim of that same kind of sneering.

When we do confess to be followers of Jesus Christ, we might feel like "aliens" in the world as it is now. In a way, we should! Who can really feel at home in the world as it is?

Not everyone thought that Jesus' disciples were out of their minds. Many were dissatisfied with the way they were living their lives. Others were very upset about the situation of the world in which they lived. For too long they had been on the lookout for a change, for something new. When they saw the joy of those first Christians they came to them and asked: "What must we do? Can we join? We would like to put aside the lives we have been living."

Their question may put our doubts to rest. Yes, it is a good thing to be a kind of "resident alien" in the world as it is. If no one felt themselves alien and uncomfortable with the world, there would be no desire or hope of changing it. We must turn things and ourselves around, change the world, and live the gift of our new life.

Miracles

"They were all astonished and perplexed at what happened...."
Acts 3:1-10

Equipped with their new risen life, Peter and John met a cripple who asked them for some money. They did not have any. They healed him instead. Peter said: "I will give you what I have; in the name of Jesus Christ, walk!" A miracle! Peter's first one.

Newly baptized African Christians wonder about those miracles. I knew that almost every talk I gave to newly baptized Christians, especially when they were young, would end with the same question: "Why can't we work those miracles? Why aren't there any miracles any more in the church?"

What was the miracle in the case of Peter, John, and the lame man? His healing, of course. But that was not all. It was not the main thing that happened. It was a miracle that Peter and John paid attention to the lame man at the gate and stopped to help him. Without their new life from Jesus neither Peter nor John might even have noticed the lame man at the gate. At the instant they did, they gave a sign of being equipped with Jesus' spirit. The healing followed from that. They paid attention to the man as Jesus would have done. Jesus lived in them.

This kind of moral miracle has never disappeared from the Christian community. Every time we open our hearts, every time we reach out to someone in the name of Jesus, his spirit is at work in us. These miracles fill the lives of our Christian communities. These miracles still happen, day after day.

In Jesus' Name

"...it is the name of Jesus which, through faith in him, has brought back the strength of this man...."   Acts 3:11-26

We often hear that we should pray. The impression is frequently given that this means we have to look for a chapel or church, a book or a hymn. There are many forms of prayer. There is the prayer "within" ourselves. It is like an attitude, an attention, a constant awareness, something that resembles being in love. Everything around you reminds you of the one you love. Everything you see, hear, smell, feel, or touch makes her or his name sing in your heart. She or he is your song!

It is this constant, loving awareness of the new relationship to Jesus that makes the apostles and the first Christians live and act the way they do. Their first thought, their first reaction was Jesus' thought and Jesus' reaction to what he saw in the world. That is why the lame man at the beautiful gate immediately reminded Peter of what Jesus would have done to him. So he said: "In the name of Jesus Christ of Nazareth, get up and walk!"

Later on Peter reiterated: "It is the name of Jesus which, through faith in it, has brought back the strength of this man you see here (healed)." If only we carried Jesus' name in our hearts as Peter did!

Mother Teresa

"If you are questioning us today about an act of kindness...."
Acts 4:1-12

The whole world knows Mother Teresa. She and her sisters specialize in working among the poorest of the poor. When you see her in one of the many videotapes made of those activities, you wonder how they do it.

You must wonder, too, about less dramatic, but no less heroic situations. A husband who has been taking care of a disabled wife for years; a son nursing an ailing mother; the mother of a seriously disabled child accompanying it on its journey day and night; a professional faithful in his or her service.

We are surrounded by miracles that go against the grain of a greedy and self-indulgent world. By what power do they work those miracles?

They often ask Mother Teresa the same question. She gives the same answer Peter and John gave when they were asked in court how they worked miracles. "It is the Lord," Mother Teresa says, "who fills us with God's love!" It is the power of the risen life of Jesus given to all of us. It is a force that is tapped when we contact a needy world in faith, a power that is present not only in those who believe in Jesus' name. It is not something exclusive. The love of God is inclusive. God's drawing love keeps us all together. It is a love manifested in the love Jesus had for all, especially those who needed that love most.

Lay Women and Men

"They were astonished at the fearlessness shown by Peter and John considering they were uneducated lay men."   Acts 4:13-21

It was not only the new life of the first Christians that amazed the leaders in Jerusalem; the self-assurance of the Christians was another reason for their consternation. They had been surprised in the case of Jesus, because he came from Nazareth, an insignificant town. Now they were surprised by his followers, whom they called uneducated lay women and men. Luke puts it in a striking way: "The rulers, elders, and scribes were astonished at the assurance shown by Peter and John, considering they were uneducated lay women and men." God was not supposed to act like that. It would upset their whole order of things. This type of lay theology did not fit in with their schemes. No wonder Peter asked them to believe what they saw and heard.

Later when the community grew Peter would have the same difficulty. Often he could not believe his own eyes and ears. How was it possible that others, even aliens, were under the influence of God's Spirit?

Bishops sometimes have the same difficulty with "their" pastors, pastors with "their" faithful, and parents with their children. It is difficult enough to accept the spirit of Jesus alive in your own heart and mind. It is even more difficult to accept that presence in those you live with.

God's Spirit does not dwell in a precious few. God's Spirit dwells in all of us.

Small Community

"The whole group of believers was united, heart and soul...."
Acts 4:32-35

When the risen Jesus appears to the apostles, he meets them as a community. When Thomas happens to be absent, he has to wait until the next time Jesus appears to their community.

The new risen life brings believers together. Christians have always known and felt this. Christians first met to worship in their own houses, then in market halls; finally they built special places in which to worship and to break Jesus' bread and share his wine. These communities formed a kind of oasis for a new style of human life in the world. Believers felt like new immigrants in an old world. They started to use the word "parish" for their communities. ("Parish" comes from a Greek word meaning something like resident alien.)

Parish remains the name we give to our worshiping communities, communities that not only organize liturgical celebrations but provide service in so many other ways.

At the moment, something is happening to parish communities the world over. It is happening in countries where the church is young, as in Africa, but also in countries where Christianity is much older. Christians are rethinking their structure, forming smaller communities. People come together to pray, to reflect on the gospels, and to try to make their risen life in the Spirit a more concrete reality in their lives. They tell each other their experiences, their spiritual stories; they assist one another in their outreach to those who need them. They are united heart and head in Jesus Christ, just as in the days described in Acts.

Grace

"...help your servants to proclaim your message with fearlessness...."
Acts 4:23-31

"On their release Peter and John went back to their own people. [Together with them] they raised their voices in prayer."

Dismissed from court, Peter and John hurried back to their community, to their support group. They began to pray, not as you would expect, that they would be spared from further persecution or difficulties, but for courage and grace.

They prayed to be able to heal the world and spread the good news. They prayed for the spirit of Jesus. They prayed to be able to witness to him with boldness.

It is grace Christian communities need, because our world needs the message of Jesus so badly. Many priests change a prayer in the canon of the Mass just after the community has prayed the Our Father together. The text reads "deliver us from all anxiety," but they add a word to that "anxiety" and pray: "free us from all *needless* anxiety." There is a certain type of anxiety that is absolutely necessary—the anxiety that helps us to spread God's truth about humanity and this world. Pope John Paul II, in his encyclical on our mission, wrote that the world has a right to hear the good news from us.

We have to pray for the grace needed to advance that news. And then will happen to us what happened to them: "When they ended their prayer, the building where they were assembled rocked, and all were filled with the Holy Spirit and spoke God's word with boldness" (Acts 4:31).

Communality

"...everything they owned was held in common...." Acts 4:32-37

In those early days being one in spirit and heart was not only a question of praying together. They assisted one another materially. We might be struck by the radicalism of their approach: "The whole company of believers was united heart and soul. No one claimed any of the possessions as his or her own; everything was held in common....there was no needy person among them" (Acts 4:32, 34).

Wondering about the way they organized themselves, we might overlook the point Luke is making. His point is not so much *how* they organized their communal welfare, but the fact that they *felt* socially responsible for one another. In this way they set a model for all communities to come.

Luke describes different ways that they organized this mutual assistance. In one instance they shared all they owned in common. In another case they sold everything they had and then distributed the proceeds according to their needs.

Luke does not describe one set way for all time to come; there are many ways of organizing social responsibility. But they did organize it! In a recent essay Larry Woiwode made a remark regarding our Christian mutual responsibility that might make us reflect: "Surely it's at least partly the failure of the contemporary church to provide for its own that has caused its members to turn to the government as benefactor."

Witnessing

"...tell the people all about this new life." Acts 5:17-26

The angel who opened the prison doors for the jailed apostles told them: "Go and stand in the temple and tell the people all about this new life" (Acts 5:20).

No easy task, neither in their world or in ours. Just pay attention to what it sometimes costs others to be faithful to the risen life. Trace it in the lives of those dear to you, in the struggle of your own kith and kin; track it in the life of your parish; trace it in your own life also!

The risen life, or the life of the spirit, has to enhance and vivify our whole human existence. It should be an activating force in all we do and decide not to do.

Did you ever sit down to consider how your professional activities should exemplify this presence of the spirit of Jesus in you?

Here is an example. In a small town, the mayor, trying to restore the discipline and behavior of his police force, asked some experts to identify the good and efficient troopers. His idea was then to identify what made these officers so excellent, and to start a training course for the whole force. In a scheduled interview he asked one of the officers selected what made him think that he was so efficient and well appreciated.

The officer responded that he tried to be a police officer in the spirit of Jesus Christ.

Do you ever relate your profession to the risen life of Jesus in you? Consider discussing this with some of your colleagues or friends.

Identity

"We are witnesses to this, we and the Holy Spirit..." Acts 5:27-33

The conversation at a party turned to religion. Many gave their opinion on a whole series of contemporary issues. One person kept silent. Then one of the guests asked him: "By the way, what are you?" In the context it was clear that he was asked what religion he was affiliated with. He said: "Oh, I happen to be a Christian!" You could tell by the way he said it that either he did not take his religious conviction seriously, or he did not want to admit it if he did.

How different from those Christians in Acts! They had no difficulty in describing or defining themselves; they had no identity problems. They would say things like: "We are witnesses to all this, we and the Holy Spirit whom God has given to those who listen" (Acts 5:31).

They did not just "happen to be" Christians. They *were* Christians, by conscious choice and commitment. They knew why they were. They had opened their hearts and minds to the presence of the spirit of Jesus.

They not only witnessed to Jesus by professing what had happened to him; they witnessed to Jesus by living as he lived. They lived in a way that attracted many others.

Family Prayer

"Every day they went on ceaselessly teaching and proclaiming the good news of Jesus Christ, both in the temple and in private houses."
Acts 5:34-42

The new communities met in private homes. Only once in the whole book of Acts is a hall hired, and that was because they could not find a house that was large enough. They hired the lecture hall of a man called Tyrannus (Acts 19:9).

The meeting of a small group in someone's home was very different from a meeting in a large church building. It must have been very different from the ceremonies in the synagogues and temples they were accustomed to.

Assembling in homes must have given their meetings a special flavor, an informal, homey climate, a more realistic mixture of women and men, and of old and young.

No wonder so many of us are trying it again. We invite a priest to celebrate with a group of families in a private home. It is quite different sharing Jesus' bread with others at your own table in your own dining room or kitchen.

In other cases a family will come together and celebrate the breaking of the bread and the sharing of a drink in an *agape* celebration before or after their common meal, with one of the family members—it could be the youngest, it could be the oldest, it could be anyone—presiding.

Pope John Paul II often speaks about the family as an *ecclesiola*, a small church, a group of people called together by God as one family, sharing together the gift of life and love. Families are the smallest units, living cells in the church, the body of Jesus Christ. They are the places where the life of the Spirit begins its interaction with our world.

Soup Kitchen

"...the Hellenists made a complaint against the Hebrews; in the daily distribution their own widows were being overlooked...." Acts 6:1-7

The first communities would not be much of an example to us if they hadn't had their problems. One problem was the distribution of food to the widows of the community. They started what we would call a soup kitchen. Followers of Jesus have always been organizing them, and they are still doing so. The soup kitchens of our Christian organizations go far back in Christian history, down to those first days.

Parishes that do not organize soup kitchens as such will organize their food care for the poor in other ways. Hardly any parish worth its salt is without that outreach. They organize "loaves and fishes" Sundays when food and money are collected to feed those who are hungry.

The name "loaves and fishes" explains at the same time where the dynamic to do this comes from. It comes from Jesus. He began this process by feeding the hungry around him and by identifying with them, telling us that even a cup of water given to someone who needs it will be considered by him as given to himself.

The difficulty that crept in was discrimination. "The Hellenists made a complaint against the Hebrews: In the daily distribution their own widows were overlooked." The Hebrew widows got the best of the food, while the Greek widows got the leftovers.

This is an issue that often hits at the very heart of our communities today. How does your parish receive strangers, especially if they are poor immigrant refugees who don't speak our language? Is your Christian family community ready to welcome them as warmly as they welcome others?

They appointed Stephen as director to settle this intolerable discrimination. They chose him because he was full of the Holy Spirit. It led to his death!

Unshaken

"...for with him at my right hand nothing can shake me...."
Acts 2:14, 22-28

After studying at one of the best theological schools in the country, a priest chose to minister to a poor rural community somewhere in the Andes mountains. After some years there he returned for a well-deserved leave. His former school invited him to speak to the students and the faculty about his experiences.

He was grateful for all he had learned. "Yet," he said, "I would like to make one observation. The theology I learned here was based on the resurrection. And rightly so, but that theology was of little help to the people I was with. They had trouble identifying with the risen Lord. They suffered so much that they preferred to identify with the suffering Jesus. This was most obvious during the Holy Week celebrations. They came in great numbers to the Good Friday celebration, while there was less interest in the Easter service. On Good Friday many came with a ball of cotton wool soaked in olive oil, which they used to 'cleanse' Jesus' wounds on the cross. Some even swallowed the cotton afterwards."

He suggested in a friendly way that the school should pay more attention to the reality of human suffering in the Christian (and all other) communities of this world.

This story reminded me of what a Polish woman once told me. She showed me a painting of Jesus sitting alone on a rock after his scourging. Then she related how poor farmers coming home from their hard labor in the fields would sit in front of that picture and contemplate it.

In those Christian communities in the Andes and Poland, and all over our suffering world, Jesus remains with people at their right hand, just as God remained with Jesus. "I saw the Lord before me always, for with him at my right hand nothing can shake me" (Acts 2:25). Always.

Peacemaker Stephen

"You are always resisting the Holy Spirit, just like your ancestors used to do."   *Acts 6:8-15; 7:51-8:1*

Stephen did what he was asked to do. He stopped the discrimination against the Greek widows. A great thing to do. A miracle! Stephen worked great miracles, indeed.

We are often impressed by physical miracles. When we speak about miracles, we frequently think about healed and restored organs and limbs. We often overlook moral miracles, such as conversion, reconciliation, and making peace. Stephen's task was to work such a moral miracle, to bring people together, to overcome racial strife.

It is a miracle we need in our midst: bringing each other together, breaking ethnic barriers, undoing racism, forming a world where all feel at home with God and each other, where we are all sisters and brothers who are friends.

Some people did not like what Stephen did, even some members of his community. They betrayed him. People were paid to give false witness against him. He was arrested.

An old story. The story of Jesus himself. Isn't it a story we all know from the world in which we live?

Though Stephen might have escaped his persecutors, he would not accommodate them. He had been asked to end the discrimination and to bring people together in the name of Jesus. He would not change his course or give in to their ways. Doing so would mean "resisting the Holy Spirit." That is what he himself accuses his accusers of. They resisted the Holy Spirit.

When he accused them of this, they must have known that he was right, otherwise they would not have become so angry. That is why they stoned Stephen, our first martyr.

Lay Apostles

"Once they had scattered, they went from place to place preaching the good news." *Acts 8:1-8, 26-40*

People who move because of their employment sometimes end up in a spot where they live miles and miles away from a church, where there is no church in the neighborhood. This situation can be a blessing in disguise. From the beginning it has been the way the Christian communities spread. When a great persecution broke out against the church at Jerusalem after the execution of Stephen, all except the apostles were scattered over the countryside of Judaea and Samaria. "Those who were scattered preached the word wherever they went" (Acts 8:4).

It seems a reversal of roles—the apostles at home and the others in the mission field, but it happens all the time. Many churches started in a similar way. Some people of the same denomination came together and began to worship in a home, a coffee house, or some other place. Preaching the Word takes place in our everyday life at home.

It happens in Africa. The adults I have baptized heard the Word from others who witnessed Jesus. When they came to ask for baptism, it was because someone had preached the Word by the way he or she lived. Have you ever preached the Word that way?

It can happen at the roadside, in a plane, in a train. It happened just that way to that Ethiopian Minister of Finance two thousand years ago who was in his chariot reading a prophecy from Isaiah that referred to Jesus: "He was led like a sheep to the slaughter, like a lamb that is dumb before the shearer; he does not open his mouth." He wondered what it was all about and complained, "How can I understand unless someone explains it to me?"

How many people pass us every day who have never received a relevant explanation of God's Word? I don't mean the self-serving Bible pushing of a fanatic out of touch with the reality of our world; I mean the good news of the risen life as it should be lived in this world.

[111]

Heart of Jesus

"Saul, Saul, why are you persecuting me?" Acts 9:1-20

We all know the pure drama of the story of Saul's conversion.

> Saul, still breathing murderous threats against the Lord's disciples, went to the High Priest and applied for letters to the synagogues at Damascus authorizing him to arrest any followers of the new Way whom he found, men or women, and bring them to Jerusalem. While he was still on the road, suddenly a light from the sky flashed all around him. He fell to the ground and heard a voice saying: "Saul, Saul, why are you persecuting me?" "Tell me, Lord," he said, "who you are." The voice answered, "I am Jesus, whom you are persecuting" (Acts 9:1-5).

So far as Saul was concerned, Jesus was dead. When he heard that voice he came to realize the life-bond that exists between Jesus and those who follow his new Way.

It was the moment of his transformation. His later reflections on Jesus and his Way are all based on this first experience. It was there in the dust of the road, blinded by the brilliance of the light that struck him, that he realized how Jesus identifies with his followers, with us, with you! It was a lesson he would never forget. In one of his letters he does not even hesitate to tell those he addresses that he loves them with the love of Jesus: "I long after all of you with the deep yearning of Christ Jesus himself" (Philippians 1:8).

He loved with the heart of Jesus. We are in the same situation as Paul. We should do to Jesus what Jesus did to us. He identifies himself with each of us. You should identify yourself with him, as Paul did.

Voluntarism

"Tabitha...never tired of doing good or giving to those in need."
Acts 9:31-42

Tabitha (Dorcas in Greek; both names mean "gazelle") offers a different example of witnessing to the life of Jesus. Tabitha never tired of doing good and helping the poor. She collected robes and other clothing from those better off and repaired or remade them, giving them to impoverished widows.

It is a type of witnessing that has carried over to us from those earliest days. You find people like Tabitha in Christian communities all over the world. They work as volunteers of the Saint Vincent de Paul Society, in thrift shops, and in YMCA centers.

It is also instructive to read the details in Luke's story that show how much the community members loved each other. Tabitha's friends, who had heard that Peter was near by, sent for him when she died. To persuade Peter to do something about her death, "he was taken up to her room and all the widows came and stood around him in tears showing him the shirts and the coats that Dorcas used to make while she was with them" (Acts 9:39). Peter, moved by this demonstration of love, asked them all to leave the room, and brought her back to life.

Acts is full of details like these about people like you and me. In Luke's descriptions, giving witness to Jesus takes as many forms as there are followers of the Way.

His love is woven in the tapestry of everyone's life and profession, and all professions and occupations offer many occasions to do this. Whether you are a hairdresser or a doctor, a nurse or a cab driver, a homemaker or a postal worker, a lawyer or a salesperson, your kindness will lighten the burden of living in this world, just as the life of Jesus and his sister Tabitha did.

Jesus' Presence

"...you must know that it is in the name of Jesus Christ the Nazarene, by this name and no other...."   Acts 4:8-12

In Africa, I once ran out of gas in the middle of nowhere. After a long walk my friend and I came upon a small house with a rickety car in front of it. We asked for help. After serving a cup of tea, our African host then collected some cans and drove us about thirty miles to a gas station. He then drove us back to our car, helped us to pour the gas into the tank, and did not want anything in return. We asked him why he was so kind to strangers. His answer: "If you are asking me for a reason or motive for this act of kindness, I am a Christian."

We may have done all kinds of deep, searching studies on the mysteries of salvation, redemption, and incarnation, but, as Acts shows us, what is ultimately worthwhile all comes down to our acts of kindness.

Kindness is not a difficult issue. Everyone knows what you mean when you talk about kindness; there is no mystery about it.

That is why Peter says so perfectly to the authorities who question him about why he healed the crippled man at the beautiful gate: "If you are questioning us today about our kindness, it is by the name of Jesus Christ." It was in the presence of Jesus that something had happened to him. He had changed, because he "had been with Jesus" (Acts 4:13). Jesus' kindness had become his kindness. It was the same answer my friend gave me in a remote part of Africa! The presence of Jesus had done something to him, too.

He and Peter not only gave a touching explanation of why they did what they did, they also explained why Jesus did what he did for us. It was his kindness.

Ecumenism

"...who was I to stand in God's way?" Acts 11:1-18

Jealousy is a terrible thing. It harmed the relationship among the disciples of Jesus while he was with them. They would fight over who had the first place, over whom he liked most. And they could not stand that others, who did not belong to their group, used Jesus' name.

In the first Christian communities, some people were jealous and possessive of the gifts and the Spirit they themselves had received.

James, the brother of Jesus, who became the elder of the Jerusalem community, practically wanted to restrict the circle of followers to the family and neighbors and friends of Jesus. Peter had a hard time understanding that foreigners—even Romans—were favored in the same way he was. He needed much time and several divine interventions before he admitted that God gave them the same gift as God gave him. This reluctance to accept the fact that others possess the same gifts from God that we have is a difficulty we may still carry with us.

Possessiveness and exclusivity are temptations every group that forms itself around Jesus has to overcome. If they do not, they divide the church into the competing and self-praising cliques that Paul fought in the early church. In our contemporary church they have led to polarizations that harm our wholeness. The different gifts we receive are only charisms when they complement each other in view of the growth and development of all of us. It is no help to place yourself, or the group you belong to, apart from all the others. A "holier than you" attitude shows the arrogance Peter overcame when he said: "So if God gave them the same gift as God gave us who believed in the Lord Jesus Christ, who was I to think I could stand in God's way?" Overcoming our possessiveness will help us to be ecumenical in our approach to others.

Nicknames

"It was at Antioch that the disciples were first called 'Christians.'"
Acts 11:19-26

At first, Christians did not call themselves "Christians." Others began to do that. "It was at Antioch that the disciples first got the name of Christians" (Acts 11:26). It was probably a nickname, meaning "Christ followers." Christians soon began to use the name for themselves, along with the name they used earlier to identify themselves: "followers of the Way."

After they adopted their new name it took on a new meaning for them. Christian was the name given to those belonging to "the household of Jesus." It still has that meaning.

They were great in using nicknames. Joseph, whose name was put forward to replace Judas Iscariot, was known as Barsabbas, meaning "the one who encourages." He even had a third name, Justus, or "the just one" (Acts 1:23). Those nicknames expressed neither rank nor function; they signified a gift, or, to say it more technically, a charism.

In some communities today such nicknames are used in a similar way. Do we recognize and encourage these charisms? In a gentle way it gives a person a role and describes services this person renders.

What nicknames would you give the community members you live and work with? What nickname would they give you, besides the name Christian?

Lord-Our-Integrity

"It is like a man traveling abroad: he has gone from his home, and left his servants in charge...."   Mark 13:33-37

In Mark's gospel, Jesus tells us the parable of a man traveling abroad. He has gone from home, leaving his servants in charge, each with his own task. He tells his doorkeeper to keep awake so as not to be asleep at his return, a return that might be at any time—evening, midnight, cockcrow, dawn!

Mark uses those time indicators again in the chapter that follows this parable, the story about Jesus' betrayal in the evening in the Garden of Gethsemane, when the disciples fall asleep; at midnight when they run away; and at cockcrow, at dawn, when Peter disowns him.

Yet, the parable is not only about that betrayal. Jesus makes that clear when he says: "And what I say to you I say to all: Stay awake!" It is about all the times that we leave him alone. It is not only a matter of staying awake and praying with him in the garden, either. It is a question of being involved with him in the task he set himself in this world, the fulfillment of God's promise, the establishment of the reign of God.

The parable tells us how the master left each of his servants with a mission to be accomplished. He left each one with his own task. He expects them to be at work, establishing what Isaiah calls the building of a new city that will practice honesty and integrity, and that will be called "The Lord-Our-Integrity" (Jeremiah 33:16).

Beginning

"The beginning of the gospel about Jesus Christ, the Son of God."
Mark 1:1-8

When you open the gospel of Mark, you find at the top of the page "The Gospel According to Mark," or simply "Mark." It is followed by a paragraph title added by the editors, like "John the Baptist and Jesus," or "John the Baptist Prepares the Way." Finally you get Mark's first sentence: "The beginning of the gospel of Jesus Christ, the Son of God."

Most biblical scholars today think that all this is wrong. It gives the wrong impression. That phrase, "The beginning of the gospel of Jesus Christ, the Son of God," is neither the first sentence nor the first line of Mark's book: It is its title.

Jesus is the beginning. Jesus starts a process, a movement. Those who follow him have to continue what he started among us. At the end of Mark's gospel, Jesus' disciples are asked to go to Galilee to meet him. It is the Galilee he came from. We have to meet Jesus there. It is our turn to begin Jesus' journey from where he began his.

Mark reveals from the beginning of his book what this trip will entail. He depicts the whole scene with firm brush strokes. There is Isaiah who prophesies that this crooked world will be straightened out. John the Baptizer arrives in the wilderness of this world to announce that this straightening out is going to begin. He adds that he can't do it, he is not powerful enough. Someone stronger than John is going to come. That stronger one is powerful enough, but he is not going to do it alone. John says: "He is going to baptize you with water." It is a second hint that we have to pick up what Jesus comes to introduce.

After having twice implicated all of us in what is going to happen, Mark writes: "At that time Jesus came from Nazareth in Galilee." His life would only be the beginning—we are Jesus' follow-up!

Program

"The spirit of Lord Yahweh is on me...." Isaiah 61:1-2a, 10-11

Isaiah is the one who describes Jesus' intentions best. When Jesus presents himself to his own people in the synagogue at Nazareth, he unrolls the scroll of Isaiah and reads his agenda from that scroll:

> The spirit of the Lord has been given to me, for the Lord has anointed me. He has sent me to bring good news to the poor, to bind up the hearts that are broken; to proclaim liberty to captives, freedom to those in prison; to proclaim a year of favor from the Lord.

At that point he rolls the scroll together, hands it back, and tells them this was the reason that he came among us.

This is not the end of Isaiah's prophecy. The prophecy is not only about the poor and wretched, it is a song about Jesus himself, and all those who are with him.

> I exult for joy in the Lord,
> my soul rejoices in my God,
> for he has clothed me in garments of salvation,
> he has wrapped me in the cloak of integrity,
> like a bridegroom wearing his wreath,
> like a bride adorned in her jewels.
> For as the earth makes fresh things grow,
> as a garden makes seeds spring up,
> so will the Lord God make both integrity and praise
> spring up in the sight of the nations!

Long before the young man Jesus could sing this song about himself, his mother had adopted these themes from Isaiah: "My soul exults in the Lord!" She could do that because she, too, understood how Isaiah's words were going to be fulfilled. She must have sung this song often when she put her child Jesus down to sleep at the end of the day. What a lullaby!

Parenting

"Mary said, 'You see before you the Lord's servant....'" Luke 1:26-38

Luke describes Mary as someone full of hope and anticipation. She must have been looking forward to the coming of a Messiah. Meeting Elizabeth, she expresses her feelings. She bursts out in song.

Like so many Jewish women, Mary had been hoping that her offspring would contribute to the coming of the future Messiah. Barrenness was considered a great tragedy because it excluded a woman from that possibility.

When the angel appears to her, she is alone in her hope. She has not made up her mind as to her male partner. She asks: "But how can this come about, since I am a virgin?" She is still free, a freedom she does not relinquish without questions.

When she is assured that the son to be born from her is the fulfillment of all her desires, she does not hesitate any longer: "I am the handmaid of the Lord!"

She did not take the initiative. God took the initiative sending an angel. Yet, in a way, Mary started it all herself by desiring and imagining the new heaven, the new earth, and the new child foretold by the prophets of her people. She hoped for him so much that she was the one chosen.

Mary knew why she wanted to become a mother. She knew what she desired her son to be. She saw him as part of the realization of all the old prophecies, an achievement not yet completed. Her son came and introduced the new life his mother expected. He left his disciples the task of completing his mission—a reason for them to know what the meaning of their parenthood is. We should look forward to offspring in the way Mary looked forward to her son. We should prepare them for their mission, in the way she prepared Jesus. We should beget and rear them with a view to the realization of God's kingdom on earth. No more and no less.

Holy Family

"...and a sword will pierce your soul too...." Luke 2:22-40

As a seminarian I had to prepare a sermon on the Holy Family. It was an assignment for our course in preaching. I delivered it to my classmates, not the easiest audience. They liked it. I was proud of my sermon and sent it to my family. That was a mistake. My father read it aloud at the family dinner. Most of my twelve brothers and sisters were present; so was my mother. When I got their reaction in a letter from my father (the longest one of the very few I ever got from him), I realized that they laughed a lot. He wrote me that a family as described by me hardly could serve as an example to any existing family. He wondered, he wrote, whether the family in Nazareth was as ideal as I presented it.

Preachers often speak about the Holy Family, projecting their ideas of an ideal family, without asking whether such a projection is realistic.

The tensions in the family in Nazareth must have been great. Practically all we hear about are their problems. A betrothed man who feels jilted; words at the child's presentation in the temple that cause anxiety; a political threat that makes them refugees in a foreign country; a bloodbath in Bethlehem after their flight; living in a hideout in Nazareth after their return; a child who runs away in Jerusalem; a mother who has difficulties understanding her son in Cana; a family that declares him out of his mind and tries to get him home; even the strange words Jesus speaks to his mother and to John from the cross.

It is the way they weathered those storms that makes the family in Nazareth a model for our families. There was an underlying bond that kept mother and son together. It was God's Kingdom that kept them together. That it is why we find his mother at the foot of the cross, a great consolation to him, and a pain she was willing to bear.

[121]

Star

"We saw his star as it rose...." Matthew 2:1-12

Even the sophisticated *Washington Post* has a horoscope, predictions that are read in the stars. Using a horoscope is a custom as old as the people that have been impressed by the thousands and thousands of lights in all kinds of patterns in the sky.

This tradition—according to Matthew's story—led some wise astrologers—Magi—from the East to the child Jesus.

It is an interesting story. The astrologers must have been looking for something new when they were scanning the sky night after night. They were not only looking for a new star. They were looking for a new human life, a new way of living their old life. They must have been dissatisfied with their old ways. It is because of the old and from within the old that the new starts to attract. If you are satisfied with the way things are, you don't hope for something new. If you don't hope for something new, you are never going to look for it. If you don't look for it, you won't find it.

The astrologers were so eager to change that they packed their luggage, saddled their camels, and followed the star without any hesitation. At first they thought that they would find what they sought in Jerusalem. They were mistaken; the star led them to the child in Bethlehem, the beginning of the new Jerusalem, the new city of God and humanity.

They blazed a trail that has been followed since, the trail toward a new city, a new society. It is the trail we should follow when we feel tired and put off by our own old ways of doing things. Don't we all know that our world should change, that we should relate in a new way to each other, to the universe, and to God?

The wise travelers were warned in a dream not to return to the old Jerusalem: "They returned to their own country by a different way" (Matthew 2:12). They returned changed people.

Struggle

"...he saw the heavens torn apart...." Mark 1:7-11

You see it so often in a film, you hear it so often in real life. Someone is struck by disaster and prays to God: "O, that you would tear the heavens open and come down!" It is a very human prayer. It is the prayer of the prophet Isaiah (Isaiah 64:1).

A prayer like this was heard when Jesus was baptized by John in the river Jordan. Mark tells us that heaven tore open and a voice was heard.

When we pray that heaven might tear open, we are praying that God will intervene in our need. When heaven tears open above Jesus a voice is heard, a voice that says: "You are my Son, whom I love; with you I am well pleased" (Mark 1:11). Those words refer to old titles and names for the one who is coming to undo the powers that rule the world in order to renew it. Psalm 2 uses them: "You are my son; [the Lord] said to me, this day I become your father; ask of me what you will: I shall give you the nations as your domain, the earth to its farthest ends as your possession. You will break them with a rod of iron..." (Psalm 2:7-10).

By recalling these words Mark intends to dramatize what is happening at the moment of Jesus' baptism. A whole new world is born in the river Jordan. The fight against oppressive powers in the world has started. From now on Jesus is an alien in this old world of ours. He is an outlaw. Mark describes how "at once the Spirit sent him out into the desert....he was with the wild animals, and angels attended him" (Mark 1:12). At one side "the wild animals" of this world, and at the other side "angels." This kind of symbolism doesn't need any further explanation.

Do you now understand what a struggle we are in for when we join Jesus, the man from Nazareth?

Christf

"Look, there is the Lamb of God." John 1:35-42

Various people will each see one person differently. This is also true of Jesus. Just read the four gospels, plus Paul's ideas, to get different portraits of Jesus.

Jesus' case is particularly difficult. The gospel authors recognized the divine dimension in him as in no other human being. Jesus is God's offspring. Jesus is the anointed one, the *christos*, the Christ.

Mark, Matthew, and Luke try to show his divine dimension by describing his everyday life, telling us how he walked through this world.

John has another approach. He stresses the divinity of Jesus from the beginning of his gospel. "In the beginning was the Word, the Word was with God...." (John 1:1). Jesus is immediately recognized as the Messiah (John 1:40). (All this slightly at the cost of his earthy humanity.)

The four gospel authors struggle with an issue we call "christology." How did Jesus relate to God, and how does he relate to us? This is an important issue that responds to another question: "How do we relate to Jesus?" When others evaluate us, will they find that dimension in our lives? It depends not only on their insight but also on the way we relate to Jesus, the Christ.

Fishers of People

"Come after me, and I will make you into fishers of people."
Mark 1:14-20

We have heard some of the Bible stories so often we don't pay attention to them. We pay still less attention to their interpretation. We know exactly what the preacher or a book like this one is going to say. We have heard it all before. It is totally predictable. It makes spiritual books, magazines, and articles often an utter bore.

The question is whether a commonly accepted understanding is the only one, or even the correct one. Take the text in Mark's gospel when Jesus says: "Come, follow me and I will make you into fishers of people" (Mark 1:17). Most of us probably have the same reaction. This is a text, we decide, that applies to missionaries and people like that.

It does, but it can also be read in another, more biblical context. Prophets had spoken about "fishers" before. Jeremiah did when he wrote: "Watch, and I shall send for many fishermen, Yahweh declares, and these will fish them up" (Jeremiah 16:16). Ezekiel did: "I shall put hooks through your jaws, and pull you out of your Nile with all your fish" (Ezekiel 29:4). And Amos prophesied: "The Lord God has sworn by his holiness: Look the days will soon be on you when God will use hooks to drag you away and fish-hooks for the very last of you" (Amos 4:2). Those texts refer to fishing out the unjust and the oppressors, to a judgment and a sifting of the world. To introduce the Kingdom of God, people have to change, to convert, and the "old" has to be fished out, caught, and done away with.

Jesus asks Simon and his brother Andrew, and later James, son of Zebedee, and his brother John to leave their type of fishing and to follow him and to get engaged in his work. They leave their nets and follow him at once, ready for a new venture, a different fishing trip.

Authority

"And his teaching made a deep impression on them...because he taught them with authority."   Mark 1:21-28

The people who listened to Jesus that day in Capernaum were struck by his authority. Authority is something we all know about. Many people have exercised their authority in our lives. They influenced us in different ways. Did you ever ask yourself who influenced you most in your life? Which family member influenced you most? What teacher have you never forgotten?

Sometimes people tell us who most influenced them. They will quote their parents or a teacher or someone they grew up with. Sometimes their influence was negative. But as soon as someone says: "as my mother always used to say..." you can be practically sure that what follows is something that influenced the life of the speaker in a positive way. Those are the great ones in my life, who made me feel great, who helped me grow. G.K. Chesterton once said: "Greatness is making others feel great!"

That is what real authority does. It is growth-giving, affirmative, positive, and helpful. The word itself is an indication of this. Its root is a Latin word, *augere*, meaning "to make grow."

That is what happened to the people when they were listening to Jesus in their synagogue. Hearing him they began to understand their own possibilities. He gave them a hope the scribes did not give them, did not even want to give them. He did not talk down to them as the scribes were accustomed to do. He treated them as friends and equals. He did not flatter them. He told them to be realistic about themselves. In fact, they had to be more realistic about themselves than they had ever been before. They were called by God to greater things than they ever had thought. It did not always make life easier, but it definitely made it much more worthwhile! His authority made them do what all authority—our own included—should do: foster growth.

Priorities

"Let us go elsewhere to the neighboring country towns, so that I can proclaim the message there too." Mark 1:29-39

Some mission sisters came all the way from Europe to start a clinic in the heart of an impoverished area in Africa. They built the clinic, opened it to those who needed it, and healed more and more patients. Every morning a long line formed itself in front of the clinic. It all seemed to work very well, and yet the sisters in the clinic started to worry whether they were doing the right thing. The cases they most successfully treated were children hit by diarrhea. Mothers would bring children dying of dehydration, and the sisters would be able to help them almost overnight.

The sisters began to notice that more and more children and adults were coming to their clinic, and that often the same people had the same complaints. The sisters came together, discussed the issue, and decided that they had to do something to prevent the recurrence of those sicknesses. It was obvious that there was something wrong with the water the people were drinking, with the available sanitation, and with the whole human environment. They did not close the clinic, though they thought for some time about that. But they switched their priorities to the causes of the diseases. Some of them started visiting people in their homes and addressing community groups to introduce a whole change of lifestyle.

When the people come to Jesus to ask him whether he can't continue healing at the house of Peter's mother-in-law, Jesus says that he is not going to do that. He did not come only to heal sick people, he came to heal the world. He came to change this place in such a way that sickness would disappear totally. He asked them not to stop healing, but to look at the reasons for so much of the sickness in our society and to change our priorities as he did.

Egoism

"And at once the spirit drove him into the desert." Mark 1:12-15

Father Pierre Teilhard de Chardin once remarked on a strange temptation people have who enter into themselves and discover their own inner life. You might think that having made that discovery people would be willing to share it. Not always, Teilhard says. He says it a bit laboriously, but it is not difficult to get the gist of what he wants to say:

> An elementary temptation or illusion lies in wait for the reflective center which each one of us nurses deep inside. It is present from the very birth of that center; and it consists in fancying that in order to grow greater each one of us should withdraw into the isolation of the own self, and egoistically pursue alone the work of one's own fulfillment; that we must cut ourselves off from others, or translate everything in terms of ourselves.

He calls it a temptation. Jesus, who was like us in everything except sin, as Paul once remarked, was tempted like this in the desert after his baptism by John the Baptizer. "Make bread out of these stones for yourself; throw yourself from the temple top to be glorified; take all power for yourself!"

Jesus refused. He did not want to be alone. His reflection on his own inner self brought him out of himself to the whole world, to heal and support it.

It is normal that books on inner healing, dream interpretation, and all kinds of methods to find out about yourself abound in the bookshops of many retreat houses. But it would not be Christian if we used them to draw a circle around ourselves to be alone, isolated. It is, however, a normal and common temptation!

Transfigured

"...his clothes became brilliantly white, whiter than any bleacher could make them."   Mark 9:2-10

When Peter, James, and John looked at Jesus when he stood on Mount Tabor, transfigured, brighter than the brightest star, pure light before them, they not only saw him transfigured, they saw more than his future and risen life. Looking at him, they were looking at themselves. He showed them who he was. He showed them also who we are going to become. He showed them our future human glory and destiny, the glory and destiny of every human being.

Coming down from the mountain after this, the three started to discuss what "rising from the dead" could mean. They had just seen something like it; they had seen him as if he was risen already. Their discussion was a logical consequence of what they had seen.

This discussion has never ended as far as we humans are concerned. It is a discussion that has a wider dimension in our day. Reading the story, we hear that it is not only his body that begins to shine with the glory of the risen life; his clothes, too, become dazzlingly white, radiating light.

One of the reasons that we must respect our fellow human beings is the glory that is each one's personal destiny.

We have to be respectful, too, for the rest of nature, for the whole of creation will be taken up in glory.

We have many reasons to discuss further what rising from the dead could mean for us. We should also consider what it means for the whole of the environment we are so closely connected with, and even composed of. The resurrection of the body implies much more than we ever thought!

Labor

"We are preaching a crucified Christ: ...to the gentiles foolishness...."
1 Corinthians 1:22-25

At times Jesus is simply horrified by the prospect of his death on the cross. Just before his arrest in the garden of Gethsemane, he sweats like someone really gripped by fear and terror. At other times he says that he is looking forward to it. He is looking forward to it not because he knows what his self-sacrifice is going to mean to him, but because he knows what it will mean to us. When he sees his suffering and death as related to his love for us, they become not only bearable but even desirable.

Nobody likes the toil that is involved in practically all labor. It is often difficult to bear its burden and its boredom. That is why it is so important to be able to labor in a meaningful context. Some work for a whole year to have a nice holiday. Others toil for more altruistic reasons. They sometimes take the most difficult tasks upon themselves for the benefit of others, for the education of their children, or the care of a loved one.

Jesus lived his life and died his death for the realization of what he called the Kingdom of God among us. The Kingdom offers us the ultimate possibility of making our work meaningful, doing it as well as we can.

In his letter on human labor, Pope John Paul II wrote: "Sweat and toil, which work necessarily involves in the present condition of the human race, present the Christian and everyone who is called to follow Christ with the possibility of sharing lovingly in the work that Christ came to do."

We should now and then sit down to consider what sense the way we work and toil makes in view of the reign of God among us.

Trying to make that connection might seem foolish to many. But it is the foolishness that Paul says is wiser than human wisdom.

Work of Art

"...we are God's work of art, created in Christ Jesus...."
Ephesians 2:4-10

Late one evening in a city somewhere in a depressed but lush part of our world, dogs suddenly began to bark. They were led by some policemen on patrol through the streets. The dogs pulled at their chains to get at some very young streetwalkers on the lookout for tourists. The girls yelled and ran away. The police threatened to let the dogs loose when a man shouted to them: "Don't do that; they are human beings like you! Don't let your dogs get at them! Shame!"

That man took a risk. But what he did was an act of justice. It is what Jesus would have done. It is what Jesus did.

Paul explains why: "We are—all of us—God's work." He even adds: "God's work of art." We are all created in Christ Jesus. This truth about each one of us is the foundation of our human rights and of our obligations toward each other.

Because God loves each one of us, each of the four billion human beings living on this planet possesses an immense dignity and importance from the moment he or she is conceived. It is not only the human being in general who is "willed" by God, but each individual, concrete human being. Sharing God's love in this way, we share something in common. This should be why we don't allow ourselves any discrimination, and why we should not let any discrimination pass unchallenged in our presence. It is a risk we have to take.

Foreigners

"Some Greeks approached Philip: "Sir, we should like to see Jesus."
                                                    John 12:20-33

It starts simply. Jesus is in Jerusalem. All kinds of people are moving around him. One day some Greeks go to Philip, the apostle with a Greek name, and tell him: "Sir, we would like to see Jesus." Philip does not know how to handle this. The request is not as simple as it seems. For many scholars this incident is a real turning point, a watershed. The Greeks were perhaps the greatest danger to the Judaic culture at the time of Jesus. The Romans were political and military enemies, but the Greeks were a more subtle danger. They did not live far away geographically, but culturally they stood for everything a Jew would feel is a threat to Jewish belief and lifestyle. Greeks in their turn must have considered the Judaic way of life as very distant and strange.

So Philip goes to Andrew for advice and tells him how those foreigners want to see Jesus. They both decide to go and tell him.

When Jesus hears that some Greeks want to see him, he reacts by saying: "Now the hour has come!"

Two different worlds are coming together. Things around Jesus are becoming globalized. Everything is falling into place. "Now I am going to be glorified, and the Father is going to be glorified!" God's glory will become manifest.

Philip and Andrew must have been surprised. Maybe they were even shocked, because it is as if Jesus reacts to something like that when he says: "I tell you most solemnly, unless a wheat grain falls on the ground and dies, it remains only a single grain, but if it dies and opens up, it yields a rich harvest."

There should be no foreigners among those who follow Jesus. We must be always ready to stretch the tent, to expand the table, to open the door, and to take the next step. We need a global perspective, the one Jesus had and has.

Ambiguity

"And those who went in front and those who followed were all shouting: 'Hosanna!'" Mark 11:1-11

There is no doubt about the enthusiasm with which Jesus is received. They give him a hero's welcome in Jerusalem: flowers, branches, tapestry under his feet, dancing, singing, banners. There was good reason for that enthusiasm. Jesus showed everyone around him the kind of human life that could only be called good. He opened dimensions and possibilities hardly ever dreamed of before. Everyone shouts and sings: "Praise the Lord, alleluia!"

But his goodness also had a flip side, as all goodness does. It shows also how you should live your life. Jesus showed us our possible glory and our actual misery. Not everyone thanked him for that. I wonder whether anyone, besides some of his best friends and someone like his mother, did that.

Do you remember situations where this same kind of dynamic is at work? Situations where a new life possibility is enthusiastically greeted while many at the same time are frightened by it? Praising someone sky high, thinking at the same time: "But I don't really mean this praise; he (or she) is just too far above me!?"

No wonder that the same people who were throwing their cloaks and flowers at his feet would some days later shout: "Crucify him. Away with him!" Jesus came to reveal the truth about us. He does that in a threefold way. He shows how we could be, how we are, and what the difference between the two is. Jesus said: "You will know the truth, and the truth will make you free" (John 8:32), words that liberate and therefore frighten. We would like to be like him, and at the same time...you know! We are not so different from those people in Jerusalem!

Baptism

"While Peter was still speaking the Holy Spirit came down on all the listeners....He then gave orders for them to be baptized in the name of Jesus Christ."   Acts 10:34, 37-48

It was in Africa, during a baptism ceremony.

The candidates for baptism were surrounded by their sponsors. Most of them were adults, though several teenagers were to be baptized, too. They were all dressed in long white robes. Nothing fancy—simple and nice. The women had flowers in their hair. The singing and dancing had started long before the ceremony. The baptism was done by immersion. The candidates for baptism had asked the baptizer to keep them under water for quite some time, "so that the old will really die," they said. They wanted to start a new life, the risen life. The baptizer took their words seriously.

He kept them under for quite a time, so that when they came out, they really gasped for breath, for life, for the life we all seek, for the new life of the one who showed us by his life, death, and resurrection what it means to live life to the full—risen life, a life in justice leading to a peace only God's Spirit can give us. The life given to us in Jesus. The life that was sealed in them when they were anointed with oil: priest, prophet, and king!

They were not only anointed with an oily thumb, but with large quantities of oil, dripping all over them, while the crowd sang and danced. No wonder one American Holy Ghost Father, Vincent Donovan, wrote that he rediscovered in Africa what Jesus is all about !

Enthusiast

"...he breathed on them and said: 'Receive the Holy Spirit.'"
John 20:19-31

You can divide humanity in many ways. The old Greek psychologists divided us in four groups according to the four elements: water, fire, earth, and air. Astrologers divide us according to the stars under which we are born. One of the more popular ways among spiritually and psychologically interested people at the moment is a method developed in a mystical Muslim context, the enneagram. It divides people into nine different groups. Each group has a number. It helps to know your number to understand yourself, and to have some idea of how others relate to you.

Not all those classification systems have the same value. Some are probably pretty useless. One day at breakfast at a seminar I was participating in a young man asked me what my sign was. I told him the date of my birth, and he happily sat down next to me, saying, "I relate well to people born under that sign."

It would be interesting to try to classify Jesus in one of these ways. He definitely is a visionary, believing in the future. He is no tired pessimist who has seen it all. He does not live just for today, trying to get as much pleasure out of it as he can. He is an enthusiast, believing that there is something going on in this world and in the possibility of a new and better world, a better humanity. He believes in growth, ascent, discovery, and true human progress. For him humanity is on a journey, but has not reached its goal. He joins us enthusiastically on our safari. Following that road with him will lead us to a greater self-insight, a greater interest in others, to a wider, more spiritual human community, to a deeper intimacy with God.

Wounds

"See by my hands and my feet that it is I myself....And as he said this he showed them his hands and his feet." Luke 24:35-48

When the risen Jesus appears to his followers he often shows them his wounds. "Look at my hands and my feet; yes, it is I, indeed. Touch me and see for yourselves; a ghost has no flesh and bones as you can see I have" (Luke 24:39).

The *risen* Lord showing his *wounds.* Jesus keeps the two together. "It is written that the Christ would suffer and on the third day rise from the dead. This is what I meant when I said, while I was still with you, that everything written about me in the Law of Moses, in the prophets, and in the Psalms has to be fulfilled." His wounds would not make sense if they were not connected to his resurrection. Suffering never makes any sense without that connection. That is not only true for him, it is true for us. There are moments in life when we can't escape suffering and pain. Like Jesus, we will be wounded, too. If we live in this world the way he did, we are going to be wounded. That is unavoidable. It is a life that goes against the grain of this world. It is a life that *wants* to go against the grain of this world in order to realize an alternative, a better world.

The relation between this world and the world to come made Jesus' life possible. To remember only his suffering is one-sided. To remind ourselves only of his resurrection is also one-sided. We have to keep the two together in our lives, as he did.

Shepherd

"I am the good shepherd." John 10:11-18

Not everyone is enthusiastic about developments in our society. Many authors have been pointing at the dangers of an ever-growing individualism in our world. People are withdrawing into themselves. Books, plenty of books, have been written on the topic. They have titles such as *The Minimal Self, The Lonely Crowd,* and *Habits of the Heart: Individualism and Commitment in American Society.* They describe how almost everyone seems to be on a religious and spiritual ego trip inward. It is as if everyone considers herself or himself more and more as the very center of the universe. Pastors, educators, psychologists, sociologists, and psychiatrists all seem to be alarmed. They are not the only ones. Parents sometimes face the problem in their own children, friends in their friends, teachers in their students. Business men and women and religious face the problem in their communities.

What to do? What to say?

One pastor, Parker Palmer, suggests that we don't try to resist this tendency. Let people consider themselves as the center of the universe. Let them even deepen that inward tendency, but let them also direct and discipline it. If you are really the center of the universe, you had better take care of it. You had better be a good shepherd to it. You had better keep it together, and take care that nothing gets lost!

If you consider yourself to be in the center—and in a sense you are!—take upon yourself the responsibility of that situation, and play your role well. Be a good shepherd to yourself, the others, and the whole wide world!

Growth

"The churches...were now left in peace, building themselves up and living in the fear of the Lord; encouraged by the Holy Spirit, they continued to grow...."   Acts 9:26-31

Luke never met Jesus. Neither was he one of his disciples, nor an apostle. He was not even a Jew. Luke was a Gentile, a secularized man, well educated, most probably a doctor, well versed in writing, and quite well informed about the world in which he lived. As a doctor, he was aware that the people he treated were sick, but that the world they lived in was ailing, too. His diagnosis of the world was quite somber; he did not see much hope for healing.

Luke was in that frame of mind when, on one of his journeys, he met a Christian community. He may have been attracted by the miracles they wrought; he was definitely attracted by their lifestyle, which he describes to us in great detail. It is obvious from those descriptions that he considered those communities points of healing in a sick world. If people would all live as *they* tried to do, he was certain, the world would be healed.

Luke tried to find out why the Christians lived the way they did. He was struck that they appealed to a Spirit in them. He asked, "What about that Spirit?" In that way he was led to Jesus, the source of their kindness, their love, their joy. They had their difficulties, he realized. They were "building themselves up"; they were in process. Sometimes things went wrong; symptoms of the old sinfulness and sickness reappeared. They were growing, but were not yet where they hoped to be. They did not live the life of Jesus to the full, but they were trying. As R.E.O. White notes in *Luke's Case for Christianity*: "Out of proportion to its size, and in spite of its political naïvete, the church possessed an inner strength to expand, courage to resist, readiness to suffer, and resources to survive and to serve, that made it a force for social welfare, constructive concern, and creative idealism, as that ancient world sorely needed."

Women or Wives

"With one heart all these joined constantly in prayer, together with some women, including Mary, the Mother of Jesus...." Acts 1:12-14

The apostles were not the only ones waiting for the Holy Spirit. There were others present, waiting.

An interesting and significant point may be noted here. We have different authoritative texts of Acts that offer different versions of this reading. In one text we read that "they were constantly praying along with the *women*," like the version above. In a later (Western) text, the word "women" is changed, and the document reads "along with their *wives* and their children."

A touching detail: the apostles together with Mary, their wives, and their children. Yet, as R.N. Longenecker notes, "The Western text minimizes the independent activity of women in the early church. But Luke's mention of 'the women' fully accords with the attitude toward women as portrayed in his gospel and the consciousness within the church of the gospel proclamation."

In his writings Luke is clearly aware of the independent role of women during the life of Jesus and in the early communities. To call them women, especially considering the position of women in the world of that time, is giving them a new dignity and value. Luke names no fewer than twenty-six women participants in the story of the church, together with several groups of women. Luke saw a fairness, a dignity, and an opportunity accorded to women in the early Christian church that contrasted sharply with pagan ways and morals. In Christ a new era had dawned for women, offering liberation, equal value in God's sight, and wide social vocation; Luke would have us know it. Did he foresee that his text would be changed?

Time Warp

"In the evening of that same day.... Jesus came and stood among them....he breathed on them and said: Receive the Holy Spirit...."
John 20:19-23

Those disciples sitting together in a second-floor room in Jerusalem after the ascension were in a time warp. They were waiting and praying for something they had received fifty days before. They had to go back to their future. Jesus had breathed on them at Easter.

We are in the same situation. The spirit of Jesus is both in us and not in us. The spirit is as the Kingdom of God—it is here and at the same time has still to come. The spirit is in us like the Kingdom. It is in us like the pearl we have to rediscover, the treasure we have to dig out, the fish we have to catch again. We are redeemed, we are renewed, and we are still waiting.

It is a tension we have to solve. It is the tension that answers the question whether our belief in the redemption of humankind is not naïve. How can we say that this world has been redeemed? Think of the Holocaust, constant strife in the Middle East, the atomic bombs on Hiroshima and Nagasaki, the homeless people in our streets—a list we can lengthen endlessly without much difficulty.

We are often in the same position as those followers of Jesus in the upper room, waiting for the Holy Spirit. The seed sown in us has to grow so that it can bring forth its fruits; the yeast has to be activated so that it can make all of the dough edible; the salt has to be mixed with this world to make it tasteful. We have to become the people we really are. That is what that group in Jerusalem was praying and hoping for. That fiftieth day their reality really broke through to them. They began to act as if salted by the spirit of Jesus.

Human Rights

"...baptize them in the name of the Father and of the Son and of the Holy Spirit...."   *Matthew 28:16-20*

When we hear the names of the Blessed Trinity we spontaneously think of God. Father, Son, and Holy Spirit are the names of the divine persons. Trinity indicates life and community in the unity of God.

That is not all. Those names also tell us something about ourselves. Not only do they define God, they define you, me, and all other human beings. That is why many Christians often sign themselves when using those names: "In the name of the Father, and of the Son, and of the Holy Spirit." When we do this we indicate a relationship. We call God Father and sometimes even Mother, because we originate from God. We call God Son, believing that—as the evangelist John writes in the prologue to his gospel—we are all created together in the Son. It is together that we form God's offspring. We call God Spirit, because God is the life principle; God breathed in us from the beginning of our creation. When we cross ourselves using those names we are telling ourselves the most important thing we can about ourselves. I say something not only about myself when I sign myself in this way. This same truth applies to all around me. They, too, relate to God in the same way.

We have to respect ourselves because of our relation to God. That same respect is due to others as well. We often speak about human rights. Those rights are based on God's relationship to each one of us. We are of divine origin. All of us are carrying with us a passport, an identity card, guaranteed and signed by God. We are God's children, God's family. We share God's life. When you cross yourself, saying God's names is not only a pious gesture, it is a program for life! It influences your relationships to the people you meet on your journey through life—even in the way you greet them!

Flowers

"...I shall never drink wine any more until the day I drink the new wine in the Kingdom of God."   Mark 14:12-16, 22-26

Every week we arrange flowers to decorate altars. Yet, there are some people who have something against those flowers. They don't like them around an altar.

I once asked an older priest who likes plants and flowers why he objected to using them around the altar. I could see his point of not putting any flowers on the altar itself: The altar represents a sacrificial table or stone. But I asked him why he objected to any flowers around or near the altar.

He told me to read the story about the last supper in the gospel of Mark. I did but I did not find the answer to my question. So I asked him again. He asked me whether I had noticed how the report by Mark differs from the ones told in Luke and Matthew. In Mark's gospel Jesus does not ask the disciples to commemorate him. In fact, Jesus himself does not commemorate anything. He had asked his disciples to prepare for that meal, but when it came to it, he did not stick to the rules for the meal. He should have reminded them of the exodus from Egypt, the misery they went through, the forced labor, the bricks they made from clay and straw, the bitter herbs they ate. Jesus uses other words; he applies the celebration directly to himself. He calls the bread his body ready to be given up; he calls the wine his blood that will be poured out for many. He asks them to eat that bread, to drink that blood with him, to be as ready as he is in regard to the realization of the Kingdom of God. And in the end he tells them: "In truth I tell you, I shall never drink wine any more until the day I drink the new wine in the kingdom of God" (Mark 14:25). In Mark's gospel we are not asked to look back; we are asked to look forward to the future. We are left with the task of the realization of his kingdom. "You can't hide a mission like that behind some flowers," my friend said.

Binding Evil

"But no one can make his way into a strong man's house...unless he has first tied up the strong man."　　　　　Mark 3:20-35

One day when Jesus comes to his house in Capernaum he cannot find the privacy he is looking for. Three groups of people make this impossible: a crowd so numerous that he does not even get a chance to get to the table to eat; his family, who wants to get him back home; and a group of scribes from Jerusalem, who want to liquidate him. Those agents from the holy city accuse him of being possessed by the devil: "It is through the prince of devils that he drives devils out." They declare him to be of the devil, an accusation we still hear nowadays.

People in power often accuse those who are against them of being of the devil. Not so long ago a president of the United States called Russia the evil empire. A late leader of Iran used to call the United States the great Satan. These are dangerous accusations that lead to hatred and destruction.

Jesus overturns the scribes' accusation, saying that if he does what he does in name of the devil, the devil is fighting itself. For that is what he came to do in this world: to fight the devil who is inhabiting our human homestead. He explains his intention in a fascinating way: "No one can make his way into a strong man's house and steal his property unless he has first tied up the man. Only then can he take his house" (Mark 3:27).

Jesus comes to bind the strong man who terrorizes humanity. He comes to liberate us. He comes as a divine thief in our human night to break through the walls of the existing "order" that keeps us terrorized and imprisoned (Matthew 24:43). Binding that strong man is at the same time unbinding us.

Jesus comes to open the door through which we can come to share the spirit and the freedom of the children of God. Being unbound, however, does not suffice, nor does opening a door. We have to get up and walk into the freedom assured to the children of God.

Land

"...the land produces first the shoot, then the ear, then the full grain in the ear."   Mark 4:26-34

We all know the parables of the sower and the seed. We know them so well that we hardly pay attention to them when we hear them. Heads nod and eyes either close or glaze over, showing that we are dreaming of something else. This is a pity, because we will never discover that those stories are not in the first instance about the sower and the seed, but about something else. The title "sower and seed" was not given by the gospel authors. It comes from our Bible editors, and it is a misnomer. When you pay attention and count the use of the different words in the gospel, you will notice that another word is more often used than those words "sower and seed." The word "land" is mentioned twelve times in the three sower and seed parables of Mark.

The main theme in those stories is the land, that is to say, we are the main issue. It is a story about the enormous powers and potentialities that are conferred on us. They describe how, when we receive the seed of Jesus in ourselves, we are capable of bringing forth fruit a hundredfold! There is a verb in these stories that is used even more often than the noun "land." It is the word "listening." It is used thirteen times. If we listen to the word and example Jesus sows in us, we will be able to show ourselves and the whole wide world what we are capable of. If we don't listen we won't even know who we really are. On its own the seed can't do a thing. The land without the seed is fruitless.

Jesus' parables are about an interaction. The seed needs to be sown and the land needs to receive. The reaction to be expected is not so much a conversion, but a revelation, a disclosure. The land will never know its power until someone sows the seed—something we had better take into consideration when communicating with others.

Initiative

"'My daughter,' he said, 'your faith has restored you to health; go in peace....'"   Mark 5:21-43

She had been bleeding for twelve years. Mark tells us that she had lost her whole fortune making the rounds of various doctors, without being any better for it; in fact, she was getting worse. (Luke, being a doctor himself, does not mention this detail!)

She had heard about Jesus, and thought, "If I only can touch his clothes, I shall be healed." She elbows herself through the crowd. She touches his clothing. She feels a power invading and healing her. He feels a power going out of him.

He wonders what he felt, and asks, "Who touched my clothes?" His disciples laugh at the question, they laugh at him: "How can you ask, did anyone touch me, look at the crowd milling against you!" Their question sounds sarcastic, yet it helps us further.

The disciples were right. Hundreds of people were touching Jesus that day. But nothing happened to them. The touching of Jesus as such does not have any effect in itself. No power went out of him. That power comes when you do it in faith. It happens at the moment when you share his vision and, consequently, his person and his power.

Faith is not the consequence of the miracle. Faith is its condition. You heal because you believe, because you take the initiative and reach out. It sounds almost heretical. All seems to depend on your own initiative. But it is Jesus himself who tells her, "My daughter, your faith has restored you to health; go in peace and be free of your complaint."

Dishonored

"Where did the man get all this?" Mark 6:1-6

When he comes home to Nazareth they sneer at him. They wonder where he got it all from, he a carpenter, the son of Mary. That last remark might have been meant as a real insult. In that time people were called after their father. Who was his father? It is not the only time that people around him express their doubts about his legitimacy.

There is another thing in him they might not have liked. He had left his older mother to care for herself. He does not show too much respect for traditional roles. They don't like his fame. He is just too much for them. Instead of being glad for him, they feel offended by him. They are scandalized by his behavior. They don't believe in him.

He is amazed by their reaction. He did not expect it, though he says that he knows that a prophet is never honored among his own relations and in his own house. He leaves them and, as far as we know, he never returns there again. He leaves the old structure that wants to keep him in his traditional place, behind.

Though he lays on hands and heals some of his acquaintances, he can't work any great miracle. He is amazed by that, too. They don't have the faith to heal themselves and to break their bonds. The impossibility does not come from his side. It is their unbelief that closes them off. He is incapable of convincing them of their own potential.

Not believing in him means not believing in yourself! He always insists, "Your faith has healed you!"

The difficulty in Nazareth is not so much that he is not honored as he should have been. The difficulty is that they don't honor themselves as they should! That is why he is so amazed at them.

Pastoral Respect

"Take nothing for the journey except a staff—no bread, no haversack, no coppers for their purses." Mark 6:7-13

Jesus did not choose his disciples just so they could be with him. It is true that he wanted their company on his mission; he did not want to be alone. But he had another reason. He wanted to send them out in their turn to announce the good news and to fight evil wherever it is found.

The first time he sends the disciples out he gives them some directives, rules he never withdrew, rules that remain in force. They had to take care of their own travel. Mark says that they had to take a staff and a pair of sandals. For the rest, they are not allowed to take anything, no food, no knapsack, no extra clothing, and no money. The practical consequence of those rules is that they made themselves dependent on the hospitality of those who would receive them.

We don't know whether the apostles obeyed those rules. Because we do not always obey them we know what happens if you don't. While working as a missionary in Africa I used eucharistic bread for years that had been baked in the Netherlands. The wine we used came from Cyprus. When Pope John Paul II visited Nairobi some years ago, missionaries imported large quantities of hosts from that same bakery. We did not depend on the hospitality and resources of the host country.

This lack of trust in others, lack of dependence on others, is important not only when preaching the "good news" in far-off countries. It should concern us when we are in familiar surroundings. Just try to speak to teenagers about Jesus in terms that are not their own! During an instruction on the rite of confirmation, one teenager put up her hand, and said: "Why don't they speak in a way we can understand?" Why don't we?

Sheep

"...he took pity on them because they were like sheep without a shepherd."   Mark 6:30-34

The apostles came back from their first mission. They were tired. It had all been new for them. So he said: "Let us get some rest; we'll go to a lonely place and have a good meal and a good sleep." So they went off in a boat to a lonely place. That is what they thought. The crowd had followed them and in no time surrounded them again. They were in for the trouble they had tried to escape from, a situation all of us know too well.

Seeing the crowd, Jesus sent his disciples away to have their rest and he took it upon himself to speak to the crowd because he had pity on them, "since they were like sheep without a shepherd."

How do you listen to such a story? With whom do you identify while listening? With the disciples, with the crowd, or with Jesus?

The temptation to identify ourselves with the sheep might be great. It is not very flattering, but it is easy. It is nice to be led. Not all of us like to take responsibility for our own lives. Some leaders love to lead "sheep" like that.

Jesus is quite willing to play the role of a shepherd meeting people who behave like sheep. Not that he has anything against sheep, he has something against people who behave as if they are sheep.

He wants to change those who behave like sheep into shepherds, who in their turn change others into shepherds, and so on. That is what he does to those who follow him.

In the beginning of this story they came back from a mission he had entrusted to them. They had done things they never thought they could do: heal sick people, change hearts, announce the good news, be full of compassion for others. They hardly recognized themselves. There was nothing sheepish about those newborn men and women around him! (Our apologies to all sheep in the world; they should not be offended; they are perfectly what they are supposed to be.)

Apartheid

"Jesus, as he realized they were about...to make him king, fled back to the hills alone."   John 6:1-15

Albert Nolan is a South African priest, a Dominican. He interprets the gospels from the point of view of the difficulties in his own country in a book he called *Jesus Before Christianity*. He is especially interested in what happens when the oppressed people around Jesus want to make him their king. Jesus refuses, and when they want to seize him, he gets away from them into the mountains.

Nolan explains how the different reports of this incident in the gospels remind him of developments in South Africa. He wonders why in the gospel story so many people came together in an isolated place on the same day? Who had organized this? The reason, Nolan thinks, can only have been a secret political rally.

Jesus controls the throng by asking them to sit down in groups. It is easier to deal with sitting people in smaller groups than with a large, uproarious, standing crowd. Fearing that the crowd would want to make him king, Jesus withdrew.

The disciples themselves are another problem for Jesus. They don't mind him becoming king. They like it. They are already dividing the jobs in his kingdom among themselves! Jesus sends them away before he gradually dismisses the crowd.

He is not going to be their king, either. He would be king of one group against another group. Being the offspring of God who sends his sunshine and rain for all, Jesus simply cannot do that. Making such a choice is not divine, it cannot be divine. Jesus' divine policy is to unite people; they belong to the same human-divine family. What God has united no one should put asunder!

Even in his greatest difficulties Jesus does not allow himself to consider others as outsiders. He is against the oppression of any group. He remains inclusive in his approach.

Bread

"I am the bread of life. No one who comes to me will ever hunger; no one who believes in me will ever thirst."   John 6:24-35

As an old Chinese saying puts it, when you want to help feed people, don't give them a fish, teach them how to fish. Anyone who ever has been engaged in a food distribution organization will acknowledge the truth of that. If you offer only food, the food line will form itself every day again and again for the simple reason that filled stomachs will again get empty.

When the crowd comes to Jesus because they got all the bread they wanted from him the day before and were looking for more, he makes the same remark. He tells them that the bread he has been giving them is of no lasting use. He explains to them that the giving and receiving of that bread and fish will not solve their problems, or the problems of the world. He tells them to be interested in something that will help them more definitively, and he suggests they take him as their food and drink. He asks them to make him and his way of living their "bread and butter" in daily life.

We should eat "him." His words are true in the most literal sense. If we would accept his lifestyle and adopt it in this world, no child would ever again die of hunger, and no senior citizen of loneliness. We would be attentive to each other, using the gifts we are to each other. We would be washing each other's feet and serving at the table of the world. We would have to start soup kitchens in many places, but we would organize them as temporary measures, not as lasting solutions. We would be interested in a re-organization of our world. We would die but not remain dead, because we would have eaten of the bread of life. We would be like he was, is, and ever will be!

Drawing Power

"No one can come to me unless drawn by the Father who sent me...."
John 6:41-51

Jesus speaks of a mysterious power penetrating this whole world. It is so mysterious that we cannot see, smell, touch, hear, or taste it directly. It is everywhere. There are more of those hidden energy fields.

Early in the morning there is silence, no sound. Yet, the room is full of frequencies, waves, vibrations, and electric power fields. Pressing a button on my radio brings those frequencies to life, monks singing their plainchant in a monastery, metal hard rock from a group in London, a symphony orchestra in Cleveland, and voices, voices from all over the world. Switching on television, I tap into another energy field that connects me with events at the other side of the world in Beijing and Moscow, Pago Pago and Brussels.

All that energy was there without being visible, without being noticed. Enormous forces are hiding in nature, seeds that grow into trees, plants that turn the whole day following the sun, insects that crawl around, animals looking for a mate to perpetuate their lives, people embracing each other—even the clouds are chasing each other in the wide, blue sky.

Jesus speaks about another power, a drawing power that influences all of creation, especially the whole of humanity. It is a kind of attraction, a divine attraction. God draws all of us through Jesus toward our original and final home, an energy that draws us to God and also to one another. Protestants and Catholics, Muslims and Jews, Americans and Russians, Asians and Europeans, Christians and Hindus, aren't we all dialoguing with each other more than ever before in our world? Although we often fight with each other, the idea that we all belong to the same human family is growing among us every day.

Indeed, a power is at work among and in us. Almighty God is drawing to where we all are coming from!

Language of Love

"Whoever eats my flesh and drinks my blood lives in me and I live in that person."   John 6:51-58

You are with someone your dearly love. You would like to convince her or him to stop a dangerous habit, avoid a quarrel, forgive some bitterness, forget something from the past, or to make a decision. It might be your son, it might be your daughter, your mother or your father, a friend. She is standing there before you. He is sitting next to you. You talk, you reason, you argue, you speak. No response is given. You might as well be talking to the wall. He just stands there staring at you. She just sits there not showing any sign of real contact. You plead, "If only you would see what I see, understand what I understand. I wish I could creep into your head to make you see, into your heart to make you feel. If only we could be of the same mind in this!"

This is the way Jesus speaks in the gospel of John. He repeats and repeats: "Listen to what I am telling you. I know what is at stake. Listen to me. Try to see things as I see them. I come from the Father. Try to feel things as I feel them. Eat the bread I eat, drink the wine I drink. Drink my blood, eat my flesh!"

We know that Jesus spoke to us that way then. We can guess how he would speak to us today in our world—a world in which millions are starving while others eat too much, a world with situations like the ones in the Middle East and in Northern Ireland, in the streets of our own cities and towns. He asks us, he pleads with us to see the world as he does, to feel its hurts as he feels them. The language he would speak is the language of love, the language we use when we can't convince someone we dearly love of what we know is best for them.

Technology and Spirit

"It is the spirit that gives life, the flesh has nothing to offer."
                                                    John 6:60-69

We live in a computer era. Not everyone in the world does, but we do. Even if you have no computer at home on your desk, small computers are hidden in so many things we use. Those computers can do wonderful things. They can handle all kind of problems and issues. They are very logical in their solutions to those problems, much more so than we are ourselves. They are also fast. In a few fractions of a second they can work out problems that would take a human being months. They remain dependent on our input, but once they have it, they seem to be much more rational than we are.

That is their strength. It is also their weakness. They have nothing but that rationality. That is why they are not human. When we humans say to each other, "Now let us be logical!" we all know that something is going to happen that should not happen. A child is sent away, a marriage is broken, a business is closed, even if it causes a lot of heartbreak to those involved.

Love is different from rationality. The flesh is different from the spirit. Technique is different from the heart. Jesus says, "The flesh has nothing to offer; it is the spirit that gives life!" He does not want to condemn either our body or our technique. Nor does he want to separate them. On the contrary, he wants us to keep the two together. Without the spirit that gives life, the flesh is dead. Technique on its own is dangerous; it can be deadly. It should be accompanied by love. A merely technical or even rational consideration is never sufficient. It has led to endless disasters. Ancient Greek philosophers defined the human being as a "rational" animal. We are more than that. Our rationality is accompanied, directed, and humanized by our human spirit. It should be directed by Jesus' living spirit of love.

Purity of Heart

"For it is from within, from the heart, that evil intentions emerge...."
                                                    Mark 7:1-8, 14-15, 21-23

In a worshiping community or parish, people may get upset when something changes in the rituals. Most of us would like to stick to the traditional way of doing things. Tradition should not be changed, we think. We often complain if it is. Every so often some people write letters to complain to the authorities, or they look for another church where the old rites are respected.

Change is an abiding problem in our ever-modifying world, a problem Jesus himself faced. The introduction of a new world, the Kingdom of God, in our existing human world cannot but bring changes.

Talking with women in the street was against the traditional rules of Jesus' time. Talking with alien women, like the Syro-Phoenician woman or the one at the well in Samaria, was completely out of the question. Coming near to lepers was not done, and healing on the Sabbath was against one of their most important traditions.

One day Jesus' critics—Pharisees, scribes, and priests—comment on his disciples who do not follow all the detailed cleaning rites, and call them "unclean." Jesus uses their accusation to make his point. He explains that "purity" is neither something concerning external rites, nor does it consist merely in following old traditions. It is a question of your inner self; it is a question of your heart. And he mentions a list of vices coming out of an impure heart. His enumeration is the usual biblical one: fornication, theft, murder, adultery, greed, malice, deceit, indecency, envy, slander, pride, and an obtuse spirit.

But he adds one item to his list. In fact he begins his list with it, and his opponents, accustomed to the usual one, must have noticed that. He adds "wicked designs" or "evil intentions." He tells them that they are hypocrites. They act as if they are seeking purity, but they are after something else—they are after him! They have evil designs on him. Let us purify our hearts and reach out for holiness!

[154]

Son of Man

"Then he began to teach them that the Son of man was destined to suf-
fer grievously...."   Mark 8:27-35

In the gospels Jesus calls himself "Son of Man" 81 times. No one else
addresses him that way. They give him other names and titles, as Peter does when Jesus asks, "Who do you say that I am?" Peter's answer
is "You are the Messiah, the anointed one!" Peter is right, but he is
wrong, too. Peter gives Jesus a title that risks isolating Jesus from ordinary human beings. He becomes a special case. In a way, Peter neu-
tralizes him.

Dorothy Day, who died not long ago, is considered a contemporary
American saint by many who knew her. She started the Catholic
Worker movement, opened homes for the homeless, and community
farms for down-and-out people. She definitely was a special person.
She did extraordinary things. Yet every time she overheard anyone
saying something like that of her, she was indignant. "You say that I
am special, because you don't want to do what you see me do. You
can easily do what I do, but by convincing yourself that I am someone
special, you can escape from your own responsibility. We are not so
different. You can do what I do."

When Jesus uses the title "Son of Man," he changes our relation to
him. He changes our expectations. He does not change what we can
expect from him, but what we should expect from ourselves. Jesus
says it in as many words: "In all truth I tell you, whoever believes in
me will perform the same works as I do myself and will perform even
greater works" (John 14:12).

This is a text many overlook (many *want* to overlook). It is easier to
leave it all to Jesus, and to join him in a kind of fan club that leaves it
all to him. He did not leave us as mere spectators. We are co-
responsible.

Social Program

"He then took a little child whom he set among them...."

Mark 9:30-37

Jesus is at home. The disciples are sitting around him. On their way home they had been arguing about who was the most important. (They were doing that while Jesus was explaining that he was willing to "deliver himself in the hands of men.")

He asks them, "What were you discussing on the way home?" They all fall silent. Nobody knows what to say. They must suddenly have seen the incongruity of the situation.

In their silence they hear some children playing outside. Jesus goes to the open door and calls a child, a street child.

These are the kind of children no one takes seriously, the lowest level of the human hierarchy. Even in our world they often don't count. Just think of the little money available to help the neglected children in our own society. So many things seem to be so much more important.

He brings the child into their midst. He stands there in their circle, a bit frightened, with a runny nose. Jesus puts his arms around the child and embraces him. Then he says: "Whoever welcomes a child such as this for my sake welcomes me. And whoever welcomes me welcomes not me but him who sent me."

It is not the only time that Jesus takes children as the model for his social program (see Mark 9:42; 10:13-16). It must have been quite a shock to his disciples. What Jesus is saying is that children are as important to God and to the Son of Man as the divine persons' self. Jesus is turning their whole world and its hierarchy completely upside down. Have a look at the children around you today; look at them with the eyes of God and Jesus Christ. A child should be present at all our decision makings! The more important the decision, the more important the presence of that child, for that child is God present with us.

Arrogance

"Master, we saw someone who is not one of us driving out devils in your name, and because he was not one of us we tried to stop him."
Mark 9:38-41

During a workshop for missionaries and evangelists, the participants were discussing their work and experiences. There was one thing they all agreed on: They had found many "Christian" values in people who had never heard of Jesus.

It was John who came to Jesus with a different, yet similar, experience: "Teacher, we saw a man who is not one of us driving out devils in your name, and because he was not one of us we tried to stop him" (Mark 9:39).

It is the kind of surprise you hear often in a less obvious way. Pious Christians often say, "That person is so good, and not even Catholic!" When we say something like this, we restrict God's grace, we restrict God's presence, and we put ourselves on a special pedestal. We and those of our company are going to be the saviors of the world!

We had better pay attention to Jesus' reaction.

He starts by saying to John: "Don't try to stop him!" He gives three reasons for this. The first is a practical one: Anyone who works miracles in the name of Jesus is on Jesus' side. He then generalizes that reason: "Anyone who is not against us is with us." His third reason is the most important. Doesn't John understand that he himself will need some help now and then, if only in the form of a cup of water? And who is going to give him that help if he himself is the only one who can help? That is why Jesus adds: "Anyone who gives you a cup of water because you belong to Christ will not, I assure you, go without his reward" (Mark 9:41).

Marriage

"From the beginning of creation he made them male and female."
Mark 10:2-12

Everyone attending a marriage ceremony prays that the bride and groom will really be able to do what they promise each other: to become as one. We all know how bitter the ashes of a burned-out marriage are.

Jesus honors marriage. In John's gospel he attends a wedding. All through the tradition of his own people marriage has been considered a symbol of the final relation between God and humankind.

Mary did not forget that theme, either. When she sees her son coming to the wedding in Cana, she goes up to him to say: "They have no wine!" Did she invite Jesus to begin the final wedding between God and humankind then and there? Jesus answers: "The hour has not yet come!" But as a kind of prelude to it, he changes water into wine.

Once Jesus is asked whether a man is allowed to send his wife away. The question is not exactly about divorce, but about male domination. Jesus answers that such a male-biased approach to marriage is out of the question. Man and woman are created equal. He quotes Scripture, saying that when marrying, a man leaves his own family, that his marrying does not mean the continuation of *his* family roots. The two are equal; they are one. Marriage is a relationship where love and friendship should be the norm and ideal.

That is the love and friendship we pray for when we attend a wedding. This is the bond we should be cultivating when married. This does not mean that there will not be difficulties—any relationship experiences difficulties. The bond of married love, however, lies deeper than any of those problems.

Let us pray that that bond may exist between those who decide to marry, and let each couple cultivate it in equality and friendship. For the ashes of a burned-out marriage are bitter, indeed.

Riches

"...he went away sad, for he was a rich man." Mark 10:17-30

Lists are interesting things, as authors and publishers know. They publish books that contain only lists, lists of all kinds of items.

You find many lists in the Bible. The ten commandments, the eight beatitudes, set lists of virtues and vices. Jesus, too, loves to use those set lists. But he sometimes changes them. If he had used only the traditional lists, he would not have contributed anything new. This is a good reason to listen carefully when Jesus gives his lists.

One day a young man falls on his knees in front of Jesus and asks: "Good master, what must I do to share in everlasting life?" Jesus answers with a list: "You shall not kill; you shall not commit adultery; you shall not steal; you shall not bear false witness; you shall not defraud; honor your father and your mother."

An old list with a variant! Do you recognize in this list the odd item, the one that is unusual and new?

It is the term "defraud." In classical Greek, the word Jesus uses means "refusing to return goods that have been given in deposit or loan." In Bible Greek it means "refusing to pay the wage of a hired laborer."

The man looks at Jesus and says: "Master, I have kept all these commandments from my earliest days." Jesus looks at him, with love. He adds: "There is one thing you lack. Go and sell everything you have and give the money to the poor, and you will have treasure in heaven; then come, follow me!"

Only at the end of the story do we hear that the young man was rich. In that time and region that can only have meant that he was a landowner or a businessman employing and hiring other people. Was that the reason Jesus added the admonition about defrauding?

Ransom

"Can you drink the cup that I shall drink...?" Mark 10:35-45

A woman was explaining to a group of children why Jesus died on the cross. She said that he did it to pay a ransom for our sins. He paid the price of his blood to his Father in heaven to save us. One child in class sighed audibly, "What a goofy father!"

Children are not the only ones to have this reaction when they hear this type of theology. How could God ever ask such a thing?

Yet, it seems to be the gospel story. In the gospel of Mark, Jesus explains that he is going "to give his life as a ransom for many" (Mark 10:45).

The difficulty is not the concept of sacrifice. We all know of people who sacrificed their lives for others. The difficulty is in thinking that God would have had to wait for this ransom to be paid.

Luke narrates Jesus' death without any reference to this kind of need. In his gospel, one the robbers crucified with Jesus explains to the other one why Jesus dies: "We die because we deserve to die, because we did evil, but this man dies because he is good!" He was right.

Jesus was willing to give his life to prove to us that the newness he brought is more than a possibility. It is the only answer to our problems caused by evil and sin. In his book, *The Spiritual Life of Children* (Boston: Houghton Mifflin, 1990), Robert Coles tells the story of another child, a nine-year-old girl, who explains it beautifully: "Jesus felt sorry for us. He knew we were in trouble, so he came here to save us....He was 'too good for this world,' the nun says, and we should remember....But he didn't mind dying. He was sad, but he knew he'd live forever, and 'because he died, so will we live forever,' the nun says. That's what our church says. It's what Jesus did for us."

Called

"And at once his sight returned and he followed him along the road."
Mark 10:46-52

The last miracle Jesus works in the gospel of Mark is the one with Bartimaeus. The ideal miracle, it sums up all Mark wants to tell us about how Jesus relates to us and we to him. The story is simple. Bartimeus is blind, sitting in his cloak and with his stick on a street corner, begging. He hears that Jesus is coming and he calls out: "Son of David, have pity on me!" Those anxious that they are losing Jesus' attention tell him to be silent. He keeps calling. Jesus stops in the street and now he calls for the blind man. "Call him here!" Mark stresses this last point by repeating twice more in the text that Jesus is calling him: "So they called the blind man. 'Courage,' they said; 'get up, he is calling you.'" Once healed, he starts following Jesus.

Bartimaeus's story is the story of the ideal follower of Jesus. It combines being healed by Jesus and following Jesus. This is the miracle that should happen to all of us. It is the meeting of two energies: the one in us that reaches out to God, world, and self; the one coming from God through Jesus Christ reaching out to us.

Robert Coles's book on the spirituality of children contains this quote by Junior, a boy of twelve: "You know, I guess the Lord and us, we're all in this together: us hoping to be saved, and him wanting to save us." That is what this miracle with Bartimaeus is all about.

Good Life

"Which is the first of all the commandments? Jesus replied, 'This is the first: Listen....'"   Mark 12:28b-34

The last time Jesus meets his opponents before they come to arrest and execute him, they ask him an important question, the most important one we could ask: "What is the good life?" They ask the question in a more legalistic way: "Which is the first of all the commandments?" It is the same question nonetheless.

We know Jesus' answer. At least we think we do. First you have to love God with all your heart and soul; second, you must love your neighbor as yourself. And those two (or three) commandments are one and the same.

But that is not all he says. Before he utters those words, there is another word—a verb, a command: "Listen, Israel!"

Listening is the very first thing we should do! It has to do with the rest of what Jesus says, but it is the first thing mentioned. The most important thing for the good life is to listen, to pay attention.

Every week the *New York Times* publishes a list of the bestselling books in this country over the past week. For more than eight years one book has been on that list, *The Road Less Travelled* by a psychiatrist, M. Scott Peck. Its subtitle is *A New Psychology of Love, Traditional Values and Spiritual Growth* (New York: Simon and Schuster, 1978). As that subtitle indicates, love is one of the topics discussed in the book. For Peck, the most important form that active love takes is "to pay attention" or "to listen." You know that someone loves you when that person listens to you.

How often have you heard the complaint: "He never listens to me! I am like nothing to her!"

Listen to God, listen to your neighbor, listen to yourself! Listen to the source of life. Listen to life. No commandment is more important. Listen, and all the rest will follow.

Widow's Mite

"...but she in her poverty has put in everything she possesses, all she had to live on."   Mark 12:38-44

Jon Sobrino is a Central American theologian. Several years ago he wrote *The Hidden Motives of Pastoral Action* (Maryknoll, NY: Orbis Books, 1978). In that book he explains that often gospel stories are not correctly interpreted and preached. In other words, the preachers manipulate the stories in view of other, very often their own, interests.

One of the stories that is often used in a way that contradicts its original meaning is the one about the poor widow who offers all she has. She is so often referred to as the example of what we should do. She gave everything she had, and Jesus praised her for it.

True, Jesus praised her for her generosity. He also did something else. Just before the incident about the widow is told, he is preaching against people who devour the property of widows (Mark 12:40). That done, he sits down in the temple opposite the offering box. He is studying—that is the meaning of the Greek word used—what is happening. That is how he comes to notice the widow with two of the smallest coins available. He sees her putting the two coins in the box. He calls his disciples together, praises her, and adds: "She put in all she had to live on. All the others contributed from their wealth." Her two pennies were worth more than all the other donations.

He praises her, that is true, but it sounds at the same time like a very bitter complaint. A complaint against a temple and a priesthood that does not protect a poor widow against something like this. How can they tolerate a poor widow giving all she has to live on?

In the gospel of Mark he never goes to the temple again!

Trees

"Take the fig tree as a parable...." Mark 13:24-32

Trees are marvelous. No wonder so many people all over the world developed a great devotion to them. In many regions they are venerated, sometimes even worshiped, as symbols of God and the life God gave us. Jesus frequently compares the Kingdom of God to a tree, and says things like: "Take the fig tree as a parable."

Even in the Book of Revelation "the tree of life" grows on either bank of the river that flows through the new Jerusalem, "the leaves of which are the cure for the nations" (Revelation 22:2).

Jesus invites us to look at trees, which symbolize the abundance of creation. Looking at their twigs and branches, we will be able to gauge where we are, what life is about, how we belong together. He even says, 'I am the vine, and you are the branches.'

We need this advice more than ever before. The trees around us are no longer that healthy. Acid rain and other forms of pollution have destroyed a great many of them. Whole tropical forests are rapidly being cut down and are disappearing. Species of plants and animals are being lost. The balance of nature is seriously being disturbed. The original forest dwellers are often doomed. Sometimes it is as if you can feel the end near.

What can we do? Follow the words of Jesus in a more literal sense than humanity ever did before, as far as trees and what they stand for are concerned.

Trees give life. They feed and cover us and provide oxygen. Their wood warms and perfumes us. The paper made from them keeps us in communication with each other. We should look at them, diagnose our own environmental and ecological state of affairs from them, and learn from them, as Jesus suggested.

Christology

"It is you who say that I am a king." John 18:33b-37

In some parish churches baptism is administered during Sunday worship. It is done at the moment the creed is customarily recited. The profession of faith we say in the baptism ceremony replaces the usual recitation of the Creed after the homily.

During the moving rite of baptism the greatest hush frequently comes at the moment of anointing when the awesome words "I anoint you priest, prophet, and king" are pronounced. Through these words we express our intimate connection with Jesus. We tend to overlook this relationship.

When we say the creed at Mass or the profession of faith during a baptism ceremony we use one of the most sacred formulas of faith in our church community. It is also an old one, formulated at a time when Christian communities were trying to determine who Jesus was, how he related to God. In those older days christology—the part of theology that studies Jesus—treated mainly that kind of issue.

The issues are different in more contemporary theology. Having established who Jesus is in relation to the Blessed Trinity, we are now more interested in how he relates to us, and we to him.

The older approach ran the risk of concentrating so much on Jesus Christ that we ourselves were somewhat lost in the process. He became such a special subject of research that we overlooked ourselves, our relationship to Jesus. Jürgen Moltmann, a well-known name in theological circles, wrote in the introduction to his book *The Way of Christ* (Harper & Row, 1990): "What I wanted was not an eternal christology for heaven, but a christology for men and women who are on the way in the conflicts of history, and are looking for bearings on that way."

We have to find out how we should be the priest, prophet, and king Jesus was, is, and ever will be!

Co-Workers

"As his fellow-workers, we urge you not to let your acceptance of his grace come to nothing."   *2 Corinthians 5:20–6:2*

Paul calls us co-workers of Jesus Christ. He realizes we do not always live up to that ideal. He warns that we should not neglect the grace of God that we have received. Yet, he sticks to that description of himself and of the followers of Jesus Christ.

We are workers. We all work at something. And we can work for different reasons: for money, for pleasure, for power; we can do it because we are greedy, selfish, or in need.

We can do it for another reason too. In a recent poll taken in this country, students studying law were asked why they had chosen this line of work. They gave various answers. Many wanted a career in law for the money; others for prestige and influence; and thirty percent studied law, they answered, because they wanted to change the world to a better place.

From a Christian point of view there is even more to it than that. We can do our work to establish the Kingdom of God on earth. Nonsense, you say? Not the work you do, you think? Whatever you do, paid or unpaid, employed, self-employed, or unemployed, your work can be done with that aim. It should be. It is the work we are all supposed to be engaged in. As Paul wrote: "As his fellow workers, we urge you not to let your acceptance of his life come to nothing."

It might sound lofty. It is not. You can do the work you do, have the conversations you have, conduct your meetings and discussions— all these can be done in such a way that they bring healing to a broken world. Consider in what small ways you might daily be a co-worker with Jesus to heal the wounds of family, friends, and strangers.

Dignity

"...anyone who wants to save his life will lose it, but anyone who loses his life for my sake will save it."　　　　　　　　*Luke 9:22-25*

Jesus speaks about the possibility of losing yourself. According to him it is the worst thing that can happen to you. He says that you can't compensate for that loss by winning the whole world. Some people know this from experience. They once made hundreds, thousands, maybe even millions of dollars, and then one day discovered that they had lost themselves in the process. One day this truth suddenly dawned upon them, changing them completely.

Francis of Assisi is one of the more famous cases. He was a romantic young man, son of a rich merchant, fashionably dressed, and eager to ride his horse into battle. Coming home defeated, having lost that battle, he suddenly realized that what he was doing had little or no meaning. His life was empty. He had lost himself in glamor and vain snobbery.

He changed his way of life, left his father's shop and wealth to regain his real human dignity.

He succeeded, and what a joy he has been to the whole world ever since.

Others redirect their lives in less romantic and dramatic ways. They change jobs to be more themselves; they alter their policies; they become more critical and reflective; they join self-awareness programs, church communities, or support groups to regain their heart, soul, and humanity along with their dignity.

It is not always possible to do it the way Francis of Assisi did it. It is almost always possible, however, to redirect the work we do, to shift our interests from merely making money to more human matters that are of God. In that way we will really find ourselves.

Dawn

"Sharing your food with the hungry and sheltering the homeless poor...."
Isaiah 58:6-7

I know an older sister, a very nice person, who now and then will suddenly comment: "I don't understand how God can tolerate this world." It is what people say so often when confronted with the evil in this world. Once a secretary told me all that was going on in her family, and she made that very same statement as she wiped the tears from her eyes. How can God tolerate all that is going on? Why does God not let the divine light shine? Why does God not show power?

But the question backfires. The same question should be asked about us: How can we tolerate this world? We want God to do something about it, but shouldn't we do something about it? Listen to the prophet Isaiah: "[This is what pleases me]—it is the Lord who speaks—to break unjust fetters, to undo the straps of the yoke, to let the oppressed go free, and break every yoke, to share your bread with the hungry, and to shelter the homeless poor, to clothe the one you see naked, and not run from your own kin. Then will your light shine like the dawn, and your wound will be quickly healed over" (Isaiah 58:6-7).

We are asked to be a people after God's own heart, acting as God's love and justice in this world. It is our light that should start shining like the dawn over a dark world that badly needs light. As Teresa of Avila once wrote: "Christ has no body on earth, no hands, no feet, but yours...."

Cup of Coffee

"...I was a stranger and you never made me welcome...."
Matthew 25:35-40

She had been in the convent for a very long time and had worked hard all her life. She had met thousands of people, and often—with the help of God—had been a grace to them. Everyone considered her to be a very pious sister. She even thought of herself that way. She spent hours in prayer and devotions. She never missed any community exercises, though she did not always like them. She went to scores of stimulating conventions and fascinating prayer workshops. She faithfully made her annual retreats. She loved being quietly in an out-of-the-way place with God. She was gracefully growing old.

Then, one day, she was suddenly struck by Matthew's version of the last judgment, in particular the text about visiting and not visiting prisoners, sick people, and others. If you visit them, you visit Jesus; if you don't, it is him you leave alone.

She realized that she might fail that test. That fear was not the main reason she changed. It was because she loved Jesus. Hearing this text, she understood where she could find him. She was too old to do anything very drastic, such as going to another place. She did not do anything extraordinary, really. She started to use some of her time to visit those who were lonely in her own neighborhood. She invited them to visit her in the convent. Now and then she brought her friends together to have a cup of coffee and a piece of cake. It hardly seemed anything at all. They had very interesting conversations, sometimes even spiritual ones. There were no exaggerations. Yet her loneliness, and that of the others, was overcome. The Kingdom was forming itself around those cups of coffee and pieces of cake, and there was a new start.

Babbling

"In your prayers do not babble as the gentiles do...." Matthew 6:7,10

If you believe all they say about this world over radio and television, you can become very upset. Everything seems to be going wrong and falling apart. Talk shows speak endlessly about what goes wrong and what to do about it. Convention centers fill up every day of the week with people coming together with their laptop computers, their papers and books, studies and research results. We ourselves can attend meetings, write and read papers, talk until our mouths get dry, but what can we do?

On a smaller scale, in the family or at work, we often face that same need to come together, to talk things over again and again, until everyone is bored and some almost sick.

Jesus said: "Don't just talk, thinking that many words will help you out. They won't. Pray like this: Your Kingdom come!"

In a way, Jesus could not do very much about the world, either. Some people around him were healed and fed, but so many more remained sick and hungry. Yet God's Kingdom broke through among us in him, because he practiced it in his everyday outreach to others, and in his prayer to God in heaven. He was capable of doing what he did because he always had that prayer on his lips. Praying for it is not a question of words, or, as Jesus would say, of "babbling"; it is a question of being and doing.

If you pray "Your Kingdom come" with a sincere or open heart, you will begin to answer that prayer by your behavior. With the help of God, you will hear your own prayer and act in God's name and on behalf of God's reign. If you pray it with that same open heart together in a community or family, the same will happen to them. The Kingdom of God is not simply a promise of the future that God will overcome sin and evil; it is a Kingdom that has already begun!

Open Door

"Therefore, everyone who listens to these words of mine will be like a sensible man who built his house on rock."   Matthew 7:24-25

I was staying at a university parish in South Dakota. I had been invited to a function, so I asked for the key so that I could enter the presbytery without waking anyone up late at night. I was told that there was no key. The doors were always left open. One of the chaplains told me that was their way of expressing their openness and confidence. The people in the presbytery did not want to isolate themselves; they did not want to close the stone walls around them. Anyone who knocked would find their door open. They built their house on the words of Jesus.

This is not the only open-door policy based on the gospel. In Dublin, and so many other places, centers are open where anyone with problems can come in to ask for advice. They cannot always be helped, but the door is always open.

I heard about a parish where the presbytery is only one of the open houses in the community. They have organized themselves in a way that there is a sanctuary possibility for refugees, a shelter for homeless guests, and a division of work that makes it possible that all who need some food to get it. Centers that have all kinds of names—Christ House, Emmaus, Siloam, or whatever. They all have one thing in common: that open door. If you knock on it, it will be opened. You can be sure that the Spirit who makes people run those centers is the Spirit of the one who promised: "Everyone who knocks will have the door opened." (Matthew 7:7) They live the pattern of Jesus' life by openness to God's will in their affectionate service to others.

Family Life

"...go and be reconciled with your brother first, and then come back and present your offering."   *Matthew 5:23-25*

He was sitting opposite me, sipping his cherry soda. He did not look like a warrior, though he was dressed like one. He had signed up for the army. I asked him why. He said he could not stand it at home any more. I asked him why not. He told me stories about the endless difficulties, the fights over everything and nothing.

He was going to learn to fight as a professional, because in fact he was tired of fighting. In a sense, this professional fighter is a mild example of what frequently happens.

It is good to work at peace and justice, to work at the growth of the Kingdom in the world, but that world is not where anger and war start. Often it is at home.

We all know the names of some cruel dictators and terrorists. I do not have to mention names. You can easily make the same discovery I made. When you read their biographies or autobiographies you find out that much went wrong during their youth. In some cases you almost begin to understand them.

Once, when asked what we should do to establish peace in this world, Mother Teresa answered: "Take care to have a good family life. The anger with your father and your mother, with your sister and your brother is at the root of so much trouble."

The Kingdom first starts to fail at home. When families break down entirely, high costs are inflicted on society at large. We should do whatever we can—and that might mean that we have to ask for help—to shoulder our family responsibilities.

Shalom

"Go and be reconciled with your brother first...." Matthew 5:24

During the First World War Father Pierre Teilhard de Chardin was drafted into the French army. Since he was a Jesuit, he served as a Red Cross soldier. One day, just before one of the fiercest battles of that terrible war, he asked himself what Jesus would have thought if he had been present at the front.

As he wrestled with that question—it is not completely clear whether Teilhard tells of his own experience or that of another—he entered a church. The Blessed Sacrament was exposed there. Some frightened villagers were sitting with their priest in the badly damaged church building, praying for peace. Teilhard knelt down and looked at the host in the middle of the monstrance on the altar.

While he was looking, that host started to change. It took on different colors. It resembled a drop of oil on water. It started to spread out. He even heard a kind of rustling noise. He continued to look, full of amazement, and then he saw how the different colors took shapes and forms in the host. Finally he realized that what he saw was the answer to his question. In Jesus he sees all the warring armies and soldiers together, hand in hand.

He saw what the Jews call *shalom*, peace. It is the opposite of "pieces." As long as a sheet of paper is whole, it is shalom. When you tear it in pieces it is no longer whole, it is no longer shalom. An unbroken cup or glass is shalom; when it breaks into pieces it is no longer shalom.

We human beings were created together with the rest of creation as shalom, in one piece, in one peace.

Jesus often told us that. He did not overlook the fact that we may have enemies. He himself knew about having them! But he kept insisting that having enemies should not break us in pieces. We should love them. We should love them because we belong together: "God's rain falls on good and bad alike!"

Encouragement

"...and sends down rain to fall on the upright and wicked alike."
Acts 13:13-25

When Paul and some of his companions were guests in the synagogue in Antioch, the president of the synagogue said, "If you would like to address some words of encouragement to the congregation, please do so!"

We all know how important words of encouragement are. So often you hear the complaint that those words are not spoken.

You work and work, you even know that you are doing well, but nobody seems to notice, nobody seems to care, nobody ever speaks a word of appreciation. You are just taken for granted, and not a word of encouragement is ever heard.

Did you ever see how faces light up when you express appreciation for a meal served, repairs done to your car, services rendered?

Words of encouragement are so important to all of us. An old Latin word can be found in the middle of that term: *cor*, which means "heart." To encourage someone is to give some heart, some more heart than he or she had before. Words of encouragement are a boost. It is good not to depend on them too much, because they are not often spoken! That is what makes them extra precious when you hear them.

Even Jesus looked for those words of encouragement. He had difficulty doing without them. He was upset and said: "I never seem to be able to satisfy you. I eat and you say that I am a glutton; I don't and that is no good to you either." "I play for you on the flute, and you don't dance; I sing a funeral dirge and you don't weep. What do you really want?" He was disappointed when words of encouragement were not given, and delighted when he received them. When nobody else would give them, heaven would break open and a voice was heard saying: "You are my beloved Son!"

Jesus was great at encouraging others: "Rise and walk! Open your eyes and see! Take up your cross and bear it. I will be with you always!" Let us follow his example and encourage another person!

Abraham's Children

"...if you would like to address some words of encouragement...
please do so."   Acts 13:26-33

Jews, Christians, and Muslims call themselves children of Abraham. We know what happened to the Abram family. They made a terrific step in their lives, a step we all have to make, one that we as Jews, Christians, and Muslims should already have made.

Abram lived in a tribal context. The ethnic group he belonged to had its own tribal god. That god was theirs, and they were of that god. They lived in a narrow, closed circle around the temple of that god. In the region where Abram lived this god was called—in Abram's language—Sin.

Yahweh called the Abram family out of that circle, and they left it. It was a hard decision. As a result, they were considered to be atheists and traitors.

One day Yahweh again appeared to them and asked them to look into the sky. They saw—very vaguely—what the prophets after them would see: how all the nations of the whole world were going to come together as the one family of God. Yahweh changed Abram's name to Abraham, to indicate that what happened to him and Sarah should be repeated for all time.

Paul often recalled the story of Abraham, evoking the world as God wants it to be: the whole of humanity together as one family.

Jesus renewed that vision among us in a much clearer way than any prophet had ever done before. He not only announced it, he lived it. That belonging together of the whole world as the one family of God is the good news. It is an integral part of our salvation and redemption.

At no time since have those words been more meaningful than in our day, when people are moving all over the world, coming together more and more, even in the neighborhoods and streets where we live. Let us perceive these migrations in this light!

Joy

"My brothers and sisters, children of Abraham's race, and all you godfearers, this message of salvation is meant for you." Acts 13:44-52

We often hear the little word "but." It almost always precedes a real downer. "Everything is all right," someone will say, "but..." and you know that you just heard the good news and that the bad news is coming.

Reading the reports on those first communities of Christians in the early days, the word "but" is also heard, used in another way.

After a description of persecutions, executions, imprisonments, expulsions, and all kind of mishaps and misadventures they nevertheless enthusiastically add, "But the disciples were filled with joy and the Holy Spirit" (Acts 13:51). People plotted against them, they were expelled from their homes and persecuted, *but* they were full of joy.

That joy is an important characteristic. It is as important as keeping our "orthodoxy"! Popes, bishops, priests, and faithful will be up in arms when the orthodox teaching of the church is in danger. They seem to be much less concerned about that other aspect of our Christian set-up: joy. I agree with the person who once told me, "You are all convinced that you're saved and redeemed, but you don't look like it at all. Why do you look so sad if you believe in your salvation?" When the portrait of a laughing Jesus was painted and published some years ago it caused quite an uproar in certain circles.

Chesterton once wrote:

> Wherever a Catholic sun does shine,
> I always found laughter and good red wine,
> at least I always found it so,
> Benedicamus Domino.

Two questions should be asked from time to time in every family and community: Who is safeguarding the faith, and who is taking care of the joy?

Imitation of Christ

"...but the converts were filled with joy and the Holy Spirit."

Luke 9:23

The term *imitation of Jesus* is well known. It is the title of one of the most influential older devotional books. New translations in English and other languages frequently appear. It remains a spiritual bestseller. According to some, it is even the most read Christian book after holy Scripture itself.

Yet, though used so often, the word "imitation" is not the best term to indicate how we should relate to Jesus.

The danger is that we place Jesus outside of ourselves if we "imitate" him. It is as if he walks in front of us, and we walk behind him, the way you sometimes see a small boy walk behind his father, trying to match his stride. Or as one of the brothers of Saint Francis of Assisi did: He thought if he did exactly what Francis did, he would be as saintly as Francis was. So he mimicked everything Francis did. He ate as many spoonfuls of food as he did, prayed the same length of time in the same posture as Francis, until Francis noticed him and told him not to be so foolish.

We should do what Jesus did, but not in this mimicking way.

He sets our model, but there is more to it than that. *His spirit is in us!*

We have to live that spirit in our world, in our environment.

We have to live that spirit in our relationships with our children, our parents, our brothers, and our sisters.

We have to "invest" it in our activities and leisure, in our young years or in our senior days, in sickness and health, while alive and while dying. Let us take some time to reflect on this, and look to Jesus to find him in our own heart!

Different and the Same

"If anyone wants to be a follower of mine...." Acts 14:5-18

It happened in Lycaonia that Paul and Barnabas caused a stir when they healed a man whose feet had been crippled from birth. The people from the region thought that some gods had descended among them: "The gods have come down to us in human form." They called Barnabas "Zeus," and Paul "Hermes." The situation got completely out of control when the priests from a temple called Zeus-Outside-the-Gate started to prepare oxen for sacrifice in honor of the two. When Barnabas and Paul realized that the people meant what they said, and really thought they were gods, when they even started to prepare oxen to be sacrificed in their honor, they became—understandably—very upset.

They tried to get out of that situation as quickly as possible. They shouted: "Friends, what do you think you are doing? We are only human beings, like you!"

Yet, they had to correct themselves. They were different. They were coming to bring good news; they had recognized the fullness of God's Spirit in their lives. They had come to help others make the same discovery.

Paul and Barnabas were the same as the others, and yet different, initiated through the Spirit into the richness of the Christian community.

When the question is asked whether Christians are different from others, the answer is both "no" and "yes." Christians have discovered—and accepted—in themselves a reality that is also found in others. That is what Peter and the others experienced when the people in front of them told them: You are speaking in our language; we know what you are talking about.

Heart of Jesus

"We are only human beings, mortals like yourselves." Acts 14:19-28

The prayer group prayed "to get the heart of Jesus." A beautiful prayer, one that fits perfectly well in the context of a Christian community. It is also a delicate prayer. You really have to know what you are praying for, and what you are in for, once your prayer is heard! Paul and Barnabas encouraged the first Christians to have a "new" and "fresh" heart: "Barnabas and Paul put fresh heart into the disciples" (Acts 14:22), but they added "We all have to experience many hardships before we enter the Kingdom of God."

The "fresh" or "new" heart the text speaks about is also a good description of the role of a Christian community. That is what we should be, a new heart in the world, to be the heart of Jesus in the world. Charles de Foucauld, the saintly French ex-officer who lived for so long alone in the North African desert, hoped to be the heart of Jesus in that barren place. He carried an image of that heart on his clothes.

The old world has serious problems in accepting the new heart, a new heart in a world that is old and far from ideal. The world often gives signs of rejecting it.

Anyone who has been involved in introducing kindness and a greater concern for justice in any part of this world knows the difficulties this can cause.

We can even experience this in our own case, how our human nature resists the new heart we know it needs. If you don't believe this, just consider what great effort it takes to get rid of a vice or an addiction!

Discrimination

*"They put fresh heart into the disciples, encouraging them to perse-
vere in the faith...."*   Acts 15:1-6

No Christian community has ever been without its problems. One of
these derives from the very nature of community. Once you have
come together, organized yourself well, and developed some customs
and ways of doing things, the risk is that you close the circle to others.
The community becomes a group, and often a closed circle. Newcomers arrive, they are welcomed, but often only up to a certain point.
They should not bring in too many new ideas. They should not try to
start shifting things around.

It has been an issue with us from the beginning. What was a Jewish
Christian community going to do with those non-Jewish newcomers?
What does a white or black middle-class parish do when a number of
immigrants would like not only to be welcomed, but to share in the
decision making of the group?

Should the customs of those who were the first ones to form the
community be imposed on the newcomers? One of the issues in Jerusalem was exactly that: How should Christians from different cultures
relate to each other?

It is a difficulty that has never disappeared.

The most stifling words in a community context often are "It has always been like that; we have always been doing things this way!" Do
you remember when you last heard those words? Do you remember
using them yourself?

The community leaders in Jerusalem made a wise decision. They
did not act as if there were no problem. They did not suppress the issue. They decided to discuss the problem with the communities involved and their leaders. They made contact, dialogued openly, and
came to some wholesome conclusions.

Equality

"...after a long argument...it was decided that Paul and Barnabas and others of the church should go up to Jerusalem and discuss the question with the apostles and the elders."   Acts 15:7-21

We were sitting in an upper room in Washington, D.C. Many lobbying groups were present. They had all been lobbying in favor of certain sanctions against South Africa. We were waiting for the result of a vote in the House of Representatives. One of the black members of that House was going to come to brief us on the results. We already knew them. Our lobbying efforts had failed. They would succeed later on, but this time they had failed. The one to brief us came and explained what had happened. When he left the room he stopped at the door, turned to us, and said: "If this country learned that a couple of people were killed in the streets of an East European country, we definitely would take measures. Against South Africa we don't. Why? Because the scores of people shot in Africa are not white."

A hard truth. To accept the equality of all was the first internal difficulty the first Christian community met. Remember one group of widows was preferred to another in the distribution of food.

This always has been the difficulty in our communities. There are reports today that some parish council members are reluctant to let Christians from another ethnic background use their facilities.

Not realizing the equality God calls us to can only lead to disaster, as it has so often in church history.

Peter, Paul, and James did not mince words when they came to their final verdict: "God made no distinction between them and us....We believe that we are saved in the same way they are: through the grace of the Lord Jesus" (Acts 15:9).

[181]

Discerning the Spirit

"God made no distinction between them and us...." Acts 15:22-31

In a Baltimore parish some parish members came together about a spiritual issue, something that must be happening all over the world hundreds of times a week. This group came together because they felt the need of taking the Holy Spirit into account when making decisions in life. They felt that need not only in their own lives, but also in their own community. Should they build a new chapel? How could they solve some recurring problems in the parish school? What about a greater variety in the services offered to the parish? How do you discern the Holy Spirit? Is it sufficient to pray about it by yourself, or in community?

They all agreed on one thing: the Spirit should be discerned to find what decisions are truly of God. The communities in Acts and the apostles themselves definitely succeeded in doing this in the early days.

They were not afraid of making statements such as, "It seems good to the Holy Spirit and to ourselves...that we should do this or omit that."

It is a daring and pretentious way of stating things, so daring that we would hardly even care to repeat it.

Most probably we would not be able to say it in good faith. We don't relate to the Holy Spirit the way they did. After much prayer, fasting, discussion, and consultation, "the apostles and the elders, with the concurrence of the whole church" came to their decision. Few of us, whether in a leadership position or not, make decisions that way, but it is the only way to make decisions if you want to be sure that the Holy Spirit is in your community and in your own life!

The group in Baltimore decided to delegate some of their members to study discernment more closely. They did. They systematically read all the classical spiritual works on the issue, and they finally came out with a program that helps to form "discerners," people who can introduce persons and groups to tracing the Holy Spirit.

Spirit of Jesus

"It has been decided by the Holy Spirit and by ourselves...."
Acts 16:1-10

A theology scholar came all the way from Denmark to Nairobi in East Africa to do some research on the spirituality of East African youngsters. One of the questions she would ask them was what book in the Christian Scriptures they preferred. She had divided the Christian Scriptures into sections to get a more precise answer. One of the questions was: "What gospel do you prefer?" She expected them to answer the gospel by Luke, because it is a gospel written for people with no Judaic background. She was mistaken. Most of them preferred the gospel of John. That gospel speaks about life, and the power of life, as no other gospel does.

She then asked the question: "What book in the Christian Scriptures do you prefer?" The book most mentioned was Acts of the Apostles. The reason for this choice was the same one they gave when explaining why they preferred the gospel of John. Acts explains how the new life given by Jesus works in the concrete. Some of the students she interviewed referred to Luke's statement that Christians have the spirit of Jesus (Acts 16:7).

Paul speaks about the "spirit of Christ," and that is a beautiful way of putting it. He even states: "It is not I who live, but Christ lives in me!" Yet, the word "Jesus" makes what is happening to us all the more concrete. In this way the Spirit gets hands and feet, our hands and our feet! The Spirit, then, is not an abstract power or merely a spiritual influence. It is the life of Jesus in us.

It is the final reason, the ultimate explanation of our kindness!

We can only give a real account for our kindness by referring to Jesus.

Faith Sharing

"...they tried to go into Bithynia, but as the Spirit of Jesus would not allow them, they went through Mysia...."   Acts 16:13

Many households follow the excellent custom of praying together. A family that prays together stays together. That is true. Yet, family prayer is often not very personal. Family members may be sitting or kneeling next to each other, but often are spiritually almost like strangers. It is like this at Mass. You answer together, you kneel, stand, and sit together at the same time. You recite the creed and the Our Father together, but sometimes you don't even know the name of the person next to you.

No wonder many small groups are being formed where people tell each other about their experiences and how they live their Christian lives.

Why don't we invite others to make our common prayer more personal, more spontaneous, and to share more of our successes and failures as Christians?

Not everyone will be willing to share like that, but many might and they may encourage one another by doing it.

From the beginning, living according to Jesus' spirit has been experienced and expressed in many different ways.

It is no surprise that there are four different (and they really are different!) gospel stories about Jesus. This variety greatly enriches us. There are so many ways of living "The Way," there are so many ways of listening to the Word. To live the Way means something different in a well-to-do North American suburban area than in the squalor of a South American poverty-stricken rural region. This variety makes sharing, listening to each other, so enriching. Discussing how each of us lives the spirit of Jesus is more important than checking it against one set of customs and practices!

Women's Groups

"We went outside the gates beside a river... as this was a customary place for prayer. We sat down and began to speak to the women who had come to the meeting." Acts 16:11-15

The pages of Luke's two books are crowded with women and men, without whom neither Jesus nor his apostles would have been able to survive. It begins with Mary who, as soon as she hears that she is going to be the mother of the Messiah, hastens to Elizabeth. It is when the two meet that the full impact of what happened to them dawns on them, and they both join in song.

All through his gospel Luke speaks of groups of women. Women hail Jesus' birth, they follow him everywhere, they meet him on his way to the cross, they are the last ones to leave that scene, and they are the first ones to visit his tomb where they learn that he is risen.

Luke continues this trend in Acts. Paul meets a prayer group of women on the riverside in Philippi on a Sabbath day. He speaks to them about Jesus and the good news he is. Lydia, originally from Thyatira, who was in the fashionable purple-dye trade in Philippi, is a member of the group. She is a devout person and reveres God. She opens her heart to accept what Paul is saying. After her baptism, she invites Paul to come to her home. Her household is baptized and soon becomes the support and worship center of Philippi, the community Paul came to love most.

Lydia is only one of the twenty-six women Luke calls by name. He writes about scores of others, however, who are not named. Both Luke's gospel and Acts are crowded with women and women's groups—the group that formed itself around Dorcas to make clothing for the needy, for instance.

It is a women's movement that never stopped, and that never will stop. Think of the hundreds of sister congregations and the thousands of women's groups throughout the world who really form the heart and at the same time are the backbone of the church.

Laughter

"And the whole family was filled with joy, because they had come to believe in God."   *Acts 16:22-34*

Luke cannot stop reporting on the joy of the communities he met, the joy that came from their insight of being "people of the Spirit."

The variety of people Luke describes as exalted in spirit and consequently confident, realistic, compassionate, loving, and welcoming, is notable. They come from different ethnic groups, from various backgrounds and classes. In the family mentioned above the main person is a prison warden and his family; in yesterday's reflection the main person and her family was the well-to-do textile fashioner, Lydia.

Luke not only mentions this joy in Acts, he does the same in his gospel. That joy is the difference Jesus makes, according to Luke. In his gospel he mentions twenty-two times in twenty-four chapters that the coming of Jesus brought joy, gladness, praise, and thanksgiving. Life has not only gained meaning, it gained purpose and zest. Luke is the only one who mentions that "we will laugh" (Luke 6:21). Luke offers us scenes of a happy childhood, home, youth, health, gladness, swift feet and burning hearts, music, merrymaking, and dancing (see Luke 15:24-25).

People find their transformation in Jesus and in his spirit. They see the light. They find meaning. Their eyes light up. Their life changes. And though more often than not they remain doing the same work, they do it in another way, in another spirit, just as they become different persons, enhanced as they are by the Spirit of Jesus!

Against the Grain

*...and indeed as some of your own writers have said: We are all
[God's] children."*   *Acts 17:22-34*

When Paul was preaching at Athens, the pinnacle of human sophisti-
cation, it was a difficult time for him. He did not like the town from
the beginning. Some Athenians did not react well to his street preaching; they called him a talking bird. But some philosophers called him
over to the Areopagus, their great place of discussion and decision
making.

Luke does not take kindly to the Athenians, either. About this invitation he notes that they wanted Paul to amuse them. They liked new
fads and novel ideas. They were intrigued by Paul's belief in a resurrection.

Paul's main theme, however, was not the resurrection. The God he
preached was not the God of one group, tribe, or race, but of all people. He was preaching the God in whom all of us "live and move and
exist" (Acts 17: 28).

Paul had prepared his speech carefully, for at that point he quoted
Aratus, an Athenian philosopher, who had written: "We are all his
children." If this is true, Paul explains, then we have quite a lot to re-
pent for. If we are going to be judged according to that norm, our up-
rightness falls far short of that of Jesus. Jesus lived that truth to the
full; therefore he was raised from the dead.

It is at the mention of the resurrection that most of his audience
burst out laughing, though some others said, "We want to hear you
again."

Were they laughing at the idea of a resurrection, or did they laugh
because they did not want to accept the Way of Jesus Christ, a Way
that teaches us to love all and everyone—including our enemies—
because we are all in the same way the children of God?

It is a Way that goes against the grain of this world. It is a Way that
divides not only those who hear it for the first time, but those of us
who are used to it, and who—even when we believe in the resurrection—often have our doubts.

Lay Apostolate

"...when Priscilla and Aquila heard him, they attached themselves to him and gave him more detailed instruction about the Way."
Acts 18:18-28

It is interesting that Paul was accompanied on his apostolic journey to Syria by the business couple Priscilla and Aquila. It shows how business and mission went hand in hand. Paul had met them by chance. They were refugees from Italy, where the emperor Claudius had expelled all Jews. Paul felt immediately at home with them, because they were tent makers just as he was. The discussions the three had together went far beyond their shared trade. Paul told them about the Way, and they accepted Jesus as their guide in life. Paul stayed with them for a year and a half. They seem to have been fairly well-to-do and may even have paid Paul's passage, since they joined him on board the ship for Ephesus. They may even have paid his passage on to Jerusalem. Aquila and Priscilla were either transferring their business to Ephesus or were leaving their Corinthian operation in charge of a manager in order to open a new branch at Ephesus.

Once, long after Paul left Ephesus, Priscilla and Aquila heard a man, Apollos, speak about Jesus in a local meeting. He had been baptized by John the Baptizer, but he wanted to know more about Jesus. The two decided to instruct him on who Jesus was. They invited him to their home, just as they had invited Paul.

We are not told whether they baptized him. It seems likely, however, considering the rest of the story. Once aware of the Spirit in him and infected by the zeal of the two, Apollos in his turn left on a mission tour and was a consolation and encouragement to many.

We find in Aquila and Priscilla the kind of combination of business and mission that never stopped and may even today fit well within a Christian way of life.

Sign of the Cross

"When they heard this, they were baptized in the name of the Lord Je-
sus and the moment Paul laid hands on them the Holy Spirit came
down on them...." Acts 19:1-7

We should regularly reflect on the real core of our Christian life. The
church community reflects on it especially during Easter time, if only
because in almost every Christian community new members are baptized at the Easter Vigil.

"I baptize you in the name of the Father, and of the Son, and of the
Holy Spirit." We are accustomed to apply all this to God, who in a
mysterious way is three and at the same time one.

But let us not forget that we may also apply it to ourselves when
we make the sign of the cross, a gesture that covers the whole of our
body and person.

The baptismal formula tells us how we relate to God and how God
relates to us: the source of our being, the offspring in which we are all
created and saved, and the spirit that carries us through life. This is
true not only of myself, but of all those I associate with. It shows me
how I should love others.

Of course, we will fall short of living what we signify when we
make the sign of the cross. Christians have been falling short since the
very beginning of our communities. But they did not finally fail. Rather they succeeded. Their kindness has never died. It could not die,
since it is the kindness of Jesus himself. It is the kindness we should
continue to show in Jesus' name in our communities until all is fulfilled.

Abundance

"...in those days before the Flood people were eating and drinking...right up to the day Noah went into the ark." Matthew 24:37-44

She had worked as a volunteer in a Third World country and had liked life there. It was relatively simple and uncomplicated. But once she returned home, she quickly found that home was no longer the place she had left so many years ago. All had changed.

She told me that she noticed this most the first time she went to do her weekly shopping. Shopping had never caused her problems overseas. Sometimes there would be no sugar, or no salt—that was a nuisance, but that was all. She told me how she was totally overwhelmed when she entered a supermarket for the first time. The choices were so great that she could not make up her mind. That first time she left without buying anything at all.

In our Western world of relative abundance of goods, this is true not only of groceries, but of many things. We are surrounded by a wealth of choices. We have to sift; we have to choose; we have to sort out. We have to determine our direction. We are either sheep or wolves. We can be sound trees or diseased trees, bearing good fruit or bitter fruit. We can be gatherers or scatterers. We choose for or against ourselves. The sorting out is not going to start taking place later on, when the Lord comes. It is taking place now through our own choices.

Pope John Paul II insists continuously that we should pay attention to the seriousness of our situation. Of course, we don't really need him to make us aware of that, yet it is good to listen to his plea to use the world's abundance with restraint and with concern for the needs of others: "I wish to appeal with simplicity and humility to everyone, to all men and women without exception. I wish to ask them to be convinced of the seriousness of the present moment and of each one's individual responsibility"(*On Social Concern*, 47).

Reaching Out to Jesus

"And to the centurion Jesus said, 'Go back, then; let this be done for you, as your faith demands.'"   *Matthew 8:5-11*

It was a hot evening at a college in Kenya. The Theological Association was meeting at Alliance High School. They had invited other colleges from the area. There were over 600 students in the hall. They were obviously interested in the topic: "Healing and Miracles in Our Time." They also had a hidden agenda. The real question they wanted to explore was, Why did miracles and healing take place in the early days of the church, but do not in today's Christian communities? A good question!

Do you remember the story of the Roman officer who comes to ask Jesus to heal his servant who is sick at home? Jesus is touched by the loving care of the officer and decides to go with him to his house. The officer says that this is not necessary: "Just give the word and my servant will be cured." Jesus, amazed by the man's faith, gives the word and when the officer returns home and checks the time of the healing, he realizes that his servant was healed at the moment Jesus spoke.

The Roman officer does not do the healing. He asks Jesus to do that. Yet, if he hadn't asked Jesus, and if he hadn't believed in Jesus, his servant would not have been healed. So in a way we might conclude that the officer, too, healed his servant. How did he do it? By reaching out to Jesus. The lack of healing and miracles in our communities and in our lives is due to a lack of reaching out to Jesus! When you reach out, when you get on his wavelength, when you have faith, all becomes possible.

Childhood Memories

"I bless you, Father, Lord of heaven and earth, for hiding these things from the learned and the clever and revealing them to little children."
Luke 10:21-24

This is an amazing statement: that Jesus says that the Lord of heaven and earth revealed "these things" to "mere children." He was speaking of you and me. Not about us as we are now, but as we were long—maybe even very, very long—ago. At one time we knew what the Kingdom of God was all about.

Try to remember your first religious experience. Was it praying with your mother? Was it at your first Holy Communion? Revive it in your mind and heart. Was it when you saved your money to help the poor or a missionary in a far-off land? Revive it in your mind and heart. It will connect you to your own spiritual roots. It will help you to drink from your own spiritual well. Note it down to make it a lasting memory.

A sister once told me how as a small child she walked through a brook on a sunny afternoon. When she saw how the sun was shining on her feet under the water, she suddenly realized that God is in heaven, that all is well, and that nothing would ever ultimately go wrong. As children, we knew—just as children around us today do when they trust adults without reservation, when they share their food, shout enthusiastically when they see a flower, a bird, a horse, a cat, or a dog, and communicate with all without any difficulty.

Jesus shows a fascination with little children, those who bear the full genius of the human personality, the ones who have not yet forgotten the kingdom within, as Jean Houston wrote in one of her books. It is in ourselves that we can trace God's Kingdom. We all carry within ourselves the little child that Jesus talks about. It is a matter of finding that child in us again and freeing it, of recapturing our original joy.

Helplessness

"How many loaves have you?" Matthew 15:29-37

When Jesus told them: "I feel sorry for those people, they have nothing to eat," his disciples reacted in a way we often do in similar circumstances. They stood there wringing their hands and did not know what to do.

The poor of the world remain hungry for bread, and we Christians are still standing around wringing our hands, thinking we can do nothing. We feel powerless to help society with its pressing problems: the homeless, the runaway youth, the drug addicts, the desperate and lonely elderly.

"What might we be able to do?" you ask. "Look at what we have, hardly enough to help ourselves," you complain.

Jesus, however, asks us the same question he asked his disciples: "What do you have?" If we are willing, he will accept what we have, asking us to share it with those who are hungry, and the miracle will happen again. We will discover that there is plenty for everyone. We were only hiding what we had from each other. There is more than enough for all of us.

In *On Social Concern*, Pope John Paul II wrote: "[We] cannot but embrace the immense multitudes of the hungry, the needy, the homeless, those without medical care and, above all, those without hope of a better future. It is impossible not to take account of the existence of these realities. To ignore them would mean becoming like the 'rich man' who pretended not to know the beggar Lazarus lying at his gate" (42).

You can't solve these problems on your own. Jesus didn't. The first thing he did was to look for some company. Maybe there is a committee that is trying to solve one of these problems in your parish. Or you might join an organization that engages in helping the needy in the world. There are many of them!

Committees

"It is not anyone who says to me, 'Lord, Lord,' who will enter the kingdom of Heaven, but the person who does the will of my Father in heaven."   *Matthew 7:21, 24-27*

One pitfall we all know about is the trap of the committee and the sub-committee. Of course, there should be meetings. There should be committees, studies, and reports. Yet, if we remain in the realm of words, Jesus says we are not sensible. We are building our work on sand, which would be blown over at the slightest turbulence.

We establish ourselves in this world through concrete activities. To say "Lord, Lord" is not sufficient. Neither is writing tour plans and good intentions on sheets of paper, or feeding them into a computer.

To be with Jesus means to take over his sentiments, to live with the same single-mindedness he had, to be like he was and is. Jesus makes it clear that anyone who listens to him and doesn't draw these conclusions is foolish. Such a person is as foolish as someone who builds a house on surface soil, without any foundation.

The foundation of our faith is the living of the life of Jesus—no less and no more. If we do not intend to live that kind of life we are deceiving ourselves and others when we say that we are "his."

Everyone knows how easy it is to talk about what should be done for the poor, the homeless, the orphaned, the drug users, and even society in general. We all know how comforting it is to be counseled about problems with your loved ones, your children, your parents, your past, and your addictions. But at a certain point the talking has to give way to action. To say only "Lord, Lord!" is really not sufficient.

Blindness

"As Jesus went on his way two blind men followed him shouting:
'Take pity on us, son of David!'"   *Matthew 9:27-31*

The mother was trying to calm her child down as well as she could. It didn't help. The child was afraid of the bare white walls of the clinic and of the doctors and nurses. When the nurse came around the corner with a syringe, the child started first to scream, but then closed her eyes so she wouldn't see, as if to say, "If I don't see it, it isn't there."

This type of blindness is often found in those who are unwilling to see the situation as it is—the alcoholic who does not want to see that he is addicted, the tourist who does not want to visit the slum area of the country he visits, the patient who does not accept his sickness, the television viewer who never looks at a documentary about the poor and neglected in his own country or in the world.

When people come to Jesus to ask to be healed from their blindness or deafness, Jesus sometimes asks: "Do you really want to see? Do you really want to hear?" Do you know what you are in for when you start to see, when you start to hear? We often protect ourselves against the hopes, the griefs, and the anxieties of ourselves and of others.

John Paul II repeated something the Second Vatican Council had mentioned years before, when he wrote: "The joys and the hopes, the griefs and the anxieties of the people of this age, especially those who are poor or in any way afflicted, these are the joys and hopes, the griefs and anxieties of the followers of Christ. Indeed, nothing genuinely human fails to raise an echo in their hearts" (*On Social Concern*, 5).

It sounds pretentious, but it is well meant. The pope says that if you share in the sentiments of Jesus, then you share in the feelings of someone who is touched by any evil done to a human being, but who is also touched by any good done to someone. You can't play blind in this world and be a follower of Jesus. You will have to see with his eyes. We had better pray to be healed from our blindness, too!

Unclean Spirits

"The harvest is rich, but the laborers are few." Matthew 9:35-10:6-8

On the street I saw a small girl, cold and shivering in a thin dress, with little hope of a decent meal. You must have met her now and then, too. I became angry and said to God: "Why do you permit this? Why don't you do something about it?" For a while God said nothing, but that night God replied, quite suddenly: "I certainly did something about it. I made you! Now why don't *you* do something about it?"

We often do not accept our own authoritative power over misery, sickness, and evil. Matthew says explicitly that Jesus summoned his followers and gave them authority over unclean spirits with power to drive them out (Matthew 10:1).

We could do all kinds of things, but we don't, although so much good could come of it. It is not unwillingness on our part; it is not even lack of imagination that hinders us. Often what hinders us is the poor idea we have of our own influence, of our own weight and authority. Yet, we are charged with God's Spirit and with the mission Jesus left us to accomplish.

"At stake is the dignity of the human person, whose defense and promotion have been entrusted to us by the Creator, and to whom the men and women at every moment of history are strictly and responsibly in debt. As many people are already more or less aware, the present situation does not seem to correspond to this dignity. Every individual is called upon to play his or her part in this peaceful campaign" (*On Social Concern*, 47).

We are put in this world as participants and executors in God's creative and salvific project. We have to execute this project first in the place and situation where we are engaged as parents, educators, doctors, postal workers, priests, or retired senior citizens. And then we might also want to take into account that there is always a great demand for volunteer workers.

Reborn

"No, we were never even told there was such a thing as the Holy Spirit."   Acts 19:1-8

When Paul arrived on his mission journey in Ephesus, he noticed something strange about the Christian community. So strange, in fact, that he asked them: "Did you receive the Holy Spirit when you became believers?" They answered: "No, we were never even told that there is such a thing as the Holy Spirit."

The Ephesians who spoke like that to Paul had only received the baptism of John the Baptizer. Paul told them, "John's baptism was a baptism of repentance. He told the people to believe in the one coming after him, that is, in Jesus." When they heard this, they asked to be baptized in the name of Jesus. That is what Paul did, and the Holy Spirit came upon them.

There are many Christians, too, baptized in the name of Jesus, who never seem to have heard that there is "such a thing as the Holy Spirit." Some of them even speak about a "second baptism," about being "reborn," when they discover the Spirit. There is a lot of confusion about this.

We don't need a second baptism. None of us was baptized only by John the Baptizer. All of us are baptized in the name of Jesus. What we do need is a better understanding of what happened to us when we were baptized, how we were initiated in the risen life and into the life of the spirit of Jesus. It is a real grace to be reborn in that conviction!

Not being aware of the Holy Spirit in our lives does not mean that the Spirit is not in us. It means that we are not living from within, from the divine power that dwells within us. It is in our prayer, entering into ourselves, that we will find the Spirit. Once found, that Spirit will manifest itself in all the good works we do.

Jesus' Way

"And now you see me on my way to Jerusalem in captivity to the Spirit...." Acts 20:17-27

At the end of his life with Jesus Christ, Paul decides to go to Jerusalem. He says: "Compelled by the Holy Spirit I am going to Jerusalem" (Acts 20:22). Paul feels that the Holy Spirit is asking him to go to Jerusalem. He also knows that the Holy Spirit is warning him that if he goes to Jerusalem he will be arrested. He is going Jesus' way. Jesus, too, knew that he had to go to Jerusalem and that he would be arrested there. Jesus' disciples asked Jesus not to go. Paul's friends do the same (Acts 21:12).

Paul's story follows the pattern of Jesus' story. The journey to Jerusalem is the final one. Jesus and Paul both began their journeys reaching into their inner self. Jesus did that before he came out of Nazareth, and while he was in the desert after being baptized by John the Baptizer. Saul did it when, being struck by the Lord at Damascus, he turned into the Paul we know. Both Jesus and Paul then continued their journey through life reaching out to the people they met around them, and both Jesus and Paul decided that going to Jerusalem would be the final part of their journey, bringing all they had experienced and rallying all those they had met. All his life, Jesus was on an *inner* journey, an *outer* journey, and a *centering* journey. So was Paul, following the way of Jesus.

If we are faithful in the world in which we live, our story will be like theirs, perhaps not as dramatic, but just as real. Any time we enter into ourself in prayer we will discover that we are called to reach out and bring the whole world with all its people together in the Lord. This is the way Jesus went, and Paul, and all those who lived the Way before us.

Jesus' Affection in Us

"There is more happiness in giving than in receiving." Acts 20:28-38

Paul gives us a glimpse into his own personal dynamic when he says: "I showed you that by this kind of hard work that we must help the weak, remembering the words Jesus himself said: 'It is more blessed to give than to receive'" (Acts 20:35), a saying of Jesus that does not occur in any of the gospels.

With those words Paul gives an account of the kindness he showed his friends, of the hard work he did among them. His imitation of Jesus Christ is the key to his life. In all he does he is led by the remembrance of the life and the words of Jesus. In one of his letters he would write even more outspokenly: "God can testify how I long for all of you with the affection of Jesus" (Philippians 1:8).

This is a mild translation of what Paul says. Other translations of the same words are more blatant: "I long after you all in the bowels of Jesus Christ!" We would say, I love you with Jesus' heart, because we think the human heart is the center of emotion. Paul considered one's bowels to be the center of emotion and affection.

We are no different from Paul. We have the same Spirit; we have Jesus' affection in us. We have to tap into these sources of loving concern and kindness. We should be in accord, in harmony, in concert with him—of the same mind and heart. We should ask ourselves: What did Jesus feel and think? What would he feel and think in our situation? His life vibration should throb in us. His energy should become ours. Our imagination should be plugged into and be charged by his vision. Jesus asked us to follow him. He did not mean a literal mimicking, but an inner process of being vivified by the same Spirit that enlivened him.

That is what Paul did.

Support from Heaven

"Next night, the Lord appeared to him and said, 'Courage!'"

Acts 23:6-11

Once in Jerusalem Paul's freedom of movement did not last long. In no time he was recognized, assaulted, and brought to the military fortress. The man in charge there allowed him to speak to the crowd. They listened to him up to the moment that he proclaimed that God's grace is given to the whole of humanity. At that point they started to shout: "Rid the earth of the man! He is not fit to live" (Acts 22:22).

It was the same thing that had happened to him in Athens. The Athenians, too, had been willing to listen up the moment when Paul announced that we all are children of God.

This is almost an exact repeat of what happened to Jesus. When Jesus told those in Nazareth that the year of grace he came to bring was not only for them but for everyone, and when he even gave some examples of graced "pagans" to illustrate this, they jumped up and hustled him out of their synagogue trying to kill him.

They brought Paul to a military barracks where soldiers must have milled around him. Paul must have been disheartened as he awaited the next turn of events in the prison. The second night there the Lord appeared to him and said: "Take courage! I will be with you!"

It is a promise given not only to Paul, but to all of us as well: "I will be with you always." This divine assurance should help us to be the master of all tensions and events, rather than their victim. God's support is always there for us.

Risen Life in Us

"...they had some argument about a dead man called Jesus whom Paul alleged to be alive."   Acts 25:13-21

When you read the report of Paul's arrest you get the impression that he was arrested and condemned because he believed in the resurrection. Luke reports, "His accusers had some argument with him...about a dead man called Jesus whom Paul alleged to be alive" (Acts 26:19).

The difficulty his enemies had with Paul was not only because he alleged that "a dead man Jesus" was alive, although the Roman official who arrested him might have thought that that was the case. The difficulty Christians have experienced in recent times has not only been because of belief in the resurrection, either.

Think of some recent martyrs: the three nuns and the one laywoman in El Salvador in 1980, the six Jesuits and their cook and her daughter there in 1989. They were not killed because they believed in the resurrection as part of Christian doctrine. They were killed because Jesus was alive in them. Living his risen life and bearing his spirit, they witnessed to justice, peace, integrity, and God's kindness to all and everyone. Witnessing to the risen life brought them to their deaths.

The American bishops once wrote: "We cannot celebrate a faith we do not practice....We must...continue to move from strong words about charity and justice to effective action." The same can be said of our belief in the resurrection: We can't celebrate the resurrection without expressing the risen life of Jesus in our own lives.

This truth applies not only to those who die a violent death for this practical faith in the risen life. It applies to anyone who in his or her daily life expresses Jesus' love and goodness to all, beginning with those who are nearest to us, the ones we meet as "neighbors" in our family, at work, or wherever we are.

Abiding Spirit

"On our arrival in Rome Paul was allowed to stay in lodgings of his own with the soldier who guarded him." Acts 28:16-20, 30-31

The book of the Acts of the Apostles has no end. The narrative closes with Paul under house arrest. We do know Paul's end, however. He was beheaded. Luke must have known that when he finished writing Acts, but he does not mention it. Instead he reports that Paul spent those last two years welcoming "all who came to visit him, proclaiming the Kingdom of God and teaching the truth about the Lord Jesus Christ with complete freedom and without hindrance" (Acts 28:30).

The book remains open-ended.

Luke closes, noting with a sense of relief and triumph that the Word was spreading even to Rome. It is strange that he does not even mention what happened to Paul. But Paul was not really the topic Luke was interested in. His topic was the continuing activity of the Holy Spirit in the world

There is really no end to his story! The Acts of the Apostles will be continued forever, until humanity and creation find their fulfillment in Jesus. You and I, all of us are involved.

What is described in Acts is, in a way, our acts. We live the same risen life as the first Christians did; we live with and by the same spirit of Jesus. We do this at another time, in a different world. We have to do in our world *now* what those Christians did *then*. It is now our turn to witness to the resurrection of the Lord by the lives we live.

Solidarity I

"And now some men appeared, bringing on a bed a paralyzed man whom they were trying to bring in."   Luke 5:17-26

Jesus was teaching in a packed house. People stood outside around the small openings in the wall that served as windows. A larger group of men and women were standing in front of the entrance to the house. When some new arrivals came with their paralyzed friend on a stretcher they could not enter. Nobody gave way. They were not willing to give up their places. It was not even fair to expect that.

They climbed on the roof and managed to push and pull the roofing aside and to make a hole big enough to lower the stretcher through. It dangled for some moments rather dangerously in the air. But then it came down just in front of Jesus.

"Seeing *their* faith he said: 'My friend, your sins are forgiven you'" (Luke 5:20). There's that little word "their" in this gospel story from Luke. Jesus forgave and healed the crippled man, because he saw *their* faith. He saw the faith of the paralyzed man together with the faith of his friends who brought him and who were so insistent on having something done for their disabled friend that they did not hesitate to break through the roof above Jesus' head.

Jesus must have been amazed at what he saw. It must have been another sign of hope to him. He saw there signs of a greater justice, a growing human solidarity everywhere.

He often healed people who were brought by others. Even more often, he healed people who were introduced to him by others. In today's text he explicitly forgives and heals because *they* together brought to him a man who needed healing.

To Jesus it was a sign that conversion is possible, that differences can be overcome, that forgiveness can be granted. It was their togetherness, their solidarity, that prompted Jesus to forgive and heal.

Solidarity II

"Suppose a man has a hundred sheep and one of them strays; will he not...go in search of the stray?"   Matthew 18:12-14

Jesus asks the disciples about the good shepherd who lost a sheep: "Will he not leave the ninety-nine?"

We are so accustomed to the answer Jesus gave to this question that it does not strike us that in real life the answer might be "No." Doesn't the shepherd put the ninety-nine at risk? Would it not be more logical for him to take care of them? Should he leave all those others behind because one got lost? Is leaving those ninety-nine not only absurd, but even irresponsible?

It is Saint Augustine who recommends that we should have a closer look at numbers when we read the Bible. Numbers have a deep meaning. Sometimes their significance escapes us because it is too foreign to us. In this case that meaning is not too difficult to grasp. Even for us 100 is a special number. It indicates completeness. It is a rounded-off number.

The number 100 has the same kind of importance in the Bible. It is a serious matter when the whole number is broken. It only takes one to break it. So, in a way, it does not even matter whether one is missing, or sixteen, or thirty-four. Losing even one means losing completeness.

Humanity, God's flock, belongs together like the number 100. If even one is lost or marginalized, *we* are no longer complete. That is why Jesus came to find the lost and marginalized one. We human beings belong together, and should reform our attitudes accordingly. Jesus came to find us, to bring us together, and to lead us all home.

Solidarity III

"Come to me, all you who labor and are overburdened, and I will give you rest."   Matthew 11:28-30

You can listen to sayings of Jesus in different ways. You *should* listen to them in different ways. In today's text Jesus invites us to come to him with our burdens and sorrows. So we should go to him and, indeed, we will find our rest.

There is also another way of understanding this saying. We are like he is. Haven't we received his spirit in us? We should be to others as he is to us. We should be the ones to say to others: "Come to me, all you who labor and are overburdened, and I will give you rest."

Jesus does not mean this in just a vague way. He means what he says. People did come to him and left him refreshed, having found new meaning in life, and new ways of living. He restored their human dignity, helped them to overcome crippling obstacles, healed, and forgave them.

John Paul II put it in a different way: "[Solidarity] then is not a feeling of vague compassion or shallow distress at the misfortunes of so many people, both near and far. On the contrary, it is a firm and persevering determination to commit oneself to the common good; that is to say, to the good of all and of each individual, because we are all really responsible for all...a commitment to the good of one's neighbor with the readiness, in the Gospel sense, to 'lose oneself' for the sake of the other instead of exploiting him, and to 'serve him' instead of oppressing him for one's own advantage" (*On Social Concern*, 38).

If anyone starts to tell you of her or his worries, don't shrug them off. Take your time, offer a cup of tea or coffee, and listen. Show them your solidarity. Be an oasis in the desert of their lives, just as Jesus is in yours.

Jesus' Questions

"Jesus began to talk to the people about John: 'What did you go out into the desert to see?'"   Matthew 11:7-15

The first thing we hear about Jesus is that as a child of twelve he asks questions in the temple. Then there is a great silence about Jesus in the gospels for about eighteen years. The first thing we hear of him after that silence is that he is again asking something. This time he asks John the Baptizer to baptize him.

The people ask John what they should do, and he tells them that they should reform. He even tells them that they should share their second pair of sandals and their overcoat with those who have none.

Asking questions seems to be a harmless thing. "I am only asking a question," we will say. But asking a question often changes the way things are. As long as no questions are asked, things will remain the same. "The most subversive thing that could happen in this society is for someone to ask a question" (Joan Chittister, O.S.B., *Salt*, March 1989).

Jesus never stopped questioning us: "There are many millions who are deprived of hope due to the fact that, in many parts of the world, their situation has noticeably worsened. Before these tragedies of total indigence and need, in which so many of our brothers and sisters are living, it is the Lord Jesus himself who comes to question us" (see Matthew 25:31-46) (*On Social Concern*, 13).

We often pray asking favors, without checking what we are really asking for. We ask for "our" daily bread, and don't seem to wonder why others go without enough to eat. Some more questions would not do this world any harm. To start with, we could listen better to the ones our children, friends, and parents ask us.

Joining In

"...you wouldn't dance...you wouldn't be mourners."
Matthew 11:16-19

The American bishops have been taking on many issues. There have been many letters on peace and disarmament, on the economy, on poverty, and on mission. All kinds of deeds have been added to those words. The emergence of the Catholic peace organization Pax Christi, the RENEW programs, the RCIA programs, hundreds of national networks, and all sorts of action groups and activities on a local level are signs of a change. More and more Christians see their professional skills as talents to be used on behalf of God's reign. The percentage of those who join these groups, however, still remains relatively low.

Too many don't dance with the Lord when the Kingdom makes some progress, and many more don't mourn with God when the Kingdom in this world is betrayed and people suffer. As Jesus said:

We played the pipes for you
and you wouldn't dance;
we sang dirges
and you wouldn't be mourners (Matthew 11:17).

Wouldn't it be wondeful if, considering the many people in need, we did dance and did mourn and harnessed all the faith and all the energy there is, just starting with ourselves?

This is what the American bishops and the pope are hoping for: "There is no justification for despair or inertia. Though it be with sorrow, it must be said that just as one may sin through selfishness and the desire of excessive profit and power, one may also be found wanting with regard to the urgent need of the multitudes of human beings submerged in conditions of underdevelopment, through fear, indecision, and, basically, through cowardice. We are called, indeed obliged, to face the tremendous challenge of the last decade of the second millennium, because the present dangers threaten everyone" (*On Social Concern*, 47).

Structures of Sin

"...he will set everything right again." Matthew 17:10-13

Any visitor to a large city can't help being struck by the differences between the rich and the poor. Who does not agonize over the panhandlers in our midst, and who does not feel embarrassed when we cannot give money to all who ask?

There are masses of needy in crowded streets, neglected people in need of more than money can buy—a smile, a word of kindness, eye contact, a helping hand, some hope, a moment of patience, a prayer, a sign of compassion, but also political action and societal reorganization.

Things are not as they should be. We are caught in what Pope John Paul II calls the "structures of sin" (*On Social Concern*, 37)—the worship of money, ideology, class, and technology.

Jesus did not come into this world to comfort only some of us; he came to comfort all.

"The motivating concern for the poor—who are, in the very meaningful term, 'the Lord's poor,' because the Lord wished to identify himself with them (Matthew 25:31-46) and takes special care of them—must be translated at all levels into concrete actions, until it decisively attains a series of necessary reforms. Each local situation will show what reforms are most urgent and how they can be achieved. But those demanded by the situation of the international imbalance...must not be forgotten" (*On Social Concern*, 43).

One day his disciples asked Jesus when Elijah would come again. Jesus said that he had come already, and he describes what Elijah came to do. This is at the same time a description of his own role, one for which—as he said—he would suffer greatly: "He came to see that everything is once more as it should be" (Matthew 17:12).

Refugee

"...the good news is proclaimed to the poor...." Matthew 11:2-11

He was in a new country as a refugee and for those first days he didn't know what to do. He was afraid and looking for something he could identify with. That's why he went to a church that first week-end. He was a Christian, a Catholic. Among the few documents he had with him was his baptismal certificate. He was a first-generation Christian who had been baptized when he was about twenty-two years old. He was now very glad he had been baptized. Even in this strange land he knew he belonged to a community.

He stayed in the back of the church. He didn't understand everything that was said, he didn't know any of the hymns, but he knew what was going on. He joined in the movements he was accustomed to in his own country, kneeling, standing, bowing his head, crossing himself. It was like a slow but familiar rhythm and dance. He went forward to receive Holy Communion.

After the service he went to the priest at the entrance of the church. He walked up to shake hands as he saw the others do. He wanted to introduce himself. After all, he was a member of the Christ's community, too. He was the last one. The pastor paid no attention. He tried to show the priest his baptismal certificate, but the door closed in front of him. Yet, the good news had been preached to him. He had been told that he had been baptized in the one body of Christ. That day the reality fell short of the message.

Born of Woman

"His mother Mary...was found to be with child through the Holy Spirit."   *Matthew 1:18-24*

Like all of us, Mary was connected with nature in a thousand ways. There were not only the connections with all those who made up her ancestry, there were also the links with the water and the air, the sun and the earth, the plants and the animals that supported and formed her existence. Martin Luther once said, speaking of woman, that we should never forget that from her Christ was born. You could also say that of the whole of nature. No wonder that reflecting upon her dignity we came to the conclusion that Mary was taken up bodily into eternity.

I have read that the chances that a deep breath inhaled today will contain a molecule from Julius Caesar's breath are 99 in 100 (*Harper's Index* #167, 1989). That would be just as true of Jesus' and Mary's breath.

The natural world is sacred; it is God's creation. The cosmos demands respect. It always has, but we seem to have lost that respect. We've violated nature too often, simply using it for our own economic needs. We've forgotten that many of its resources are not renewable; we have seriously polluted our environment. We must learn to respect the sacredness of the natural world around us. The dominion granted to us by the Creator is not an absolute power, nor can one speak of a freedom to "use and misuse," or to dispose of things as we please. Jesus was, like all of us, born from the womb of a woman, and through her from the womb of nature. Many of us have to regain the respect and reverence due to the cosmos out of which we were born.

Unbelief and Prayer

"How can I know this?" Luke 1:5-25

We often think of Thomas when we are full of doubts. But Zechariah, one of Jesus' uncles, is another who offers a good example of unbelief. When Zechariah—who must have been praying endlessly to father a child—heard from the angel that John would be born to Elizabeth, he could not believe it. That seems strange because Zechariah had really been praying for it. The angel even mentioned those prayers: "Zechariah, don't be afraid, for your prayer has been heard. Your wife Elizabeth is going to bear the two of you a son" (Luke 1:13).

Zechariah is not the only one to pray for an intention he doesn't believe will be heard. We sometimes even pray hoping *not* to be heard. It is said that Saint Augustine once prayed for chastity, but added: "But not yet!"

We pray for peace, yet we remain dependent on the manufacture of arms. We pray for an end to air pollution, yet we use our car to go and buy a paper at the newsstand around the corner. We pray for a more just world, but we don't share the surplus we have with those who haven't enough. We pray to be protected against sickness, but refuse to buy unsprayed apples if they look less perfect than the sprayed ones.

Zechariah was silenced because of his unbelief. In fact he silenced himself. What do we say when we are caught in the act of praying for things we do not believe in and are maybe even not hoping for? We, too, had better keep our mouths shut, and start praying again when we have overcome our unbelief in what we are praying for.

Mary's Blessedness

"...blessed is she who believed." Luke 1:39-45

Sarafina is the title of a very moving musical about the Soweto uprising of South African students against apartheid. It has played for over a year in New York City to full houses. One of the most moving songs is entitled "Freedom Tomorrow."

The whole musical is about that future. In it Sarafina and her fellow students are so sure about freedom *tomorrow*, that they dedicate themselves fearlessly to it *today*.

The Blessed Virgin Mary believed that way. She dreamed of a more human and divine future for all of us, a future she knew about only in the promise made her. She was hope's incarnation in this world. She was so sure of that future that she was giving herself to it by bringing Jesus into this world. Her belief made her willing to take God's promise into account in her daily life, and into her own body. Luke's first beatitude is dedicated to her belief: "Blessed is the one who believed that the promise made her by the Lord would be fulfilled" (Luke 1:45), a beatitude said of all of us who believe that the promise made to us will be fulfilled.

Mary's faith made her dedicate herself to the fulfillment of the promise she believed in. She did this even before she had experienced the resurrection of her son. In a sense she had less to go by than we have. Her dedication was radical. She educated herself and her son to the fulfillment of humanity's most inspired hopes. So should we. We should take care that her hope and blessedness are passed on to the people around us, and to the generations that will follow us.

Akin in Faith

"And I tell you that many will come from east and west and sit down... at the feast in the kingdom of Heaven."   Matthew 8:5-11

An older missionary told me about his experiences, the same story so many missionaries had told me before. He had gone to bring God's word to others, often risking his life to do so. He could tell you about lions and snakes. Sometimes he exaggerated, but most of what he said must have been true.

One thing had really struck him, he told me. Every time he told people a gospel story, they understood what he was talking about. It was as if all those stories were already in their heads and hearts, and that they only needed to be reminded of them. Then he said something that hit home: "It is so obvious that we relate to each other in the same faith!"

He said he learned as much from them as he taught them. They made him discover things he never discovered in his own surroundings. He had often been thoroughly amazed, because when he went to that African country he thought—so he told me—that he knew it all.

It is what Jesus discovered during his lifetime. Meeting a Roman officer he said, "Nowhere have I found faith like this!" Meeting a Syro-Phoenician woman he made the same remark. He was amazed by the conversation he had with the Samaritan woman at the well. All those times he drew the same conclusion as that missionary: We are akin to each other in our faith and hope. All men and women find in the depth of their consciences a law written by God on the human heart. In our desire for healing and wholeness, we of the east and the west, the north and the south will one day come together in peace, taking our places with Abraham and Isaac and Jacob at the feast in the Kingdom of heaven (Matthew 8:11).

Parish Groups

"All must put on sackcloth and call on God with all their might...."
Jonah 3:1-10

Jesus did not speak only to individuals, though he did that from time to time. He organized those individuals into groups. From the beginning he was followed by a core of twelve, a larger group of seventy-two, and an even larger group of some hundreds. He planned with them; he sent them in groups of two; he discussed matters with them before they went out. After their return he debriefed them and they evaluated the results of their mission.

The change and conversion Jesus is looking for is not only individual or personal but generational, something like what happened when the prophet Jonah went to Nineveh. He announced that the city was going to be destroyed because of its amoral state of affairs. Their sins cried out to heaven. The king of Nineveh, hearing the prophet, took the warning seriously. "He then had proclaimed throughout Nineveh, by decree of the king and his nobles...that all must put on sackcloth and call on God with all their might; and let everyone renounce their evil behavior." The whole of Nineveh's society got involved. All had to review and change their evil ways. They did, and the city was saved.

You can't organize a change of the world on your own. You need a network, cooperation, a group, a community, a church, a whole generation.

In many parishes, groups are organized to cover almost all parochial needs: liturgies, eucharistic services, music and singing, mourning and celebrating, visiting the sick and shut-ins, and preparing doughnut breakfasts.

Would it be feasible to help to start an organized attempt to Christianize the professional activities of the parishioners in a concerted way, so that our community starts to turn around toward the ideal Jesus gave us?

Prayer I
Pray Alone

"...go to your private room, shut yourself in, and so pray to your Father...."
                                                                  Matthew 6:6

A senior citizen went to her pastor with a problem. She told him that she did not know how to pray. Every time she tried, so many thoughts cropped up in her head that she never managed to put herself in the presence of God. That is how she put it.

He listened to her carefully. When she had finished, he gave her this advice. He asked whether she ever did anything restful, an activity to relax. She said she did. She liked to do some knitting from time to time. Nothing complicated, simple things like a pair of socks, sometimes even a sweater. She liked the rhythm of the clicking needles and the feeling that something was growing from within her hands.

He told her that next time she wanted to pray, she should not try to get in the presence of God. He told her to take the piece of knitting she was busy with and sit down comfortably in an easy chair, maybe next to a window. He told her to start knitting, quietly remembering that she would like to pray, and see what would happen.

She must have done that, because some time later she told him that she had followed his advice. After some time, clicking her knitting needles, looking now and then outside into the sky, seeing some birds fly past and hearing some voices of playing children in the distance, she felt the presence of God.

He may not have told her exactly what Jesus told us to do when we want to pray by ourselves alone. Jesus said: "When you pray, go to your private room, shut yourself in, and so pray to your Father who is in that secret place, and your Father who sees all that is done in secret will reward you" (Matthew 6:6). The private room Jesus speaks about could be a private room in your house, but he might also have meant the private room of your heart. Both possibilities are covered in that pastor's advice!

Prayer II
With Two or Three

"...Where two or three meet in my name, I am there among them."
Matthew 18:19-20

From the beginning of the formation of Christian communities Christians did not only pray alone. All through Acts we see and hear them praying together. Though we often hear that Jesus went into the mountains or in the wilderness to pray alone, we also hear that he often prayed together with his friends.

Jesus pays special attention to one type of "community" prayer. It is to the prayer of two or three together. He might have experienced its power at home doing it with his mother. He himself practiced it. Think of the scene of his agony in the garden just before he is arrested. Twice he comes to ask three of his disciples to pray together while he is praying. On other occasions, too, we learn that he is praying with one or two others. Think of the deaf and mute man he takes apart from the crowd, and how he prays together with him.

Praying in twos or threes is especially blessed by him. "In truth I tell you once again, if two of you on earth agree to ask anything at all, it will be granted to you by my Father in heaven. For where two or three meet in my name, I am there among them" (Matthew 18:19-20).

Simone Weil, the French mystic, once wrote: "Two or three, and there should be no more!" She did not want to exclude praying with a larger group, but she wanted to insist on what Jesus said himself, that when two or three come together to pray, such a prayer has a very special power. Anyone who has ever prayed like that at a sick bed, at one or another happy, glorious, or sad occasion knows this. A father and a mother, a sister and a brother, a friend with a friend—every time when two or three pray together, you will notice Jesus' presence! It is the type of prayer we often overlook, but it will show us how good the Lord is—and how present.

Prayer III
All Together

"Alleluia! Praise Yahweh, all nations; extoll Yahweh, all peoples...!"
Psalm 117:1

On several occasions we hear how Jesus prays with larger crowds. He did that when he went as a child with his parents to the temple services in Jerusalem. According to Luke he did it every Sabbath day during his stay in Nazareth.

To be together with the others in a parish liturgy can be a real joy. It should be! It is the type of prayer and worship in which we discover the wide horizon of praying together with one another and together with Jesus himself. It is a prayer rhythm that helps us to look at the world with the eyes of the Father, to see it with the vision of the Son, and to vivify it with the breath of the Spirit. It is a rhythm that will carry us to the peace and the joy of a new world, where bread is broken, wine is shared, wounds are healed, and God is praised. Rejoice to meet your brothers and sisters in the presence of the Lord. Rejoice that so many come together to praise the Lord with you, and express how they are inspired by God's Spirit.

Some might object that I don't know about the worship in your parish church, that if I did know, I wouldn't be speaking so enthusiastically about it. That is true, I don't know, but let me tell you what I once read in a rule for a congregation of brothers: "Let yourself be renewed in your faith, hope, and love. Don't let yourself be distracted by accidentals. Try to understand God's Word even in the mouth of a bad reader. Don't be irritated by the brother who sings off-key. The forms are only important to the extent that you know how to see through them" (*Rule for a New Brother*).

Prayer IV
Difficulty of Prayer

"...he threw himself on the ground and prayed that, if it were possible, this hour might pass him by."   Mark 14:32-42

Again and again we tell each other that we can't pray. It is a strange complaint, because we use prayer techniques in our life every time we need each other.

We know how to get something done by others, even if others are not inclined to help us. We greet them. We tell them that we are at a loss, we wouldn't know what to do without them, they are the only ones who can help us, they are known to have helped others, we are grateful for the help they gave us before, we are sorry for former misunderstandings, and so on. We all learned those techniques in childhood. We wouldn't have survived without them. They belong to our human survival skills.

If you analyze what you do when you need something from somebody else, you will find out that you use all the traditional forms of prayer. You ask, you praise, you thank, and you ask for forgiveness.

Praying is not difficult because we lack the skills, or because those skills demand a lot of training. Prayer is difficult for another reason, a reason we can easily trace in the lives of people who prayed. Every time they prayed and listened to God, God addressed them, too. They got to hear what God expected them to do. It is the story of Abraham, Moses, even of Jesus. It was while praying in the garden that Jesus understood what faithfulness to his mission would mean. It is while praying that we will hear what our mission in life is.

If you have ever really prayed, you must have experienced this. It is that knowledge that makes prayer so difficult!

Prayer V
Distractions

"...Peter went to the housetop at about the sixth hour to say his prayers. He felt hungry and was looking forward to his meal, but before it was ready he fell into a trance...."　　　　*Acts 10:9-23*

Another common complaint about praying concerns distractions. I can't pray. I can't seem to put myself in the presence of God. Every time I try to do that hundreds of thoughts crowd in between God and me.

Did you ever hear the experience of Teilhard de Chardin during the First World War? He was a Red Cross soldier in the French army. Just before a fierce battle he desired to be as near to Jesus as possible, so he gave himself Holy Communion. He had a kind of vision. In that vision he saw how the consecrated host was not really with him. It was in front of him, beckoning him to get it. He tried and succeeded several times. Every time he caught the host, the host turned into something else, into something he had to do as a priest/soldier. Again and again the host turned into a task and then escaped from his hand. It was only when this had happened several times that he understood what was happening to him. Jesus made it clear to him that Teilhard could only be united to him on condition that he fulfilled his charitable task at the battlefield.

When we sit down for prayer to be with Jesus or with God, the distractions that occur are often not distractions at all. They are often concrete invitations to reconsider our daily chores and relations in the light of Jesus. They are invitations to pray for ourselves and for others. They are signs to relate our daily tasks to God's Kingdom.

Prayer VI
Pray Always

"Then he told them a parable about the need to pray continually...."
Luke 18:1

To pray continually, to pray always: how is that possible? Can anyone do that? What could Jesus have meant?

Of course, he did not mean that we should be on our knees all day praying. Even the monks in the desert in ancient times could not do that.

If the ideal of praying the whole day is realizable, Jesus must have been able to do it. He, too, was not praying all the time in that formal way. How, then, did he pray all the time?

When you read the life of Jesus in any of the four gospels, it becomes obvious in any of them that Jesus had the ability to see anything that happened around him from the perspective of the Kingdom of God. Whatever he experienced, saw, smelled, tasted, or touched betrayed the presence of that Kingdom. It is as if he managed to look all the time through this world into that other world. Fish, snakes, foxes, sparrows, gnats, lillies, grass, mustard bushes, vines, clouds, sunsets, playing children, a found treasure, the stories and the news he heard, the rich and the poor, saints and sinners, camels, and thunderstorms—he saw them all in the context of the Kingdom.

This is what it means. It is the kind of attitude in which someone is simply in the presence of God constantly.

It is often called the prayer of simplicity. You need some formal prayer to reach that stage and to keep it up, but it is possible for anyone to learn to pray constantly.

Not One-Dimensional

"Watch yourselves, or your hearts will be coarsened by...the cares of life, and that day will come unexpectedly, like a trap."
Luke 21:25-28, 34-36

Some years ago it was fashionable to call the Western world and Western humanity one-dimensional. Those who did so wanted to indicate that modern people often live as if the only thing that matters is their material welfare. They don't think of anything else. They have no further perspective in life. They conveniently forget where they came from, and where they are headed. They live a life according to the old pagan saying *carpe diem*, which means "seize the day"—enjoy it and forget about the rest.

This is a pagan approach to life, an impossible approach for a follower of Jesus. A Christian cannot forget what Jesus told us about the meaning of our lives. We don't just live for the day of today. Jesus depicted the real depth of our lives several times.

Jesus speaks about our lives against a background of final things that are going to happen, when in the end the sun and the moon will darken, the whole of human history in the world as we know it will come to a close, and we will be swept into the world to come. Those who believe in his words will be able to stand this changeover fearlessly; those who never understood this dimension of our existence will be full of fear. They will not know what is happening to them. We do: Jesus has told us. We should live each day aware of that revelation. Our acts and omissions are not just one-dimensional. They count here and in the world to come.

Final Trumpet

"...even now the axe is being laid to the root of the trees, so that any tree failing to produce good fruit will be cut down and thrown on the fire."
Luke 3:1-9

For many, the early 1930s were disastrous years, years of crisis and the great depression. Hardly anything went well. One of the exceptions was a show on Broadway. The show was called *Green Pastures*. It played 1635 times during those terrible years, up to the time that the man who played God in the show—the seventy-year-old Richard B. Harrison—collapsed during a performance and died. The show was so popular because it was a source of hope and inspiration to many.

During the show the archangel Gabriel, confronted with the misery and sinfulness in the world, asks God repeatedly: "Can I give the end signal, may I blow the final trumpet? Look at what they are doing over there in the world!" But again and again God refuses to give him permission.

John the Baptizer would have loved to blow that trumpet. He did, in a way. He announced the end of the world as he had known it, speaking about the axe that is already at the roots of the tree of all life, about a fire that is going to cremate all, and about a final sifting out of everything.

John did not know that the end of the old world would not come in this way, or that the end would come by the change Jesus was going to introduce. John did not believe in healing. He thought in terms of terminal surgery. Jesus proved John wrong. Jesus proved wrong all those like John who have given up hope on this world, by revealing the healing that is taking place, a healing that those who believe in Jesus should be engaged in.

Conversion and Follow-Up

"...he will baptize you with Holy Spirit and with fire." Luke 3:10-18

Mark Twain once noted in his journal that a revival mission visited his town. He noted that everyone but himself converted. He added rather sarcastically that within a week all had again turned into sinners.

Conversion alone is not sufficient. Some Christian churches preach the need of conversion every week, a necessary but insufficient preaching. It is necessary to break with the past, but you also have to foresee the future. You have to change and begin a new life. You need a fresh approach, a new spirituality.

John the Baptizer is a good example of all this. When he baptized people they asked him what they should do next. His advice was radical: They should be honest and fair, which meant that if they had any extra clothing—two overcoats or tunics—the second one should be given to someone who had none. When people looked at him to see whether he was serious, he admitted that this was asking much, and that he really could not give them the power to change their lives so radically. But he added that someone else would come after him who would baptize them with fire, enabling them to really change their lives and their world.

John was speaking about Jesus, who would come to baptize us with the Holy Spirit, the Spirit of fire. Jesus not only spoke about conversion, he equipped us with his spirit to live new lives that would make a difference in our world, a life of bearing witness in a world that needs that Spirit so much.

Mary's Privileged Place

"Of all women you are the most blessed...." Luke 1:39-45

Pope John Paul II can't write a letter without mentioning the Blessed Virgin Mary. Theologians can't stop speaking about her. Millions of faithful visit her shrines in Lourdes, Fatima, and Medjugorje. The well-known priest/sociologist/novelist Andrew Greeley holds that Mary is a central figure in the Roman Catholic religious imagination.

No wonder that you seem to touch a sensitive nerve when you speak about Mary in Catholic circles. Such was the case even during the Second Vatican Council, when the council members had to decide whether or not to dedicate a special document to the Blessed Virgin. It proved to be the closest vote of the whole meeting. While in practically all cases the majority was about 94 percent, in this case the majority obtained only seventeen votes more than those who were in favor of a special document. Mary was not going to get a special document dedicated to her. She would be mentioned—and with great honor—in the document about the people of God, in the document on the church. The idea was to give her a special place among the faithful, among us.

Somewhere in Australia a parish council expressed this intention in a beautiful way. They had a new statue of Mary made. The statue was made so that it could be placed in a place of honor in the front pew in the church. It is an original way of expressing about Mary what Elizabeth said of her when the two met after the annunciation. "Blessed are you among all women, and blessed is the fruit of your womb!" Mary is called blessed because she could say of Jesus in a very special way: "He is of my body, he is of my blood!"

God's Solidarity

"Indeed, from his fullness we have, all of us, received...." John 1:1-18

Older ones among us might remember how every Mass used to end with the opening of the gospel of John. Nowadays we hear that gospel only rarely. It is one of the gospel choices at Christmas, but it is not always heard even on that day, because it is more attractive to read the Christmas gospels from Matthew or Luke. Those two gospels are full of interesting details like shepherds and sheep, angels and stars, gifts, and lots of other people.

The beginning of the gospel of John sounds heavy and abstract. "In the beginning was the Word; the Word was with God and the Word was God" (John 1:1).

Experts tell us that these words are the beginning of an ancient christological hymn sung by people who used the term Word (*Logos*) in a special way. That does not help us much, however. It all sounds pretty abstract, at least until a bit later in the same hymn when we are told that the Word became flesh and lived among us (John 1:14). The Word became deed. God's offspring became one of us, God lived with us.

That living with us was a sign of God's solidarity. It is something we can illustrate from our own human experience. We can talk endlessly about solidarity with the poor, but only when we share our lives with them will they be able to say: "Now you are really one of us!" It is at such a moment that our words become deeds.

God became one of us. There is no human experience that is foreign to God. Jesus was born as one of us, he lived as we do, he even died our death. By rising from the dead he assured us life for all time to come. His solidarity will last forever and ever!

Mary, Mother of God

"...they hurried away and found Mary and Joseph, and the baby lying in the manger." Luke 2:16-21

Chinua Achebe, the well-known Nigerian author, made an interesting remark about men and women in his book *The Anthills of the Savana.* He tells us how in both our biblical and his African traditions women are blamed for all that went wrong in the world. In our case it is the familiar story of Eve. In Achebe's tradition women were the reason that God, who once lived very near to his human creation, left it. God was so near that the women who were pounding their millet into flour hit God. God warned them against this. They would be careful for some time, but then would start to chat again, forget about the divine presence, and hit God again. Finally, God gave up and left.

In both cases, Achebe writes, men told these stories. They knew that they were not true stories, and because they felt somewhat guilty about them, they added another story in which they relate that final salvation will come through a woman, different from all other women, who cooperates with God. Achebe warns us to be careful about those stories. They might be told as a patriarchal conspiracy to keep women in a secondary place.

That is why it is good to consider that every woman is invited by God to be like Mary, cooperating with God to give birth to God in themselves and in the world in which they live.

It is what Jesus himself said when a woman in the crowd around him shouted one day: "Blessed the womb that bore you and the breasts that fed you!" But he replied: "More blessed still are those who hear the word of God and keep it." (Luke 11:27b-28).

No doubt Mary is the mother of God. She became his mother by doing something all of us can and should do: "hearing the word of God and keeping it."

Jesus' Baptism and Ours

"...while Jesus after his own baptism was at prayer, heaven opened...."   Luke 3:15-16, 21-22

Luke's report on Jesus' baptism is different from the same story in the other gospels. In those stories heaven opens at the moment that John baptizes Jesus, but not in Luke's account. John baptizes Jesus without anything special happening. Luke writes: "Now it happened that when all the people had been baptized and while Jesus after his own baptism was at prayer, heaven opened and the Holy Spirit descended on him in a physical form like a dove. And a voice came from heaven, 'You are my Son, today have I fathered you'" (Luke 3:21-22).

Of course, Jesus did not become God's son at that moment. Yet, something changed in his life. He did not return to Nazareth. It is as if a new light suddenly dawned upon him, as if he became better aware than ever before what he himself, the Son of God, was about.

Though at another level, this is what baptism should do to us. God doesn't become our Father at the moment that the water flows over our heads. We are not at that moment created in the Son, and the Spirit does not then become our life. All those relations were already there. It is at the moment of our baptism that those relations are formalized by those who brought us—most probably as babies—to a Christian community to be baptized. We have to formalize those relations for ourselves, too. We have to become more and more aware of them and accept them in our lives.

We should do what Jesus did immediately after his baptism. We should enter in prayer now and then, meditating upon what happened to us in our baptism. Heaven might open to us, too, and we might come to a greater understanding of who we are.

August 11 _____

Cana and Mary's Help

"...and the mother of Jesus said to him, 'They have no wine.'"

John 2:1-12

What did Mary think of when she went to Jesus to tell him: "They have no wine"? Biblical scholars and theologians have been speculating on that for centuries. Isaiah once used the metaphor of Yahweh being the bridegroom of humanity: "Like a young man marrying a virgin, your rebuilder will wed you, and as the bridegroom rejoices in his bride, so will your God rejoice in you" (Isaiah 62:5). Did Mary think that this final wedding feast between God and humanity was going to start when she saw Jesus arriving at Cana? Is that why Jesus answered her: "My hour has not yet come"?

We don't know. We can only guess. One thing we can be sure of is that God loves us with a love that resembles our most intimate and passionate human love.

Andrew Greeley uses this theme in his numerous bestselling novels. He once said that he writes those novels neither to entertain nor to educate or indoctrinate his readers. He writes them to fascinate, thrill, and entice them in such a way that they will understand and feel what the realities and possibilities of God's love for us are if we believe what the prophet Isaiah foretold—a love shown to us by Jesus, who was willing to give his life for the sake of us, his friends.

It is nice to think of the two young folks sitting at their wedding feast at Cana. We don't even know their names. Maybe those names are not mentioned because they stand for all of us.

Did those two realize, when they were drinking the new wine Jesus made for them, that they stood as a model for the love that came to us in Jesus?

Jubilee Celebration

"He has sent me...to proclaim a year of favor from the Lord."
Luke 4:16-22

In Nazareth they had heard about his baptism by John the Baptizer. They must also have heard about the miracles he had already worked in Capernaum. It is understandable that they were slightly upset. So would we be, if we had been living in Nazareth then. Why had he not immediately returned to Nazareth to heal the sick there?

They all came to the synagogue the weekend he was home. They expected him there because, as Luke notes, it was his custom to come there for the sabbath celebrations.

As the moment for the reading came, Jesus stood up to read. They handed him the scroll of the prophet Isaiah. All eyes in the synagogue were fixed on him. Unrolling the scroll he read how the prophet foretold that the year of favor, the year of the jubilee, would start. He rolled the scroll up, returned it, and said: "This text is being fulfilled today." To understand what happened, we must know something more about that year of the jubilee. Every fiftieth year priests were to sound a horn, called a *jobel*, to begin the jubilee year. Slaves should be freed, debts forgiven, and all property—especially land—should be re-divided. The intention was to avoid an ever-growing gap between the rich and the poor, and the reorganization of a just equity.

It is not certain whether the Jewish people ever practiced that divine directive. That is why prophets like Isaiah foretold that one day Yahweh would start a jubilee year, a year of grace.

No wonder the people in Nazareth grew excited when they heard that justice and equity finally were going to be restored. It would be quite something even today. In fact, it is what Pope John Paul II has asked for several times, advising us not to forget that the goods of this world are meant for all.

Jesus Threatened

"They sprang to their feet and hustled him out of town...intending to throw him off the cliff...."   Luke 4:23-30

It is instructive to note at what point in the gospels Jesus' life is threatened for the first time. In Luke's gospel it is at the beginning of his public life, when he addresses his own neighbors at home in Nazareth.

They were enthusiastic when he proclaimed the year of grace that was going to begin. However, they got very upset when he explained that this year of grace was not going to be for them alone, but for all others as well. He did that by referring to some pagans—outsiders like Naaman the Syrian and a Sidonian widow.

It is at the mention of those aliens that they jumped up, hustled him out of the synagogue, and tried to throw him off the cliff.

It is a dynamism we constantly find in the gospels and in Acts. The real difficulty is always the same: As soon as it becomes clear that God loves the whole of humanity without any preferences, believers get upset.

When Stephen tries to combat discrimination in Jerusalem he is arrested and murdered. When Paul preaches God as the one in whom we all equally move, exist, and have our being, the Athenians leave him.

It is an issue that leads to murder and death even in our day. The Reverend Martin Luther King, Jr., was killed because he fought for equal rights. Bishop Oscar Romero was murdered because he defended the rights of the poor. The fact that God loves all of us in the same way remains the most difficult issue for most of us. To express it in our own lives remains even more difficult!

Ichthus, Fish

"...he said to Simon: 'Put out into deep water and pay out your nets for a catch.'"   Luke 5:1-11

Why did Jesus choose fishermen as his first disciples? Many explanations are given. John A. Sanford, an Episcopalian priest/psychologist, says that a fish is the symbol of what is swimming around in our inner depth: possibilities, riches, expectations, potentialities, combinations, creativities hidden from our eyes because they are swimming in the dark—silent, mysterious, and unfortunately unseen. The disciples are called fishers because, once confronted with Jesus, they fished those possibilities up from within themselves and helped others to that realization.

Jesus feeds the crowd around him with fish, he fries fish for them at the breakfast he eats with them after his resurrection, and eats some to prove that he is not a ghost.

In the earliest African communities Jesus was symbolized as a fish, the symbol for the totality of our inner possibilities brought to light by Jesus. Julius Africanus wrote: "God's well produces a continuous flood of water, a stream in which there is one fish, caught on a divine hook, feeding the whole of humanity." It is in the presence of Jesus—the *ichthus* or "fish"—that all of us can discover who we are.

No wonder that fish plays such an important role not only in the life of Jesus, but also in the life of so many Christians, who eat fish instead of meat on the days of abstinence during the forty days of Lent.

Mysterious, indeed. Symbolism is the matter our dreams are made of. In that matter the "fish" plays an important role!

Mary's Assumption

"And Mary said: '...the Almighty has done great things for me...his faithful love extends age after age...!'"   Luke 1:39-56

It was after the Second World War that Pope Pius XII decided to solemnly declare that Mary, the mother of Jesus, was assumed into heaven, body and spirit, after her death. Many theologians wondered why the pope did this. Catholics had believed it traditionally, and a new dogma about Mary might complicate relations with other Christians.

Pius did it for a good reason. It was his way of reacting against the horrors of the wars he had lived through during his lifetime. The First World War claimed ten million people, the Russian Revolution cost forty million human lives, the Holocaust killed millions of Jews, fifty million people were lost in the Second World War, a war that ended with the explosion of two atomic bombs.

It is in that context that Pius XII wanted to say something not only about the body of Mary, but about the body of all of us. He must have hoped that the celebration of the Assumption of Mary would teach us new respect for the bodily presence and history of each human being here on earth.

The pope was not the only one who wanted to do that. Everyone who understood the horrors of those wars, and the almost total disrespect for the bodily and earthly life of human beings, agreed with him wholeheartedly. Our body, too, will remain integrated in our own personal history, now and for all time to come.

Our body deserves our respect, and we have to pay it to ourselves and to our fellow human beings. We are not allowed to destroy or neglect either our own bodies or those of others.

What happened to Mary will in the final instance happen to all of us. We will be integrated in the glory to come, as we are, body and spirit.

Empowerment

"Having exhausted every way of putting him to the test, the devil left him...."   *Luke 4:1-13*

When Jesus comes out of the desert he is in a vulnerable position, not because he has been fasting for so long, but because he is about to make a new beginning in our old world. No wonder that Satan, the great opponent to anything really new, is present to tempt him. At first, the temptation is simple: make bread. (Later people will come to ask him for bread.) He is tempted to become a political ruler. (Later people practically try to force him to become their king.) He is tempted to perform a great stunt, jumping from the pinnacle of the temple. (Later the crowd will constantly ask him for a sign, a great miraculous sign.)

In all cases Jesus refuses. He does not give in. He refuses to take over. He refuses to rule them. He refuses to perform tricks for them. If Jesus had not overcome those temptations, none of us would ever have found our own words in our own mouths, our own feelings in our own hearts. We would have remained children, asking for bread. We would have remained powerless.

One day one of the students of Rabbi Mosche Leib von Sassow asked his master why God tolerates atheism. The old rabbi answered, "So that you would never be able to allow somebody to die, while consoling him with God in heaven. You yourself should help him, as if God did not exist. You and nobody else. That is why God allows atheism to exist."

In no way did Jesus come to take over from us, though he was tempted to do so. He came to empower us. And that is just what he did.

Life's Journey

"...they were Moses and Elijah and they were speaking of his passing which he was to accomplish in Jerusalem."   Luke 9:28b-36

Luke describes the life of Jesus as one long journey, one lifelong safari. This is true not only of Jesus: The others in his story are also on the road nearly all the time. Mary hastens to Elizabeth. The shepherds come to greet the child. Joseph and Mary go to and from the temple.

In Luke, these journey stories continue even after the resurrection. Jesus walks with the two to Emmaus. And as soon as they recognize him, they in their turn are back on the road to the others in Jerusalem.

In Acts, Luke calls the mission Jesus left us "The Way" three times. Before Jesus left his disciples he ordered them to travel to the ends of the earth. Luke himself traveled all over his world from Macedonia to Syria, from Malta to Italy. Acts is one long travelogue of the disciples, of Peter, Paul, and the others. Together they covered practically the whole of their known world.

One of the shorter trips Jesus asked Peter, James, and John to make was the one to the top of Mount Tabor, where he was transfigured before them. There, with Moses and Elijah, Jesus discussed his *passing*, which he was to accomplish in Jerusalem. The Greek word Luke uses is *exodos*, the same word the Hebrew Scriptures use to describe the journey from slavery in Egypt to freedom in a new land, the same kind of "exodus" we are invited to make with him, from the old sick world we live in to the new and glorious one we are destined for.

It is good to think in those "journey" terms during our daily commuting to and from work, school, and family. Whether we like it or not, we are almost always on the road. We seem to be drawn by something that is still to come.

The story of the transfiguration is a forecast of the glory that is awaiting us when we follow his Way.

Healing and Growth

"'Sir,' the man replied, 'leave it one more year and give me time to dig round it and manure it: it may bear fruit next year....'" Luke 13:1-9

Luke was a doctor. He made Jesus one as well. It is Luke who reports that Jesus says of himself: "No doubt you will quote me the saying, 'Physician, heal yourself'" (Luke 4:23).

According to Luke the world is sick, and so is humanity. Humanity should be healed; in many ways Luke describes Jesus' work among us as that of healing.

Yet, Luke is a good enough doctor to know that healing has to come from within the one who is sick. If any sick person asks a doctor, "Can you heal me?" the wise doctor will say, "No, I can't heal you. I can help you to create the conditions under which you might heal, but the real healing has to come from within you." It is what Jesus says after practically all of his healings: "Your faith has saved and healed you!"

It is like the parable Jesus tells about the fig tree without any fruit. Its owner will come, dig around it, manure it, and water it. That is all the owner can do. The rest is up to the tree. It is only from within the tree that the fruits will come. Without the cooperation of the tree nothing will ever happen.

Luke describes in his gospel what fruits we should deliver to be healed. We have to convert, to change. According to Luke, that change is the aim, the high point, and the summary of Jesus' presence among us—conversion, the forgiveness of the past, and a healed existence.

The questions of how and why we got into our present state are much less important than that other question: How are we going to get healed?

Self-Forgiveness

"...we will celebrate by having a feast, because this son of mine was dead and has come back to life...." Luke 15:1-3, 11-32

He was telling me the story about the prodigal son. He did not tell me the story, of course. He knew that I was no stranger to it. He told me what had happened to him when he was meditating on it during a retreat. He had really needed that retreat. He had to change his life, if only to be able to continue it.

While meditating on that story he had used an etching Rembrandt once made of it, with the father embracing his lost and found son. He told me that he really felt like the younger son. Suddenly the drawing took a new meaning. All at once he understood and felt that God forgave him. More important, God still loved him in a very real way.

At that point he jumped up. When I asked him what hit him he answered that he had just then discovered something else, something he hadn't even thought of during his retreat. He suddenly understood, he told me, that not only did the father forgive his son, but the son at that same moment forgave himself! At that very moment the son must have accepted his shadow side, deciding to do something about it, but nevertheless loving himself as the father loved him.

While he said this, tears were streaming down his face. I didn't know what to do. I offered him a cup of coffee. He did not need that, he said. Before he left we prayed together. We never forgot that evening. That evening he did what is probably the most difficult thing any of us can do. It is difficult to forgive others; it is much more difficult to forgive oneself. It is one of the greatest healing gifts we can receive!

Taking Sides

"Go away, and from this moment sin no more." John 8:1-11

One day they almost forced Jesus to take sides against someone, the woman caught in adultery. He refused to take sides against anyone. What he did was express his belief in her inner goodness. He told her not only to go home, but to change her life.

He did what the prophet Isaiah once foretold God would do: "No need to remember past events, no need to think about what was done before. Look, I am doing something new, now it emerges; can't you see it?" (Isaiah 43:18-19).

It is not only the woman who goes home a better person when he tells her: "Neither do I condemn you; go away, and from this moment sin no more" (John 8:11). Her accusers and molesters, who did not throw their stones, also go home better persons.

Jesus healed all of them by awakening something in them that is greater than they are.

Jesus refuses to discriminate between the "good" and the "bad" in the story. He refuses to take sides in that way. The side he chooses is that of unity and cohesion, and of the ultimate goodness hiding in each one's life. A choice that is against anything that tears human life apart, makes it impossible, or kills it. Jesus did what he helped the woman and her accusers to do: "Don't condemn. Go home, and don't sin."

It is an invitation, a piece of advice, or, better, a command we should apply in our own lives. It is no good condemning ourselves or others. It is better to get away from the past and change our lives.

Oscar Romero's Death

"This is my body given for you; do this in remembrance of me."
Luke 22:14-23:56

In 1970 a small Christian community formed itself in one of the slum areas of San Salvador. They had no water, no gas, no electricity, no school, nothing. The population was hungry, desperate, and consequently often drunk. Some men and women began a prayer group. They reflected together on the gospel of John. They were intrigued by his theme of light and darkness. The group increased slowly, and slowly they began to get their despair, their drunkenness, and their debts under control. They became sufficiently self-confident to start a credit union. They got more and more influential. They began a Building Society; they fought to be connected to public services like electricity and water. They succeeded. They fought their own greedy and egotistic behavior together.

They were accused by the authorities of being progressive and dangerous. Arrests and interrogations followed. Three priests in the community, Rutillio Grande, Alfonso Navarro, and Ernesto Barrero were killed between 1977 and 1978. Their bishop, Oscar Romero, convinced that those priests were no bandits, condemned their murders. He himself was killed March 24, 1980, while presiding at the Eucharist. He was shot by someone from the back of the church. Some days before he had said: "I often receive death threats. I have to confess that as a Christian I don't believe in death without a resurrection. If I am murdered I will rise in the people of El Salvador...if they execute their threats I sacrifice my blood to God for the salvation and the resurrection of El Salvador."

His prophecy is fulfilled. Visitors to El Salvador tell how his portrait hangs everywhere—in shops and living rooms, in churches and market stalls.

No one can opt for the poor and against oppression without suffering. Even Jesus couldn't.

Business and Breaking Bread

"...he took the bread and said the blessing; then he broke it and handed it to them. And their eyes were opened and they recognized him...."
Luke 24:13-35

J.A. Fitzmyer, a great expert on the gospel of Luke, notes that the disciples report they recognized Jesus not by seeing him, but in the breaking of the bread.

Luke was speaking about the two who walked with Jesus from Jerusalem to Emmaus. But he was not just speaking about them; he was speaking about what he himself had experienced. Luke recognized the healing Jesus brought into this world, not because he heard about it, or saw Peter and Paul. He recognized the healing spirit of Jesus in the breaking of bread and sharing of wine in the communities he met.

Luke explains this in the beginning of his gospel when he writes to Theophilus that he is reporting on "events that have taken place among us." Luke is thinking not only about what happened to Jesus but what happened to his followers. They were the ones breaking their bread and sharing their wine. It is good to ask ourselves whether our own Christian communities would lead someone like Luke on the path to Jesus.

That is not so much a question about the quality of our Sunday liturgy. It concerns the quality of our human and professional life. In his 1991 encyclical, *Centesimus Annus*, Pope John Paul II extends this idea of a Christian community even to business enterprises. He suggests that they be organized as Christian communities, interested in the welfare of their members and cooperators, but also in the larger community they serve. Shops, hospitals, studios, service stations, family businesses should be organized in that way, he suggests.

Definitely something to think about!

Thomas's Doubt

"Unless I can see... I refuse to believe." John 20:19-31

Thomas is the one who did not believe, the one who doubted. Because of this he generally gets a rough deal. People who doubt are still called after him.

Thomas did not believe that the others had seen Jesus. Why didn't he believe? Was it because he found the others still sitting in their safe upper room after having seen him? Would it not have made more sense if they had left that room immediately after his appearances to announce that astounding good news to the world? Why was it that seeing him did not change their whole lives?

Maybe we touch here on the deepest ground of unbelief in the world around us. It is not difficult to believe in Jesus. They say that even Karl Marx had no difficulty in believing in him. It is much more difficult to believe that his *followers* believe in him.

If we really believed in Jesus, wouldn't we live different lives? Are we really so different from those who don't believe in him?

Did you ever hear the story missionaries and evangelists tell in all kinds of variations? It is the story of the old Indian or the wise African who says: "If what you say about Jesus is really true, why did you wait so long before coming to tell us?"

All of us are surrounded by people like Thomas, people who wonder how we can say that we saw him, and yet behave in the way we do. They expect us to act the way we tell them Jesus did, and to live as he lived, putting himself on the line for a greater justice and a lasting peace.

Jesus' Last Breakfast

"...there was some bread there and a charcoal fire with fish cooking on it."   *John 21:1-19*

Every Christian is able to tell what the last supper was about. It is an unforgettable meal, one that is commemorated in most Christian communities in one way or another. We very rarely hear about that other meal Jesus had with his disciples after his resurrection, his first breakfast with them.

Evening meals are generally nice. They occur at the end of the day, everyone is in a good mood. The day is over, the work done. Breakfast is a different issue. It is at the beginning of the day; the work has to be started, organized, and divided. When people come together for breakfast, it is often for a working breakfast.

That is what happened that day. Peter and some others had gone out fishing. They hadn't caught anything. When they approached the lake shore they saw a man who asked them for some fish. When they told him that they had not caught anything, he suggested they throw the net out once more. They did, and caught 153 big fish. By that time they had recognized Jesus, and they were surprised to be invited to a breakfast for which he had already baked the bread and some fish. It was after the breakfast that he asked Peter, "Do you love me?"

After that breakfast they got to hear with Peter what loving him would mean—going out to the whole wide world taking care of his sheep and his lambs.

On the shore was that strange number of fish—153. Experts have puzzled over that number. It probably represented the different varieties of fish observed in that region at the time. If so, Peter and company must have understood that the number symbolized their mission to the world. Plenty for them, and us, to do!

Messianic Secret

"If you are the Christ tell us openly." John 10:27-30

It is a cold morning, John writes, when they come again to ask him whether he is the messiah. "How much longer are you going to keep us in suspense? If you are the Christ tell us openly" (John 10:24).

In the original text their question sounds like a threat, and it is. They suspect he is the messiah. They are right, but they have their own idea of what the messiah should do. According to them, as messiah he should be for them and against others. That was not Jesus' idea.

If he had said, "Yes, I am the messiah, the one you are expecting," it would only aggravate the confusion. He wanted to keep it a secret for the time being, until they grew in insight.

He did not come to divide, he came to bring together. He did not come to scatter, he came to gather.

He answers their question with his parable about the shepherd to whom all the sheep belong, and who has to take care of all of them.

This parable not only says something about him, but about us. If we are with his spirit, his role in the world is our role, his mission our mission, as he told his disciples after his resurrection and before he left them: "As the Father sent me, so I am sending you."

The secret of his identity is out. There should be no secret about who we are and what our intentions are, either. He entrusts us with his "Good Shepherd's Project."

Friends

"It is by your love for one another that everyone will recognize you as my disciples."   John 13:31-35

In 1891 when Pope Leo XIII wrote his encyclical "On New Things" (*Rerum Novarum*), which started a whole new chapter in the church's social teaching, he wrote that the foundation for a Christian social order could only be "friendship."

We Christians often say that we are each other's sisters and brothers. That is not what Jesus said. He uses the word brother when he asks us to forgive each other seven times seven times.

He asks us to be sisters and brothers who are friends.

Later popes used other words for the same issue. Pius XII used the phrase "social charity," Paul VI spoke of a "civilization of love," and Pope John Paul II champions "solidarity." But in his encyclical *Centesimus Annus* ("Hundredth Year"), which celebrates the centenary of *Rerum Novarum*, John Paul comes back to that word "friendship."

Christians should be the friends of all, real friends; and Jesus makes it clear what real friends are willing to do for each other. They are even willing to lay down their lives for each other. Let us pray that we will never be asked to do that in the literal sense of the word, but let us in any case be more willing to see those around us with the eyes with which he would see them.

That is not an easy task in our world, a world where we are getting more and more ethnically mixed, with all the consequent difficulties and tensions.

Let us be friends, let us be kind, let others say of us: "Look how they love!"

Holy Spirit, In-Between God

"...the Paraclete, the Holy Spirit, whom the Father will send in my name, will teach you everything...."   John 14:23-29

One of the oldest controversies in the Christian community surrounds the Holy Spirit. It is the reason that Eastern and Western Christianity have been torn apart for more than a thousand years. The question is a theological one, and it turns around one word we find in our Western Creed, *filioque*. The question is how the Holy Spirit originates in God, and how the Holy Spirit is given to us.

Though the difference seems a mere detail, it makes all the difference. In the Eastern churches one believes that the Holy Spirit is first given to the community and, consequently, to the individuals. In the Western churches we believe that the Holy Spirit is first given to the individual and consequently to the community.

This mere detail points up a difference that is so deeply rooted in the two sides that it betrays itself at the most unexpected moments.

When President Ronald Reagan and Soviet leader Mikhail Gorbachev addressed the world on New Year's Day some years ago, that difference showed up. Reagan, addressing the Russians, stressed his interest in guaranteeing them the individual and personal freedoms and rights Western people take almost for granted, while Gorbachev, speaking to the Americans, emphasized that "we" would have to work together to guarantee world peace.

The two opinions belong together; they complement each other.

John gives the Holy Spirit a name, *paracletos*, a name that means counselor, advocate, consoler, but also *mediator*. That last translation is perhaps the best one. The Holy Spirit is the "in-between" God, the force and energy that should bind us together, to realize a peace only God can give.

Total Vision

*"But Stephen, filled with the Holy Spirit, gazed into heaven and saw
the glory of God, and Jesus standing at God's right hand."*

Acts 7:55-60

People who have been through near-death experiences report that just
before they thought they were dying their whole life passed before
them. They suddenly saw all that had happened to them, and they
went through all their experiences in one flash of insight.

Stephen must have experienced something like that when he was
kneeling outside of Jerusalem being stoned to death. He had been witnessing to Jesus Christ in the court before the judges and others
present. But now, just before he died, he suddenly saw it all.

Heaven opened and he saw Jesus taken up in glory. Now it is no
longer only a question of words. He sees for himself. All the pieces fall
together into place. Heaven and earth are connected. Jesus is not only
in heaven, because Stephen sees him from earth. He prays as Jesus
prayed, expressing the unity he sees: "Lord, do not hold this sin
against them" (Acts 7:60).

It is the same prayer others prayed facing death. Martin Luther
King prayed: "Do to us whatever you want, we will still love you."

It is the prayer of Etty Hillesum on her way to the extermination
camp, who refused to allow her world to be divided into friends and
enemies.

In all those cases people facing death keep the world and humanity
together. What human beings do to the world cannot undo what God
did and does to it. They all pray as Jesus prayed.

They all remain faithful to his command: "Love your enemies."
They all remain faithful to the vision of the world and the human family as willed by God. We belong together. It is a vision we all carry in
our hearts.

August 29 _____

Our Own Mother Tongue

"How does it happen that each of us hears them in our own native language?"
                                                            Acts 2:1-11

What message could Jesus have for our time and age? He lived so long ago, in a region so foreign to most of us, in a very different environment...we might continue this kind of argument endlessly.

It is nothing new. The foreigners who visited Jerusalem as tourists or as business people in the time of Jesus might have said the same thing. It is true they were his contemporaries, but they came from so many different regions and cultures, from Asia and Africa, from the Middle East and Europe.

When Luke describes the Pentecost crowd in Jerusalem, he gives us an idea of that variety: Parthians, Medes, Elamites; people from Mesopotamia, Judaea, and Cappadocia, Pontus and Asia, Phrygia and Pamphylia, Egypt, and the parts of Libya round Cyrene; residents from Rome—Jews and proselytes alike—Cretans and Arabs. The whole of Luke's world was present.

They filled the street when Peter and the apostles spoke for the first time under the influence of the Holy Spirit. And though so different, they all heard what he said in their own mother tongue. They spoke the language of the Spirit, the language of Jesus, and everyone recognized it.

Jesus was no stranger to them. How would they have been able to recognize him, if what he stood for did not echo from within their own hearts? In the apocryphal gospel of Thomas, Jesus once said, "Don't be amazed about what bubbles up from within me; listen to yourself, and you will hear it come from within yourself."

After all, we are all created after the same pattern, the image of God.

At Play Everywhere

"I [Wisdom] was beside the master craftsman, at play everywhere on his earth, delighting to be with the children of humankind."

Proverbs 8:22-31

Around 1846 two German missionaries opened a church in what is now Kenya, in East Africa. It was not the first church in that region. Hundreds of years before a Christian community had flourished around Fort Jesus in Mombasa, but it had disappeared completely due to a persecution that finished it off.

The first day of the new church the two invited the local population of Rabai. Only fifteen persons turned up, all men, not a single woman or child. The evangelists worshiped with them in a solid Western church service, with solemn, translated European hymns, prayers, blessings, and a sermon. They knew the local language, so that was no problem. Yet, after the service when they asked whether the fifteen intended to come back the following Sunday, they answered that they did not plan to do so. Their reason was simple. They did not think much of the service. It had been too dull for them. They were accustomed to worship in another way, they said. They were accustomed to much livelier singing, with drums and other instruments, dancing, eating, and drinking afterwards. The two missionaries wrote in their diary that they were upset about this reaction. They wrote that they even felt "humbled."

It is a discussion that never ended in Africa, and that spread to our own country. Shouldn't our liturgy be more festive?

Should it not only be called, but really be, a celebration with music and dance, at least from time to time?

Was it not once said that God delights in being with us, playing together with us over the surface of the whole wide earth? Why is our worship often so dull? Why don't we express our joy in the Lord?

Discipleship

"The disciple is not superior to the teacher, but the fully trained disciple will be like the teacher." Luke 6:39-45

Once an Indian disciple asked her master: "Maharajah, Sacred Scripture says that a guru, a teacher, is needed to make progress. Is that true?" The Swami answered, "It is necessary in the beginning; after that it is the teacher in yourself who can play the role of guru."

The teacher Jesus intended something like that when he told us that he was going to the Father, and that we would discover ourselves to be with his spirit. There is a divine spark in us. It is the Pentecost event. Those little tongues of flame disappear inside us to be with us forever and ever.

That does not mean that all will go well with us from here on. We all know stories about disciples who became as powerful as their master, but who did not use that power in the way their master did. One of the stories in Acts concerns Simon the witch doctor, who wanted to buy the power of the apostles to earn money and get rich, not to build up a Christian community.

Perhaps this is the reason that Jesus at times plays out the relation between master and disciple in very dramatic ways.

Take the instance when he washed their feet at the last supper. Having done that he says: "You call me Lord and Master and rightly so, I am. If I, then, the Lord and Master, have washed your feet, you must wash each other's feet. I have given you an example, so that you may copy what I have done to you" (John 13:14-15). Or as Jesus says in our Scripture for today: "The disciple is not superior to the teacher, but the fully trained disciple will be like the teacher" (Luke 6:40).

Jesus' Amazement

"I tell you, not even in Israel have I found faith as great as this."

Luke 7:1-10

In 1988 the International Association of Mission Studies met in Rome. The discussion in one of the working groups began with the missionaries exchanging personal experiences. They had much in common. One of the participants said: "When I left my seminary I had not been told that I would meet God working with the Hindus. From my theological training I expected the contrary. It was a great surprise for me to discover that they, too, walked with God."

He and the others had discovered that God is wider than the Christian circle.

Jesus seems to experience something like that himself when he expresses his amazement about the faith of the Roman officer. In fact, Jesus does not meet that officer himself, because when he approaches his house to heal the officer's favorite servant, the man sends him the message: "I am not worthy to have you under my roof, and that is why I did not presume to come to you myself. Let my boy be cured by your giving the command. For I am under authority myself, and have soldiers under me; and I say to one man, 'Go,' and he goes; to another 'Come here,' and he comes; to my servant 'Do this,' and he does it."

When Jesus expresses his amazement about the officer's faith, Luke uses the same word he used for Mary's faith at the beginning of his gospel, a faith not restricted to the Jewish circle, just as our faith in God is not restricted to the Christian circle. God is not just with us, God is with all of humanity, in many different ways.

September 2 _____

Death and Hope

"And the dead man sat up and began to talk, and Jesus gave him back to his mother."   Luke 7:11-17

One gospel text that is often read at funeral services, especially for young people, is the story of the widow at Naim who was burying her only son. In those days, her son was probably also her only hope and livelihood. Jesus was struck by her grief, stopped the funeral procession, and returned the dead son alive to his mother. At first hearing, the text seems an almost cruel choice for grieving parents. Parents should not be burying their children. When they do, it is because of something tragic—cancer interrupting a young life, an accident tearing someone away from his loved ones.

What consolation does such a text offer? Jesus is not present now and the miracle is not going to be repeated. We human beings can do a lot, but we can't bring back those who die.

It is exactly at this point that the story about the young man at Naim makes sense. We can't do anything about death, but God can. At Naim God breaks through the hopelessness of this world. God opens new possibilities. The road is open to new life, life assured!

The story is about that hope, a hope that counts not only at the physical death of a child, but of all death: the death of a marriage, when a couple gets divorced, the death of a job when it is lost, the sad death of your plans for life. The hope revealed in this story about Naim does count at those moments when we are confronted with the apparent deadliness of death.

Forgiven and Accepted

"It is someone who is forgiven little who shows little love."

Luke 7:36-8:3

During the party a rich Pharisee gave in honor of Jesus, a woman came in. Those present recognized her; she had a bad name in town. She went to Jesus and waited on him; she wept, and at a certain point she knelt at his feet and anointed them with the oils she had brought. Even before Simon, his host, could make any remark Jesus addressed him: "I tell you her sins, many as they are, have been forgiven her." It is strange that he tells this to Simon, even before he says anything to the woman anointing his feet.

That woman already knew.

She is not forgiven because she is anointing Jesus' feet, showing her love. She anoints Jesus' feet because she is forgiven! "It is someone who is forgiven little who shows little love."

From our own human experience, it is not difficult to grasp what happened here. It is the case of someone who is despicable in her own eyes. Everyone despises her. She is a nobody to others. She is not anointing his feet to be forgiven. In that case forgiveness would have depended on her initiative. She understood and felt that Jesus forgave her, that Jesus—unlike all the others—accepted her.

She knew that he was willing to recognize her as a person notwithstanding all that had happened to her. She remained valid in his eyes. That is why she came in with her perfumes and oils. She anointed him because she loved him, and she loved him because she knew that he loved her.

Christ of God

"It was Peter who spoke up. 'The Christ of God,' he said."

Luke 9:18-24

People around Jesus are always asking, "Who is he?" It is a question asked from the very beginning of his life. He is obviously someone who touches everyone, someone who causes a strong reaction, either favorable or unfavorable. There are all kinds of rumors and ideas about him. Why does he do the things he does? Why does he always seem to be on the side of the sick, the poor, and the abused?

He himself asks that question. "Who do the crowds say I am?" There are two answers: the one from Peter, who says: "You are the Christ of God, which means you are the anointed of God"(Luke 9:20), and his own, "The Son of Man" (Luke 9:22).

He then describes what this means by using four verbs: "to suffer, to be rejected, to be put to death, and to rise."

Why would that be? Why does it still happen day in and day out to those who follow him?

It has everything to do with the divine dynamic in our world, a dynamic described in the main event of the Hebrew Scriptures. The God of the exodus is an "ethical" God, a God who takes the side of the oppressed poor. To opt for the poor implies the willingness to do something about this world, to convert, change, and heal it. It is an option that is not well received by those who are interested in the world as it is at the moment, and who are powerful in it.

Consequently, to opt for the healing of the world is dangerous. It means being gripped by God's dynamic in this world. It is what he asks his followers to do and be. It is the cross all of us have to carry. It is the task we face in the exercise of our daily work and skill.

Jerusalem, the Bride

"Rejoice with Jerusalem, be glad for her, all who love her!"
Isaiah 66:10-14

Jerusalem is not just the name of a town, it is the name of a woman, a name in which the word *shalom* is heard—"Possessor of Peace," "Home of Peace," "She in whom Peace is at Home."

Of course, it is also the name of a town, a town that is like a human body energized by a mighty spirit, where all creative and developmental forces and powers come together.

Jerusalem is a beautiful, lively bride on the lookout for her bridegroom, who is on his way to her.

Jerusalem is the name of humanity waiting for God; she is the bride who is saying, "Come" (Revelation 22:17). Jerusalem stands for the fulfillment of the divine-human history. It is another name for the Kingdom of God. It is the name of heaven. Jerusalem has always been praised by the prophets as the ultimate, the eschatological aim of the human journey. Jerusalem is the mystical destiny of the whole of humanity.

It is in Jerusalem that the whole of humanity will come together, and where the Kingdom of God will be realized. No wonder that the geographical Jerusalem played such an important role in the life of Jesus. In his heart and mind, Jerusalem is the only place where the new life should break through the old one.

You can't avoid poetry when using the name Jerusalem. So many images are connected to and with it. Jerusalem is the ultimate, the absolute. You can't get any further, or deeper, or wider, or higher. Everything has to give way to Jerusalem.

Jesus had to go there even though his own disciples told him not to go. In Luke's gospel it is the final and most decisive choice he makes. It determines all the rest.

We, too, will have to face that choice, choosing in favor of the Jerusalem of all the prophets and of the Book of Revelation, or against it. "Yes" or "No"—there is no compromise possible.

Seventy-Two Means the World

"...the Lord appointed seventy-two others and sent them out ahead of him...."
Luke 10:1-12, 17-20

Luke is the only evangelist who reports the mission Jesus gives to seventy-two disciples. There is another mission given to the twelve, but the report of the mission of the seventy-two is exclusive to Luke.

Bible scholars wondered what the number seventy-two referred to. They all agree on the twelve. Those twelve indicate that Jesus' mission extends to the twelve tribes of Israel. There might be something in the fact that Luke is a Gentile, the only non-Jewish evangelist. Another clue might be that he is writing for Gentiles.

Bringing these hints together and looking for a corresponding number in the Hebrew Scriptures, many scholars now agree that the number refers to the seventy-two grandsons of Noah, who left their grandfather's homestead, spread out all over the world, and thus became the origin of all the peoples that live on the earth.

The twelve refer to the whole of the Judaic nation, the seventy-two to the whole of the world. The good news is that together we form one family, one father, one brother, and one spirit. In the Book of Revelation, the last book of the Christian Scriptures, John describes how he sees all the nations coming together to the New City, the New Jerusalem, each one bringing its own treasure to it. It is the movement started by those seventy-two. It is the movement that was symbolized from the moment of his birth, when the magi from the East came to bring their gifts to his cradle in Bethlehem. All of us are taken up in that movement as well.

In Your Heart

"Jesus said to him, 'You have answered right, do this and life is yours.'"   Luke 10:25-37

A lawyer comes to test Jesus. He asks him, "What should I do?" Jesus does not give him the answer. In the gospel of Luke Jesus rarely gives answers. Instead, he returns the question. He asks his interrogator, "What do you think you should do?"

The lawyer gives the correct answer: You have to love God with all your heart and your neighbor as yourself. So why did he ask? The man asks another question to justify himself: "Who is my neighbor?"

Again Jesus does not give a direct answer. He tells the story of the good Samaritan. When the story is told he repeats his examiner's question: "Who was the neighbor in that story?" Again the lawyer gives his answer.

Jesus often dodges questions. He does not want to answer. He leaves the answer to us. He is not going to take over. He respects us too much for that. He tells stories and parables, he gives examples and poses riddles, but it is up to us to make up our mind. Jesus does not write encyclicals or pastoral letters. In the whole of the gospels he wrote only once, and then in the sand, so the wind had blown away whatever he wrote in no time.

Jesus is faithful to the ancient text in Deuteronomy: "For this law which I am laying down for you today is neither obscure for you nor beyond your reach. It is not in heaven...it is not beyond the sea....No, the word is very near to you, it is in your mouth and in your heart for you to put into practice" (Deuteronomy 30:11-14).

September 8

Perfect in Christ

"...it is Christ among you, your hope of glory...." Colossians 1:24-28

In June 1985 a sixteen-year-old Australian girl, Ruth Henderson, was sitting in a hijacked TWA plane next to Robert Dean Stethem, a young American marine. Robert had been tortured.

Some years later Ruth testified in court against the hijackers. "His head was bleeding and his back. His wrists had been bound together so tightly that he had no feeling any more in his hands. His knees and his ribs hurt him. We talked about trivial things, like diving and Greece. Talking about those ordinary things seemed to relax him, and it made him forget his pain. It helped both of us not to think about the nightmare in which we were caught...He told me that maybe it would be better if he would be killed. He was convinced that in any case one of the American Marines—there were six Marines on board—was going to be killed. He said that the best would be that they would kill him, because he was the only one who was not married. He talked about all that very candidly. He thought the best would be that he would die, so that the others could live." Later Robert Dean Stethem was killed and thrown from the plane.

What an amazing story of compassion and solidarity! This is the attitude of Jesus Christ, of whom Paul wrote in his letter to the Colossians: "The message which was a mystery hidden for generations and centuries and that now has been revealed to his holy people...it is Christ within you, your hope of glory" (Colossians 1:25,27).

Prayer VII
Not What But How

"Father, may your name be held holy, your kingdom come...!"
Luke 11:1-13

The famous theologian Karl Barth once wrote that praying is nothing but reminding God of God's promises and holiness. That is how Abraham prayed. When God tells him that Sodom and Gomorrah are going to be destroyed, Abraham reminds God of God's promise: "Is the judge of the whole world not to act justly" (Genesis 18:25).

This is what Jesus does when he teaches his disciples how to pray: "Father, may your name be held holy, your kingdom come!" It is on that foundation that you ask for a new start in your life and for everything you need for that life. You also have to ask God to forgive you for all you did wrong in the past, and don't hesitate to remind God that you are doing the same, that you are forgiving anyone who might have harmed you.

And ask not to be misled, but to be guided in the correct way.

Jesus does not tell us *what* we should pray, but *how*. No nonsense, no long prayers—just straightforwardly tell what you expect from the one who put you in this life, and whom you trust in everything.

In Luke's gospel, after giving them the Lord's Prayer, Jesus tells the story about the man who asks his friend for three loaves in the middle of the night. He gets those loaves, not so much because of his friendship, but because of his persistence. The word Jesus uses is the Greek word *anadeia*, which really means "shamelessness." To be too timid when praying to God is no sign of confidence. On the contrary, ask God to stick to the promises given!

Capital and God's Kingdom

"...for life does not consist in possessions, even when someone has more than one needs."   Luke 12:13-21

Luke writes eighteen times in his gospel about wealth and its dangers. Mary sings about the difference between the poor and the rich even before Jesus' birth. Luke is the only one who mentions that the (poor) shepherds are the first ones to hear about Jesus' birth. He notes that Jesus belongs to the poorer class and that they brought the sacrifice of the poor to Jesus' circumcision in the temple. He is the one to tell us that John the Baptizer asked those who had two shirts to give the second shirt to those who had none.

Yet, Jesus is not against wealth as such in Luke's gospel. He definitely does not center his message directly on a redivision of goods. The essential thing is to be with Jesus, to be Christ-like. That is the real treasure, the genuine pearl. To be like Jesus leads to a new type of life, a life that leads unavoidably to love and care, to justice and peace, and to the development of anything that would bring those qualities about. Our wealth, our gifts, and our talents should be used to build the Kingdom of God. In certain situations, that can be done by giving alms.

That, however, is neither the only nor probably the best way to tackle the problems of the world.

In Washington, D.C., a famous Christian community has many rich and influential members. They formed a "Ministry of Money" group. They meet regularly to discuss how to invest and use their money in view of God's Kingdom. For instance, they might invest in the research on sicknesses of the poor that would otherwise be left unresearched and untreated, the sort of research that is usually not interesting for the shareholders of the pharmaceutical industry.

The medical doctor Luke would have no problems with that use of wealth!

Sojourning

"Wherever your treasure is, that is where your heart will be too."
Luke 12:32-48

"Your treasure is in heaven," Jesus says, "because my Father gave you his Kingdom." This saying puts us in a strange position. We have it, and we have it not. We have arrived, and we haven't yet arrived. We are here, and we are not here.

This is the situation in which Abraham and Sarah found themselves, recognizing that they were strangers, sojourners, and nomads on this earth (Hebrews 11:13). They set out for a country they had seen high in the sky between the stars, but they did not know exactly how they were going to get there. "By faith they sojourned looking forward to the well-founded city, designed and built by God" (Hebrews 11:10).

Sometimes the reality of the Kingdom breaks through in our actual lives, when we live the life we are going to live forever and ever when our journey is over.

Sometimes it happens only in sign or symbol. In 1968 a young woman, Koosje Koster, was arrested in the main street of Amsterdam. She caused an obstruction to the traffic, the police report stated. She had been distributing currants from a brown paper bag to the passers-by. People surrounded her and began to ask her questions. That is how she ended up at the police station.

When the police asked why she had been doing this, she replied: "To make them eat at least for once out of one and the same bag." When reporters asked her why currants (in Dutch *krenten*), she answered that the sound of the word reminded her of Corinthians, and of Paul's letter that we should, in the name of Jesus, eat together and be faithful to the breaking of the bread Jesus left us.

Our treasure is in heaven, in the togetherness with God and each other for all time to come. Let us sojourn with faith in that direction.

Dove or Hawk

"Do you suppose that I am here to bring peace on earth?"

Luke 12:49-53

Pacifists, or the doves among us, are often deadly serious people.

This is understandable; once you have chosen against violence, there is no place for compromise.

The same is true for the hawks among us, the ones who believe in the use and the efficiency of violence.

All that seriousness has a negative side. There is hardly any space left for some playfulness, for some humor. If you lose your sense of humor you will definitely have trouble with Jesus' words about peace.

Did Jesus come to bring peace? If he did, why then did he say, "Do you suppose that I am here to bring peace on earth? No, I tell you, but rather division" (Luke 12:51). But if you say that he did not come to bring peace, a whole new set of difficulties arises.

The correct answer is, of course, yes, he did come to bring peace. That was his intention, that is why he came. But that was not how it had worked. His presence alone brought tension, tore families apart, as it still does. Some favor him, some are against him.

He did not come to conquer the world with violence. He did not come to force us.

He left us the word *shalom* as our greeting. It is the Hebrew word for peace, for wholeness. It is this kind of wholeness Jesus came to bring to the whole of humanity, a peace that asks for a choice. You are in favor of it, or you are against it—dove or hawk!

No Number of Saved Ones

"Sir, will there only be a few saved?" Luke 13:22-30

To find the right question is often more difficult than finding the answer. If you have all the answers but don't know the questions, you haven't learned very much. Saying that someone knows all the answers is no compliment.

Sometimes Luke groups together a set of answers that Jesus gave at different times. Luke does that by introducing a question. For example, Luke uses this literary device when he introduces a voice from the crowd that asks: "Sir, will there be only a few saved?" (Luke 13:24). A whole set of answers follows.

Jesus speaks about a narrow door; a householder who keeps his door closed; about people who come in from the East and the West; about how the last ones will be the first ones and vice versa, and so on.

But he does not directly answer the question of how many will be saved. What he is willing to tell is how to be saved. He does not want to play the number game, or give a body count. He is only willing to tell what kind of people enter. He tells us how Abraham, Isaac, Jacob, and all the prophets are there.

It is a pity that he doesn't mention any women, at least not by name. He mentions them indirectly by indicating the type of people you find in heaven, those who dedicated themselves to the Kingdom of God here on earth.

If you are busy here only eating and drinking, producing to consume without any further perspective, you don't belong to the Kingdom of God here on earth. You are saving neither yourself nor anyone else. The correct question to Jesus' answer is not: "Will there be many?" It is: "Are there many here who are saved?"

Option for the Poor

"When you have a party, invite the poor, the crippled, the lame, the blind...."
Luke 14:1, 7-14

Many theologians today use this text to justify the church's "option for the poor," but few seem to draw the conclusions of this option. It really is quite a radical choice!

You can develop all kinds of theories about the existing structural injustices in the world. It is a fact, however, that this injustice has to do with the way our economic, political, informational, and religious life is organized.

Almost everyone is engaged in those structures. According to certain statistics 40 to 50 percent of the working population is part of the bureaucracy and almost all the rest of the working population works for it, directly or indirectly.

It is difficult to expect that either of those two groups will be eager to "rock the boat." As soon and as long as the economy goes well, even trade unions have trouble keeping their members.

The change has to come from another direction, especially from those who at the moment are not part of the process: the sick, the homeless, the poor, the crippled, the marginalized, and, in many cases, the women.

That is why Jesus' option for them is very significant. So would our "option for the poor" be, if we followed his example. It would help to change the world.

Price to Pay

"No one who does not carry his cross and come after me can be my disciple."   Luke 14:25-33

Crowds of people are following Jesus. He is a celebrity by now.

Some come because they want to be healed, others just to see and hear him, others again because they are really touched by what they see and hear.

At one point Luke tells us that Jesus turned around. That means he suddenly faced them. That must have created some confusion. Now there is a kind of confrontation, the confrontation we all need.

In his writings, the Danish theologian and philosopher Søren Kierkegaard tells a story about a Sunday service somewhere in Denmark. They are all singing about their willingness to receive Jesus: "Come, O Jesus, come!"

Suddenly the sacristan comes out of the sacristy to whisper something in the ear of the minister, who turns to them and says: "Jesus heard our prayers, he is in the sacristy, and he would like to see each one of you."

One by one they go the sacristy, every woman and man. They are still singing when they knock nervously on the door. And indeed, there is Jesus, who has the same question for each one of them: "Are you really my disciple?" Nobody dares answer the question. But as soon as they are safely in the church again, they sing again with all the others.

In Luke's story, Jesus turns to them and says: "No one who does not carry his cross and come after me can be my disciple." He speaks about the price they must pay to be considered one of his followers, a price that is pretty high; it is paid for with life itself.

Lost Coin

"...what woman with ten drachmas would not, if she lost one, light a lamp and sweep out the house...?   Luke 15:1-31

Saint Gregory of Nyssa offers an explanation that could have been written today of Jesus' parable of the woman who lost one of her coins. It is almost a piece of modern depth psychology. He explains that the woman in question is looking for her lost humanity. He thinks that the lost coin represents her heart and soul, and that the woman stands for all of us.

When she lights a lamp, that lamp is "without any doubt our consciousness, throwing light on our deepest depths." (*Against Eunomius*, XII) The lost coin can only be found in our own house, that is in our own self.

Gregory goes even further when he adds that "the parable points at the image of our King, not yet completely lost, but hidden under the trash of our existence."

According to Gregory, Jesus is that king, the one who came to redeem us, but who in his turn has to be "redeemed" in us. If we don't find and free him, we will never be who we are supposed to be.

That loss—becoming a lost sheep—would not only affect us, it would affect the whole of humanity, the whole of the flock. Jesus, the treasure of God's Kingdom, is hidden in every one of us.

We, too, need a lamp to light up the house, and a broom to stir up the trash to find God's reign in us.

Recycling and Waste

"There was a rich man and he had a steward who was denounced to him for being wasteful with his property." Luke 16:1-13

A steward was denounced as being wasteful. His master called him and said, "What is this I hear about you? Draw me up an account of your stewardship because you are not to be my steward any longer."

In Jesus' parable the careless steward takes the accusation from his boss very seriously. He takes great care to arrange his affairs in a way that he will get out of his difficulties. He doesn't use the most honest of methods. His boss will later call him "unjust," but he praises him at the same time for having learned his lesson and for being so "astute" as to rearrange his affairs.

If only, Jesus then sighs, the children of light would be as astute as the children of this world.

This parable takes on new significance in a time when we are accusing ourselves and each other of wasting our environment and our resources.

It will not be news to anyone to hear that all of us could be accused of being wasteful stewards. The trashbags in front of our houses once, sometimes twice, a week give ample proof of the quantity and quality of the things we throw away, week in and week out.

The way we use and waste paper and plastic, energy and water, glass and aluminum, food and drink cry out to high heaven and ask for better management.

We have to follow the example of the steward in Jesus' parable. If not, we, too, will simply be dismissed as mere wasters of God's gifts.

Even recycling is a spiritual issue. Asceticism always was!

September 18

Rich and Poor

"...between us and you a great gulf has been fixed, to prevent those who want to cross from our side to yours or from your side to ours."
Luke 16:19-31

"Chasm" is a word used in the translation of Pope John Paul's 1991 encyclical on the social teaching on the church, commemorating the one-hundredth anniversary of Pope Leo XIII's encyclical *Rerum Novarum*—the encyclical that is considered to be the beginning of the church's modern social teaching.

John Paul uses the word "chasm" to describe the distance that existed a hundred years ago between the rich and the poor, a word that still can be used. It is the word some translators use when translating Jesus' parable about the rich man with Lazarus at his door.

Once the two are dead, the rich man in Hades sees Lazarus being comforted by Abraham, and he shouts to them: "Father Abraham, pity me and send Lazarus to dip the tip of his finger in water and cool my tongue..." Abraham replies, "My son, remember that in your life you had your fill of good things just as Lazarus had his fill of bad. Now he is being comforted here while you are in agony. But that is not all; between us and you a great chasm has been fixed, to prevent those who want to cross from our side to yours, or from your side to ours" (Luke 16:23-27).

The chasm Abraham speaks about is the distance the rich man himself had fixed while he was eating and drinking while Lazarus suffered at his door. It is a kind of eternal consequence of the life he had been living here on earth.

The conclusions to be drawn from this parable are hard, when you consider that so many at our doors are hungry and helpless. You don't even have to think of the so-called Third World when thinking of them. In a city like New York 150,000 people are said to be homeless.

Obviously no one of us can do anything to bridge that chasm between them and us, but, organized together, we definitely can.

All Is Given

"We are useless servants: we have done no more than our duty."
Luke 17:5-10

Some years ago the film *Amadeus* was quite popular. For months people lined up in front of movie theatres all over the country to see a film whose theme is a theological issue.

The film is about a confession. Salieri, a contemporary of Mozart and also a composer, confesses that he is probably the cause of Mozart's death. He wanted to murder him because there was something he never had understood. How was it possible that Mozart, according to Salieri a vulgar and superficial person, was able to write such beautiful music so effortlessly? All Mozart had to do was sit down and the most magnificent melodies flowed from his pen.

And he, Salieri, a serious man who had dedicated his whole life to God and lived an almost ascetic life, had such difficulty in getting music on paper.

It is about that total gratuitousness of God's gifts that Jesus speaks when he says: "When you have done all you have been told to do, say, 'We are useless servants; we have done no more than our duty'" (Luke 17:10).

All we can do comes from God. All is given, everything is gratuitous. Where does the poet get his words, the painter his colors, the architect his shapes, the sculptor his forms, the doctor his healing power, the mechanic his skill, the computer programmer his creativity, and the author his inspiration, if not from God?

If we are honest about ourselves we will have to admit, even after all we might have done and the awards we have received, "We are useless servants; we have done no more than our duty."

Remembering Jesus

"Remember the gospel that I carry, 'Jesus Christ....'"
2 Timothy 2:8-13

It is impossible to imagine that Jesus could be forgotten. Yet, he himself must have been afraid of that when he asked them at the last supper to remember him. Paul must have been afraid of the same thing when he writes Timothy not to forget Jesus and the gospel.

Many have forgotten Jesus. A religion teacher in a British primary school noted some years ago that only a few children in her London class knew that we celebrate Christmas because Jesus was born on that day.

He can be and often is forgotten. Everything can be forgotten. The Bible tells how the Jewish people after the exile had forgotten the whole of the law, until Nehemiah recovered the scrolls and read them to the people.

Something forgotten does not function any more in our conscious life. It plays no conscious role in our decision making. If it appears to us in a dream it is not understood.

It is wise to keep old memories alive, our successes but also our mistakes and disasters. Events like the Second World War, the Holocaust, the atomic bombs over Hiroshima and Nagasaki should never be forgotten.

An expert on African affairs was asked what he thought the most important issue in Africa was. His answer astounded most of those present. It was "forgetfulness." He explained that in some African countries people got so accustomed to solving problems with violence, they forgot that in their own tradition problems were always solved nonviolently by dialogue, consultation, and compromise.

"What Africa needs," he said, "is to remember those old democratic ways!"

Prayer VIII
Holy Spirit in Us

"Then he told them a parable about the need to pray...and never lose heart."   *Luke 18:1-8*

Luke is interested in prayer. He is especially interested in the prayer in which you contact the Holy Spirit. It is the first thing he mentions when writing Acts. "You are going to be baptized with the Holy Spirit...you will receive the power of the Holy Spirit which will come on you" (Acts 1:5,8).

Luke mentions the role of the Holy Spirit eighteen times in his writings. According to Luke praying is making and keeping contact with the Holy Spirit in you.

That is what Jesus does from his baptism to his death on the cross. In four of the parables Luke recounts, Jesus speaks about prayer. He tells us that we should pray constantly, that we should pray for the coming of the Kingdom of God and against temptations that might make us forget that kingdom, and that we should pray especially for the Holy Spirit.

Those intentions relate to each other. The realization of the reign of God among us is the reason that we should remain in contact with the Holy Spirit, and it is the Holy Spirit who pushes us towards that fulfilment.

That is not all, however.

There is another aspect to the presence of the Holy Spirit in us. That other aspect is the Holy Spirit's presence itself. Wherever we are, whatever happens to us, we are always "at home" with that Spirit. A terrific reality, one that we don't take sufficiently into account. Its realization would change our whole life!

Snob

"I thank you, God, that I am not... like everyone else." Luke 18:9-14

The great American theologian John L. McKenzie calls the pharisee in the temple a religious snob when he prays: "I thank you, God, that I am not grasping, unjust, adulterous like everyone else, and particularly that I am not like that tax collector there" (Luke 18:11).

We don't know where the word "pharisee" comes from. We don't even know what its root is, though some think that it means something like "the special ones."

In our own contemporary vocabulary it is far from a compliment to be called a pharisee.

I don't think anyone hearing Jesus' parable wants to identify with the pharisee. But the only other person in the story is the tax collector. Though he prays well—and is even praised by Jesus because of it—identifying with him causes some problems, too. Jesus does not say that the pharisee is lying about himself. He is faithful and pious. It is the way he prays that is wrong. So should we better identify with him and not with the tax collector?

Jesus' parables are often filled with this kind of ambiguity. In a way he teases us in them. The best solution is probably to admit that we have something of both the tax collector and the pharisee in us.

At the same time we stand with the pharisee in front of the temple, and with the tax collector in the back. What a story! And Jesus is the laughing third one!

Jesus' Humor

"He kept trying to see Jesus, but he was too short and could not see him for the crowd, so he ran ahead and climbed a sycamore tree...."
Luke 19:1-10

Jesus' humor often escapes us. This is because we make religion and piety such serious issues. Even now laughing in church seems to be somewhat uncouth, though we do it more and more. Yet, when you read the stories about Jesus it is obvious that the crowd around him must have laughed because of his examples and metaphors. Don't you think they laughed when he compared John the Baptizer—that grim prophet dressed in the skin of a camel—with a blade of grass in the wind, and with a dandy at a royal court? And what about the beam in your own eye and the splinter in the eye of your sister or brother? Not to mention the suggestion of lighting a lamp and putting it under a bed or bucket.

Our church meetings hide the fact that the rowdy crowds around Jesus must have enjoyed his stories immensely, and that pharisees and security guards must often have been upset when everyone around him burst out in hearty and loud laughter.

Tell the story about Zacchaeus once to children, and you will see that they will be struck by the comical aspects of it: that he is a small person (all children identify with someone like that!) who climbs in a tree to see Jesus (and at the same time to hide from him!), who is called down to be his host. Consider the almost comical way Zacchaeus reacts to Jesus: "Look, sir, I am going to give half my property to the poor, and if I have cheated anybody I will pay him back four times the amount!" (Luke 19:8). The crowd around them must have been roaring its appreciation.

Jesus looked at Zacchaeus, saying: "That is exactly why I came!"

Afterlife

"...the dead do not marry because they can no longer die...."
Luke 20:27-38

One day they confront Jesus with the question of what happens to a married person after death. They tell him a story about a woman who consecutively loses seven husbands. What is going to happen to her in paradise?

That story reminds me how years ago I used to bring Holy Communion to a very old widow. She lived on a farm that disappeared long ago. She was always in bed, one of those old-fashioned high wooden beds. On the wall in front of her hung a large photograph of her husband. That photo was old, too. It was yellowish and all kinds of small insects had crept in it under the glass. As in many old photos, her husband looked straight into the lens of the camera, and there was no hint of a smile on his face. Taking a photo in that day and age was a serious business.

The last time I brought her communion and gave her extreme unction—as it was called in those days—she pointed at the photo and said: "I am going to him." Heaven definitely meant more than that to her, yet she went to him.

Jesus would have no difficulty with that, but he said something about it that is worth reflection. "Those worthy of a place in the other world and in the resurrection from the dead, do not marry, because they can no longer die, for they are the same as the angels" (Luke 20:35-36).

It suggests that people marry because they die. They marry because it is no good to remain alone. They marry to survive in this world, and to overcome death. They marry "until death do us part."

In the other world, there will be no death any more, no loneliness, and no separation. The two that were together will be together again. Paradise means being all together. That widow was right, but in a different way than she thought.

Sun of Justice

"But for you who fear my name, the Sun of justice will rise with heal-
ing in his rays...."   Malachi 3:19-20a

The prophet Malachi is prophesying the coming of Jesus, the sun of
justice who will heal the world. When prophesying this he not only
spoke of Jesus but of all those who would walk in his footsteps. There
are thousands and thousands of individuals and groups that are healing the world because they are following Jesus. In the first communities they helped the poor; as monks they changed the face of pagan
Europe; as religious women and men they built hospitals and started
schools; as volunteers and in their professional lives they are actually
at work all over the world. They were and are still often persecuted,
and many have died as witnesses to this sun of justice.

It is a healing community that is touching the lives of more and
more people, a healing movement that is constantly developing. You
can notice that in the papal and other pastoral documents that accom-
pany us on our journey through this world.

For over a hundred years the popes have been insisting in ever
more precise terms on the need to change the social structures in this
world. Pope John Paul II has recently been pleading for an alternative
to war and violence to solve the world's problems. Over the last decade those documents have been speaking not only about a good "human ecology," but also about a change in our use of minerals, plants,
and animals. This is not a new agenda. Its implications are now better
seen than ever before. The sun of justice is becoming more and more
visible, its healing rays more healing. All of us should shine with its
light!

Royal Road of Love

"Jesus, remember me when you come into your kingdom."
Luke 23:35-43

When Jesus is hanging on the cross between two murderers the crowd is looking on. They are listening, too. In Luke's report they don't mock Jesus. They see how the soldiers fix a notice above his head, reading: "King of the Jews" in three languages of the region—Latin, Greek, and Hebrew. The crowd, but also the women and the few men who who remained faithful to him till the end, must have asked themselves how he would be able to realize his kingdom. The word "king" must have sounded ridiculous in that situation.

It was not. One of the murderers was aware of that. He asks Jesus to be allowed to be with him in his kingdom. He is a bit vague about the timing when he asks that. He says, "Jesus, remember me, *when* you come in your kingdom."

Jesus is not vague at all. He says: "I tell you, today you will be with me in paradise." Not *when*, but *today*.

There is another one who looks through all the misery of the moment. A stranger—but who is a stranger to Jesus?—the commanding Roman officer. Luke says he gave praise to God, saying, "Truly, this was an upright man!"

God always wanted to show God's glory and love for us, a glory and a love so magnificent that it would blind and burn us, had it not been filtered through Jesus' humanity.

His suffering and pain was his royal road to us. It was in his giving up his life for us that he showed us God's glory and passionate love.

There was no other way. There is no other way but along the royal road of love.

Prayer IX
Asking for Help

"My Lord, our King, the Only One, come to my help, for I am alone and have no helper but you and I am about to take my life in my hands."
Esther 4:17

Queen Esther is in serious trouble. The story is too long to be told here, though it would be worthwhile to do so. It is one of the more dramatic stories in the Hebrew Scriptures.

Through all kinds of intrigues a man called Haman had organized the extermination of the whole Jewish nation in the land of King Ahasuerus, which stretched from India to Ethiopia. Esther, the king's favorite wife, is Jewish. She would like to do something about this, but she is not allowed to approach the king without having been summoned. "Anyone, man or woman, who approaches the king in his private apartments without having been summoned there, must die, unless the king, by pointing his golden sceptre toward him, grants him his or her life" (Esther 4:11). She had not been summoned to the king for the last thirty days. Going to him without being called was practically suicidal. "She prayed, 'My Lord, our King, the only one, come to my help, for I am alone and have no helper but you, and I am about to take my life in my hands'" (Esther 4:17).

She is not asking Yahweh to take over from her. She is asking for help. She herself—with Yahweh's help—will take the risk and do the job.

It is not that we pray too much. We don't. More often we pray in a way that allows us to hand over responsibility.

Ask and it will be given to you, Jesus says. Once we have the courage we asked for, we will have to move on with that help. God helps us to help ourselves.

Re-Adjusting

"...if you remember that your brother or sister has something against you, go and be reconciled with your brother or sister first, and then come back and present your offering." Matthew 5:20-26

Jesus speaks about those who hold something concrete against us. He speaks not only about them, but about us as well. Before we bring any offering to the altar we should reconcile ourselves with them. Hearing this we might think of sons and daughters, fathers and mothers, brothers and sisters, relatives, or those we work with every day. We should reconcile with them. There is no doubt about that.

Yet, there are those others who might be blaming us for our life-style, for our lack of interest in their lot—refugees, homeless people, neglected children, lonely and marginalized elderly people, those we waged war against, and so many others.

We can draw up a list too long to tackle, too long even to think about. How would we be able to face the altar with them? How can we keep our balance in the world in which we live?

The answer lies in our willingness to be attentive to the situation and to organize ourselves in our work and life in such a way that we make things better, not worse.

We can begin doing that by relating our celebrations of the euchar-ist to the issues of justice and reconciliation in our daily life.

Pacifism

"...love your enemies and pray for those who persecute you...."
Matthew 5:43-48

The discussion on pacifism has been endless even in circles devoted to Jesus. Would Jesus have used violence if he had been in situations where many of us would have no hesitation to do so? This is a difficult question. It arises not only in the context of international or civil conflicts, but at any level where we harbor violent, defensive, or revengeful feelings against others in our own family, business, or other affairs.

Evangelii Nuntiandi (*The Gospels to Be Announced*) states: "The church cannot accept violence—especially the force of arms which is uncontrollable once it is let loose—and indiscriminate death as the path of liberation, because she knows that violence always provokes violence and irresistibly engenders new forms of oppression and enslavement" (37).

You can respond to evil with evil, and before you know it you are taken up in a cycle of ever-increasing violence. You see it around you: One child hits another, the other hits back, and so on until they both end up frustrated and crying.

Jesus presents us with the only way out of the issue. Respond to evil with love. Love your enemies, and pray for those who persecute you. A hard lesson, and a difficult one, it is the only way out to break through the circle and cycle of violence. It is a lesson opposed to the way we usually arm ourselves against the other, verbally and physically, internationally and nationally, and personally.

Peace can only be made by peace.

Empathy

"Be compassionate just as your Father is compassionate."

Luke 6:36-38

We can feel sympathy or antipathy for someone. Everyone knows what that means. It is something that often spontaneously bubbles up in you when dealing with someone. It is also something you notice in others when they deal with you.

There is a third "pathy"—empathy, when you feel tuned in to a situation in the same way someone else is. It is a response in which you feel and react like the other, a situation in which you can honestly say, "I share in your feeling."

When Paul writes that he loves with the love of Jesus, or that the life of Christ became his life (Galatians 2:20), he means something like empathy. It has something to do with solidarity and compassion. The suffering of another becomes our suffering.

That person becomes flesh of our flesh—a solidarity Jesus traces back to the fact that we belong to the same family.

According to Pope Paul VI, it is a feeling and awareness that is growing: "Men and women are growing more anxious to establish closer ties of brotherhood and sisterhood; despite their ignorance, their mistakes, their offenses and even their lapses into barbarism and their wanderings from the path of salvation, they are slowly making their way to the creator, even without adverting to it. This struggle toward a more human way of life certainly calls for hard work and imposes difficult sacrifices. But even adversity, when endured for the sake of one's brothers and sisters out of love for them, can contribute greatly to human progress" (*Populorum Progressio*, 79).

Global Village

"...you have only one Father...." Matthew 23:1-12

To hear that we belong to one global village is not news anymore, nor does this information greatly impress us. Though we are connected in all kinds of ways—by satellites, telephones, fax machines, radio, and many others—we remain strangers and often divided against each other.

People sitting in the same bus, train, or plane do not relate to each other because they are using the same kind of transport.

Being aware that we are flying the same spaceship, called earth, is not much help either.

Jesus gives us a reason to relate to each other, a reason that does not depend on any kind of modern inventions, a reason as old as humankind: It is our common divine origin.

"You have only one Father, and he is in heaven" (Matthew 23:9). We have one parent, we have one origin, we belong to the same family. We are all brothers and sisters. Until recently this seemed to be only talk, but human history proves it to be fact.

Get an atlas and take a good look at the world. Get acquainted with the family you have, the world we live in, the spaceship we are traveling on together.

Look at the adventures, the tragedies, the comedies, and the achievements of the human family in that family spirit that Jesus introduced you to.

October 2

Promotion and Career

"She said to him, 'Promise that these two sons of mine may sit one at your right hand and the other at your left in your kingdom.'"
Matthew 20:17-28

One day the mother of two of Jesus' disciples comes to him with a request. You get the impression that the two sent their mother. They did not dare to come themselves; they must have been unsure of their own request. Whatever the reason, she came to ask the best places in his kingdom for her two sons, one at his left side and one at his right side.

They wanted the most influence: career, promotion, climbing the ladder, winning the rat race, we all know the dynamics. Even if we ourselves are not inclined to go that way, others might nevertheless almost force us to do it. A wife might nag her husband day and night for not getting a promotion, pressuring him to get ahead.

A husband might have those same aspirations for his wife, or parents toward their children. Trying to get higher and higher, never satisfied, until we exceed our competence, and are never ever happy again.

This is what Jesus implied in his answer: "You don't know what you are asking for." They answered, "Oh yes, we do!" But they didn't.

The other disciples were no better. When they heard what the two had done, they were indignant. How could they have done a thing like that, trying to climb over their heads! Their indignation shows that they suffered from the same presumptuous ambitions. It is then that Jesus cuts the whole argument short by saying: "Anyone who wants to become great among you must be your servant, and anyone who wants to be first among you must be your slave, just as I did not come to be served, but to serve, and to give my life for others" (Matthew 20:26-28).

[280]

Responsible Consumer

"They sold Joseph to the Ishmaelites for twenty shekels of silver...."
Genesis 37:3-4, 12-13, 17-28

The story of Joseph and his colorful coat remains a bestseller. The musical based on this story is revived again and again. One of the reasons must be that the story is so unbelievable. How could his brothers do something like that to Joseph, their very own brother? It is almost incomprehensible. We would never sell our sister or brother! Would we?

The answer to that question depends on whom you consider to be your brother and your sister.

It is not a pretty question, but could they be those women and children working for paltry salaries in sweatshops in a far-off part of the world, stitching textiles together? Could they be those men working on plantation fields so often sprayed with insecticides that even they, though warm-blooded, run the risk of early death?

Remember what the Second Vatican Council once said about them: "We are filled with an overwhelming sadness when we contemplate the sorry spectacle of millions of workers in many lands and continents condemned through the inadequacy of their wages to live with their families in utterly subhuman conditions" (*Mater et Magistra*, 68).

It is difficult to know how to respond to this situation, how to improve the living standards of our poor sisters and brothers. One response is to become a responsible consumer. Several organizations exist to help us in this. We might organize ourselves better in our parish and elsewhere to profit from the information they can give us. It is part of the "new spirituality" we urgently need.

Micah's Miracles

"...grant us to see wonders...." Micah 7:14-15, 18-20

Micah is a prophet who prays to Yahweh for miracles. "As in the days when you came out of Egypt, grant us to see your wonders" (Micah 7:15). He would like a repeat of the liberation of God's people out of the hands of oppression and sin. We need prayers like that. No doubt about it. We need wonders like that, too. Yet, the danger is that one can stop at the prayer. God is so mighty that the wonders can easily be wrought.

But God did not work a wonder when the people were brought out of Egypt. They themselves had to decide to leave, they had to pack and march to the freedom promised to them. God backed them up, so to speak, in those decisions, but they had to decide to move.

In *On Social Concern*, John Paul II pleads for the same things Micah does, but he directs his prayers not so much to God as to us: "I wish to appeal with simplicity and humility to everyone, to all men and women without exception. I wish to ask them to be convinced of the seriousness of the present moment and of each one's responsibility and to implement—by the way they live as individuals and families, by the use of their resources, by their civic activity, by contributing to economic and political decisions and by personal commitment to national and international undertakings—the measures inspired by solidarity and love of preference for the poor" (47).

Pope John Paul is praying for wonders. He prays that our hearts may be moved, and that we may get on our way out of our present situation, where many, ourselves included, suffer too much.

Toil

"You remember, brothers and sisters, with what unsparing energy we used to work, slaving day and night...."　　　*1 Thessalonians 2:7-9*

At times Jesus is horrified by the prospect of his death on the cross. Just before his arrest in the garden of Gethsemane, he sweats like someone gripped by fear and terror. His mouth must have been totally dry at that moment, like it is when fear catches us.

At other times he says that he is looking forward to it, not because he knows what his self-sacrifice is going to mean for him, but because of what it will mean for us, showing us that it is possible to break through all kinds of obstacles that hinder us and keep us down. When he sees his suffering and death related to his intentions they not only become bearable, they become desirable. It is a question of motivation.

Nobody likes the toil that is linked to practically all our labor. It is often difficult to bear its burden. That is why it is good to do it in a worthwhile context.

Some work a whole year just to have a nice holiday. Others take the most difficult tasks upon themselves to further their career, to achieve fame or glory.

Jesus lived his life and died his death for the realization of the Kingdom of God among us. It is this motivation that made all his labor and toil worthwhile. It is that motivation he strengthened in his night-long prayers in the mountains and at other lonely places.

Considering the toil, the blood and sweat, the stress and boredom that often is part and parcel of our daily chores, we should sit down from time to time to reflect on what makes it all worthwhile, reflecting on our motivation so that it does not become a dulling routine, but remains or becomes again a motivated activity in which Jesus' example, message, and mission play a role.

We are sharing in the work that Christ came to do. We should do it lovingly and as joyfully as possible. The victory is ours!

Race and Color

*"There were many widows in Israel...when a great famine raged
throughout the land, but Elijah was not sent to any of these; he was
sent to a widow in Zarepath, a town in Sidonia."* Luke 4:24-30

We often forget how things change during our lifetime. The older we
get the more obvious those changes should be. Sometimes it hits you
when you clean out a cupboard or your basement, your garage or
your loft, or when you browse through your books.

You might find one of those old prayer books, one you used to use
yourself, or one your father or mother used long ago.

It is interesting to take a good look at such a devotional work. It
helps us to see the changes we are thinking of. In the preparation for
confession, for instance, check the list of sins mentioned in the examination of conscience.

A lot of sins have remained the same. That is understandable. You
will also notice that several contemporary sins are not mentioned, or if
they are it is only in the vaguest of terms.

People often used to live in such closed communities that others
who did not belong to that circle were hardly taken into account. In a
modern examination of conscience—as they are often done during
penitential services—we are asked to reflect on our behavior to those
who belong to ethnic groups or races different from ours.

The older books hardly mention things like that.

Our life has been extending, now encompassing many more than
only those living in our own circle, growing wider and wider in our
interests and concerns. The world and humanity are growing on us.
The dimensions Jesus preached are extending wider and wider. No
wonder his contemporaries were often baffled and upset about his approach.

Seventy-Seven Times

"'Lord, how often must I forgive...as often as seven times?' Jesus answered, 'Not seven, I tell you, but seventy-seven times.'"
Matthew 18:21-35

Thoughtless words spoken without malice can hurt for a lifetime. So can words spoken with malice in order to offend. Not only do individuals hurt each other, so do families and nations.

History books, cemeteries, plaques in churches, airports, railway stations, and war monuments remind us of a past that was full of hatred and revenge and far from peaceful.

Refugee camps, civil wars, riots, and shootouts show that the present is not much better. We, too, witness brother fighting against brother, sister against sister, family against family, nation against nation.

The whole world, our whole environment is filled with those negative energies. How do you make up for them? How do you make up for the past, for the word you said and regretted ever after? For the offensive words spoken to you that you never forgot?

This is one of the more sensible questions Peter asked Jesus: "How often must I forgive my brother if he wrongs me?" Jesus' answer is short, though he puts it in a longer symbolic way. His answer is: "Always, seventy times seven."

The only way to make up for the past is to forgive. There is no other way to clear the sky, to make our human environment livable.

Jesus himself practices what he says. Forgiving is the first thing he does after his resurrection. When he appears to them, his first word is, "Peace," giving them and all of us his power to forgive.

Whenever the past haunts you in a moment of depression or some bitterness, use your power to forgive "them" for what they did, and don't forget to forgive yourself in the process! Heal your past.

Sabbath Rest

"And now, Israel, listen to the laws and customs which I am teaching you today, so that, by observing them, you may survive...."

Deuteronomy 4:1, 5-9

Jurgen Moltmann is a great theologian who took the lead on many theological issues. He wrote one of the first books on the theology of creation that speaks of the spirituality of care for the earth in contemporary terms. His approach is simple.

He believes that what we have to do is consider the old life laws as found in the first book of the Bible.

One law he would like to see restored is the sabbath law, not only to guarantee every human being, every animal, and every plant a seventh day of rest, but also to guarantee such a rest to the land every seventh year.

We desperately need that kind of respect for ourselves, for others, for all that is alive and gives life, to begin to offset the ecological disasters we have allowed. A seventh day of rest, a simpler life, another order of priorities.

Another theologian who stressed this point not so long ago is Pope John Paul II in his encyclical *Centesimus Annus*. He writes that every worker has a right to that rest, not only to obtain the leisure it provides, but also because it gives us the time to reflect on who we are, on how we relate to the world and to God, the source of it all. John Paul wonders whether that human right is sufficiently respected in our industrialized societies.

Maybe it is through our ever-growing respect for animals and plants, the water and the sky, that we might rediscover a greater respect for ourselves, for our own human environment.

Was it not said and written that we should learn from creation around us!?

Scattering

"Anyone who is not with me is against me; and anyone who does not gather in with me throws away."　　　　　　　　Luke 11:14-23

We are living in a time when all seems to point to the fulfillment of the old prophecy that one day all human beings will come together. When you read the latest papal documents on mission and social teaching, you cannot help but notice this theme repeating again and again.

We all know slogans like: "One world or no world." Yet, at the same time, we seem to be more divided than ever before.

It is in our actual context that old words of Jesus take on a new meaning. We are accustomed to words like: "He who does not gather with me, scatters." These words do not engage us. We gloss them over. They do not enter our spirituality or piety.

If they did, we would be busy at the process Jesus came to introduce in our world, a process that intends to bring the whole of humanity together as the one family of God, a process he illustrated by leaving us the breaking of our bread as the symbol of his intention.

Perhaps his verdict is less a condemnation than the observation of a fact. If we are not busy gathering and bringing together, the opposite will take place.

At the same time, his words are a question to each one of us. Are you a gatherer or a scatterer in the exercise of your profession, in the way you educate the ones dependent on you, in the urban legends you tell?

According to Jesus' words, there is no middle here. You are either gathering or you are scattering.

Justice and Love

"...this is the first: you must love the Lord your God....The second is this: You must love your neighbor....There is no commandment great-er than these."
                                                        Mark 12:28-34

"The experience of the past and of our own time demonstrates that justice alone is not enough, that it can lead to the denial and destruction of itself, if that deeper power which is love, is not allowed to shape human life in its various dimensions" (*Dives in Misericordia*, 12,2). Those papal words are meant to be a warning.

But, as the pope writes, it is a warning based on experience, an experience we have all had. When you rely solely on justice without pity, and the pound of flesh has really to be paid, people suffer.

In other words, justice is not the best of bottom lines. All of us have been in situations where we neglected, offended, or mistreated others. It is hardly possible to live our human lives avoiding the betrayal of others always and everywhere. You passed one who needed your help, didn't you? And you were in a position to help, weren't you? You didn't, did you?

All of us have failed to do justice. None of us has totally clean hands. That is why we so often ask that justice should not be done to us: Lord, have mercy, Christ, have mercy, Lord, have mercy!

Jesus tells us that justice should be done, and that it will be done. Yet, he also says that there is no greater commandment than love. So love is the bottom line.

Love is the deeper power that can bring and hold us together, the deeper power that will help and motivate us to realize the justice that should be done.

Curing Children

"...A court official whose son was ill at Capernaum...asked him to come and cure his son, as he was at the point of death." John 4:43-54

In September 1990 about forty heads of state or their representatives came together at the United Nations in New York to a meeting organized by UNICEF. This was not a meeting on the difficulties in the Middle East, or a war threat somewhere in the world. It was a meeting organized not around a threat but on a fact.

Every day 45,000 children in this world die of neglect, sickness, dehydration, or starvation. Every day 45,000 fathers and 45,000 mothers of children would like to do what the official in the gospel did: find someone to whom they could say: "Come and cure my child, who is at the point of death."

It became clear at that meeting that those children could be cured and could live if the world would be willing to do what Jesus did that day.

He did not go to see the child. He healed the child by sending his healing from the place where he was, and when the father went home he found his son healed.

The world has the means, the food, the drink, the medicine to cure any sick and dying child. What it misses is the heart of Jesus.

We, too, have to pay more attention to the appeals made to us, appeals that sound like the one addressed to Jesus the day he heard that official plead: "Come and cure my child!"

Losing Heart

"'Sir,' replied the sick man, 'I have no one to put me in the pool when the water is disturbed, and while I am still on the way, someone else gets down there before me.'"   John 5:1-3, 5-16

These are words many in our society could repeat, not because they are lying at a pool with healing power like the man of the gospel story, but because they don't seem to have a chance in the world in which they live.

Let me tell you the story of someone who got involved. Never before had she been involved with a minority group. It was the first time that she had worked with inner-city kids who were not white. She told me how her experience shocked her. The teenage children she met had practically given up on life. They lost heart. The schools they went to were not as good as the schools other children went to. They blamed their lack of success on their place and rank in society. They were always going to be second, or third. Others would always get the better places and positions before them. They thought there was nobody in their own society to help them. She understood that she would not be able to help them either, except by helping them to pick themselves up and walk.

That is what Jesus did when he told the sick man at the pool in Bethesda to stand up and walk.

You might not be able to engage yourself in the way she did, but you would definitely be able to help those who are doing that kind of work, even if only by trying to get some information from them on how they are doing!

God Our Mother

"Thus says Yahweh: 'Can a woman forget her baby at the breast, feel no pity for the child she has borne? Even if these were to forget, I shall not forget you.'"   Isaiah 49:8-15

This is not the first time I have written gospel reflections. I have sometimes mentioned, as I do now, that God may be called our Mother. Every time I do that I get some letters from people who are upset and sometimes outright angry that anyone calls God "Mother." Even if I answer that Holy Scripture does so, and that the two most recent popes, John Paul I and John Paul II, have, I am called a heretic, and sometimes even worse.

In the Hebrew Scriptures it is Isaiah who, speaking in the name of Yahweh, complains: "Can a woman forget her baby at the breast, feel no pity for the child she has borne? Even if these were to forget, I shall not forget you" (Isaiah 49:15).

In our Christian Scriptures it is Jesus who compares himself to a mother. One evening he was sitting on a hill overlooking Jerusalem. He must have heard the noises of the city, the noise of playing children, and the voices of mothers calling them home. Hearing this his eyes filled with tears and he sighed: "How often have I wished to bring all of you together, just like a mother hen gathers her chickens under her wings."

When we look at the world and humanity in the way Jesus does, his tears should be ours, the tears of a mother who can't bring her children together the way she would like to.

Idolatry

"They have cast themselves a metal calf." Exodus 32:7-14

Moses heard good news and bad news on Mount Sinai. The ten commandments were the good news. They were such good news because Yahweh gave God's people a set of commands that asked them to center their lives around Yahweh, to be themselves, and to respect each other. The bad news was: "They have cast themselves a metal calf, worshiped it, and offered sacrifice to it, shouting, Israel, here is your God who brought you from Egypt" (Exodus 32:8). They did not listen, they left the way God marked out for them.

They forgot about God and, consquently, about themselves and each other. John Paul II stresses this theme again and again in all his letters and exhortations. If you forget about God, you are going to forget that you are made in God's image. You lose your self-respect and your respect for others.

It wasn't that they danced at the foot of the mountain—there is nothing wrong with dancing. They danced around a thing, around a golden calf, around profit and gain. They lost themselves dancing around that idol.

Neither God nor they themselves were the center of their lives any more, but a thing, an idol, an abomination.

This story repeats itself again and again around us, every time money is more important than anything else. It happens when a service is not rendered, though a life might even depend on it, because someone doesn't have the money to pay for it. Or when poor children die, although the world is full of food. It happens when someone's appointment book is so filled up with engagements in view of success, gain, or profit, that the owner of the book succumbs under the self-imposed load. Bad news, indeed, while the good news was that it is ourselves we should take seriously.

Door Theology

"Look, I am standing at the door, knocking. If one of you hears me call-
ing and opens the door, I will come in to share a meal at that person's
side." Revelation 3:20

The artist William Holman Hunt once painted this scene. The painting
hangs in Saint Paul's Cathedral in London. The picture has been re-
produced on hundreds of bookmarks and in thousands of illustrated
Bibles.

A well-known English theologian, John Medcalf, once wrote that it
could have been the beginning of a "theology of doors." No one seems
to have picked that up, yet doors must have played an important role
in the life of Jesus, the son of a carpenter. Later in life he even compares himself with a door, the door of a sheepfold.

The most remarkable thing about the painting is that Holman Hunt
did not paint a door handle on the outside of the door. The begging Jesus standing in front of that door and knocking on it can't open the
door for himself. It can only be opened from within. Jesus is not willing to violate our free will, to enter uninvited, forcing himself at our
table.

He is pleading to be allowed to enter, to be part and parcel of our
life. We are the only ones who can invite him in. Quite a thought to
ponder today!

Jesus' Name

"...let us cut him off from the land of the living, so that his name may no longer be remembered."   *Jeremiah 11:18-20*

About a century ago, French author Anatole France wanted to shock his readers in a story published in an anti-Christian paper on Christmas day, 1891.

The story was about Pontius Pilate, the Roman governor who gave the order to execute Jesus. The story is in the form of an interview. When Pilate is reminiscing, his interviewer mentions the name of Jesus of Nazareth, and Pilate says: "Jesus, Jesus of Nazareth? I don't remember anyone with that name."

Anatole France wanted to make a point. He wanted to prophesy that the name Jesus would one day be forgotten.

It was what those who condemned him had been hoping for, too. They had said to each other: "Let us destroy the tree in its strength, let us cut him off from the land of the living, so that his name may no longer be remembered" (Jeremiah 11:19).

Jesus' name has never been forgotten, and it will never be. Mary and Elizabeth already knew that. His name is not going to get lost. The human and divine dimensions he opened up in our human existence will remain open for all ages to come. Anatole France was wrong.

Pope John Paul II said this in his encylical *Redemptor Hominis:* "Human nature by the very fact that it was assumed, not absorbed, in him has been raised in us to a dignity beyond compare. For, by his incarnation, he, the Son of God, in a cetain way united himself with each human being" (8,1).

Like so many other papal pronouncements, this statement is difficult, yet it tells why Jesus and his name never will be forgotten. Jesus belongs to us and we to him.

Perseverance

"Why did you bring us out of Egypt to die in the desert? For there is neither food nor water here; we are sick of this meager diet."
Numbers 21:4-9

On their way to the promised land the people around their leader Moses began to complain. It was all taking too long. They wanted to get there. They wanted lasting houses, not tents. They had been living out of suitcases for too long. They wanted to get out of the wilderness. They were fed up with being in a process, part of a history, part of a slow growth.

They were like many of us. We, too, often lose our patience on our way to the promised land. It is obvious that we are on a safari that will take a long time. Circumstances, environments, leaders, and we ourselves are changing too slowly.

We criticize those in authority—president and pope, parish priest and manager—as the Jews did Moses and God. "On the way people lost patience. They spoke against God and Moses: 'Why did you bring us out of Egypt to die in the desert?'" (Numbers 21:5).

We complain about God. We lost patience. We lack perseverance. We don't realize that our lack of patience is often the sign of our unwillingness to get involved ouselves, to carry the desired developments through.

We would prefer not to have to walk the way, like small children who want to be caried by their parents.

We ought to walk it, just as Jesus did.

Inner Freedom

"So if the Son sets you free, you will indeed be free." John 8:31-42

One of the striking things about Jesus is that he was so free. He was always free to put himself at the service of others in the fulfillment of God's will.

It begins early in his life. Luke tells that at the age of twelve Jesus stayed in the temple to the great distress of Mary and Joseph. Mary asks him: "Son, why have you treated us like this?" She adds, "Your father and I have been anxiously searching for you!"

Jesus answers, "Did you not know I had to be in the house of my Father?"

Luke ends the text by informing us that he went home with them and that he loved them. Yet, one thing had become clear; even family bonds would not keep him from doing what God would ask him to do. As a young boy he had already acquired that inner freedom. Nothing was going to hold him back.

Jesus sets an example here, as he always does. But he does more than that. He shows us what a human being can and should do. In other words, by freeing himself, he sets us free. In John's gospel we even hear Jesus saying: "If the Son sets you free, you will indeed be free" (John 8:36).

"This liberation starts with the interior freedom that [we] must find again with regard to [our] goods and [our] powers; [we] will never reach it except through a genuine readiness to serve" (*Octagesimo Adveniens*, 45).

Abram and Abraham

"And you are no longer to be called Abram; your name is to be Abraham, for I am making you father of many nations." Genesis 17:3-9

One day Yahweh appeared to Abram and changed his name. "You are no longer to be called Abram; your name is to be Abraham" (Genesis 17:5). And Sarai's name was changed to Sarah. God gave a reason for this change of names. "This is my covenant with you: You will become the father of many nations."

Abram and Sarah were the first ones to see it. They had been called out of their tent and God had asked them to look in the sky. There, between the heavenly bodies, they saw a vision—the city of God and the whole of humanity. Abram and Sarah would become the ancestors not only of one nation but the ancestors of the new human destiny, a future where all peoples would come together in love and justice and peace.

Most of the prophets picked up that theme. Isaiah saw how all nations would climb together to the same sacred mountaintop.

Mary the mother of Jesus understood from the beginning that all nations and generations would bless her for bringing forth Jesus.

Jesus told us that he, the Messiah, was coming to bring this vision to its realization and that he was willing to give his life for it.

This is a movement we all should be engaged in, a development no one will be able to stop.

That is why Abram's name was changed. God added a second "a" to make his name sound repetitive. What happened to Abram should happen to all of us. When his name was changed into Abraham, our names were changed, too. We should repeat in our lives what he was asked to see and do. And aren't we "becoming more and more conscious of being living members of the universal family of humankind"? (*Pacem in Terris*, 145)

Deliverance of the Needy

"Yahweh...has delivered the soul of one in need from the clutches of evildoers."   *Jeremiah 20:1-13*

For over a hundred years popes and other church leaders have been insisting that the social order in this world should change, that too many remain not only poor, but miserable and wretched. Consider what Pope Paul VI wrote on March 26, 1967:

> All of us must examine our conscience, which sounds a new call in present times. Are we prepared to support, at our own expense, projects and undertakings designed to help the needy? Are we prepared to pay higher taxes so that public authorities may expand their efforts in the work of development? Are we prepared to pay more for imported goods, so that foreign producers may make a fairer profit? (*Populorum Progressio*, 47)

He had good reason to thus address himself to the world's Christians. According to serious research, Christians, who number only 32 percent of the world's population, receive 62 percent of the entire world's income, and spend 97 percent on themselves (Barrett, *Silver and Gold I Have None: Church of the Poor or Church of the Rich*, 1983). If we Christians would listen to our leaders, who quote the words of Jesus, we would come a long way in delivering the needy, helping them to stand on their own feet and to progress. If the rich paid decent prices for goods coming from the poorer parts of the world, if the work done there were paid for more justly, the Lord would be praised all over the world, as the prophet Jeremiah foretold when he wrote: "Sing to Yahweh, praise Yahweh, for God has delivered the soul of the one in need from the clutches of the wrongdoers!"

Fullness of Christ

"...as high priest of that year he was prophesying that Jesus was to die not for the nation only, but also to gather together into one the scattered children of God."
John 11:45-56

It was late in the evening. The chief priests had come together to discuss the latest events in the country. The main topic of discussion was Jesus, especially his resurrecting of Lazarus. That worried them. They were afraid that things would get out of hand, that there would be a popular uprising with all its consequences. "The Roman troops will come in," one of them said, "and it will be our end, the end of the temple and the end of the nation." Caiaphas spoke up. He was the high priest that year and the chairman of the meeting. He said that Jesus had to die: "It is to your advantage that one man should die for the people, than that the whole nation should perish."

At that point in the story John the evangelist takes over. He notes: "He did not speak in his own person, but as high priest of that year he was prophesying that Jesus was to die for the nation—not for the nation only, but also to gather into one the scattered children of God."

Jesus died for all, to bring all of us together in God's homestead. This truth is the foundation of our mission outreach to all others in the world. Pope Paul VI somewhat paraphrased the words of Caiaphas when he wrote:

Your vocation is to bring not just some people, but all people together as brothers and sisters...Christians know full well that when they unite themselves with the expiatory sacrifice of the divine savior, they help build the body of Christ, to assemble the people of God into the fullness of Christ (*Populorum Progressio*, 78-79).

This task is not only entrusted to those who go to far-off countries. It is a mission that concerns our neighbors in our own towns and cities.

Bible Group I
Faith Exchange

*"The first thing Andrew did was to find his brother and say to him,
'We have found the Messiah'...and he took Simon to Jesus.'"*

John 1:40-51

It seems a relatively new thing, something happening all over the
world. More and more Christians meet in groups to tell each other
their faith experience. It is done in many different contexts. Sometimes
it is as the result of a RENEW program in a parish, sometimes it is in a
Bible group, or in a RCIA context.

But it is not really a new phenomenon. In fact, you find it from the
beginning of the gospels. "The first thing Andrew did was to find his
brother [Simon Peter] and say to him: 'We have found the Messiah!'"
(John 1:41).

The disciples and people who follow him are constantly telling
each other what they felt and thought about him. It was not new in
the Judaic context, either. The synagogue had always been a center
where people told each other their experiences with Yahweh and listened to the stories of how people had dealt with them in the past.

Yet, there is something very new about this phenomenon for us. Often our religious experiences are the last ones we would speak about.
People would often not even read the Bible for themselves. Much was
left to those who were supposed to do all this professionally, and others were a bit left out in the religious cold. Many did not drink from
their own spiritual well. They drank from that of others. It is not bad
to do that, but to do only that would be a pity. Just remember how often Jesus would ask the people around him, what do you think? How
does what I say relate to your life? It is as if some don't even dare to
ask themselves those questions.

Bible Group II
Life Experience

"And at once his sight returned and he followed him along the road."
Mark 10:46-52

You can form a Bible group in many ways, and with different intentions. You can come together to study the Bible. In such a case you take the text, prepare the session by consulting commentaries, dictionaries, and textbooks, and you discuss your findings. From time to time, you might even invite an expert, a Bible scholar or somebody like that, to help you. There is nothing against that approach. It is very good and instructive. You might really get an insight in the letter and content of the Bible. It is not the only way to organize a Bible group, however.

The early Christians did not have what we call the New Testament. What they had were the stories about Jesus as told by people who had met him, and who had been witnesses to the resurrection. They listened to those stories and placed them in their own lives. They used them—though used is maybe not the best word—to get some light on their own existence and to change their own behavior. When you read Acts, you will notice what is happening in those first communities. The life, death, and resurrection of Jesus were the center of their community life, because they saw their own life in the light of the life of Jesus.

Take the story of the blind man Bartimaeus. It ends like this: "And at once his sight returned and he followed him along the road" (Mark 10:52). That was not the end of Bartimaeus's story, it was the beginning!

October 24

Bible Group III
Freedom

"Then suddenly an angel of the Lord stood there....He tapped Peter on the side and woke him. 'Get up,' he said; 'hurry!'—and the chains fell from his hands."   Acts 12:1-17

Groups that read the Bible from the viewpoint of their life experience often show great insight. The most striking descriptions often come from small Christian communities in Third World countries. In those countries people sit together to read the Bible in the contexts of their lives without the learned luggage others would bring with them. Carlos Mesters (*The Defenseless Flower*, Orbis Books, 1990) explains that this gives them a great freedom when reading the Bible. They read a story or a parable, are prayerfully silent for a moment, and then tell each other what this story means in their own lives, how it clarifies, eases, and helps them.

Reading in Acts how an angel came to rescue Peter from prison, one group member recalled how as a child she once entered the house where her bishop was imprisoned, unbeknownst to his friends. The guards took no notice of her because she was a child. She smuggled a note out of the bishop's house that informed his friends and they helped him escape. That young girl was like the angel to Peter, she said.

This freedom, reading the text and applying it, has another advantage. When you speak about your experiences, you avoid the possibility of the kinds of discussions that often arise when you look for the meaning of the letter of the text, and end up almost imprisoned by it.

You must remain free in your associations of the Bible to your own life or that of the community. It will be especially helpful when you do it in a group with different people. You will be amazed at the many ways Jesus can enlighten our lives. After all, the gospels themselves are already so different because of the communities they were written for: Matthew is homely, Mark tough, Luke joyful, and John very distinguished.

Bible Group IV
Like Jesus

"I long for you with all the warm longing of Christ Jesus...."
Philippians 1:8

In the Bible group we are thinking of you do not read the Bible on its own, you read it in the context of your own life, or in the life of your community. It is your own experience that gives what happens in the Bible new life.

This sounds presumptuous, but it isn't. Isn't what happens in the Bible infinitely more important than what happens in our lives? The answer is both "yes" and "no." The two relate to each other. To say it in a somewhat more complicated way, the Bible and our life are two frames of reference that relate to each other.

How do they relate? Paul explains that well. He writes to the Philippians that he loves them "with the warm love of Jesus." That is not exactly what he writes, but that is how most modern translators translate the text. What Paul really writes is that he loves them with "the bowels" of Jesus. We would say with the heart of Jesus, because we consider the heart to be the center of our emotions. In Paul's time people thought that center to be the bowels.

It does not matter how you translate it, as long as you see Paul's point: What vibrates in him are the vibrations of Jesus.

An example from physics might help here. When there is a well-tuned piano in a room, and someone in that room has a tuning fork and hits it so that it produces its tone, the string in the piano that corresponds to the tone produced by the tuning fork will start to vibrate, too. It will produce the same vibrations as the fork. If you silence the tuning fork, the string on the piano will continue to resonate.

Something like that happens when we hear the stories about Jesus for ourselves, but especially when we hear them in a group. It is singing his melody in so many ways.

Bible Group V
Our Own Book

"Notice what large letters I have used in writing to you with my own hand."   *Galatians 6:11*

My own father was not allowed to read the whole Bible without special permission from his bishop. He got that permission and was proud of it. No Catholic today needs an episcopal license to read the Bible in her or his own language. It shows that things—thank God—have changed. Formerly the Bible was in the hands of those who teach and rule and preach.

That time is over. It is not yet over in the hearts and minds of everyone, however. There are still plenty of faithful who don't dare to take the risk of reading the Bible on their own, not even in a group. Yet, the Bible is written for us. It is ours. We should read it. It should wake us up to the song Jesus is singing in and through our lives. As Carlos Mesters writes: "The Bible is the book of the church, the book of the community, it is the book of 'God's Family.'" What Paul writes at the end of his letter to the Galatians is true of all that is written in our Holy Scriptures; it is written to you; it is written to us.

This does not mean that those who study the Bible to explain it, put it in its historic context, and find out what those texts meant to the people who wrote them are not needed. Of course, we need them. We need their books, their studies, and their head work. But this keeps the Bible foreign to us. We can and should enter those stories with our own hearts, hands, and experiences. The Bible is no longer a book that belongs to others. It is given to us in our community, not only to them.

That is what Jesus meant when he praised God for having given his revelation to all of us, and not only to the learned!

Bible Group VI
Faithful

"And he won the approval of all and they were astonished by the gra-
cious words that came from his lips."　　　　　　　*Luke 4:16-23*

Jesus taught with a new authority, his amazed listeners told each other. Many explanations of that newness have been given. You can find
some of them in other reflections in this book.

One of the explanations is that Jesus interpreted the Scriptures from
his own viewpoint and that of his listeners. He did not leave it in the
hands of the Pharisees and the scribes. He applied it to himself and to
his listeners from the moment he talked to them.

Think of the scene at Nazareth when he reads them some verses
from the prophet Isaiah and then applies it without further ado to
himself and his own life: "This text is being fulfilled today even while
you are listening" (Luke 4:21).

His main interest is not to interpret the Scriptures, but to interpret
his own life with their help. He is first faithful to the meaning he discovers in the text for his own life and that of his listeners.

So you have to be faithful to two things: the Bible text, and your
own life and struggle. You should meditate not only on what Mary
might have felt at the moment she sang her Magnificat, you should
also meditate on what her song means in your life.

You can do that alone. It is better, however, to do it in a group, a
group that is neither too large, nor too small.

That means that a third faithfulness comes in. You have to be faithful to the others and their experience.

In the book we mentioned by Carlos Mesters, he writes that those
three—freedom, familiarity, and fidelity (as he calls faithfulness)—
belong together like coffee, milk, and sugar in the same cup. Each influences the taste of the other.

Bible Group VII
Texts

"Each day, with one heart, they regularly went to the Temple but met in their houses for the breaking of the bread...."   Acts 2:46

When you begin a Bible group one of the first problems is choosing texts. You can start with any text. You can also start with a theme, a theme you pick from this book, for instance.

You can begin with texts from the Hebrew Scriptures, a collection Christians somewhat presumptuously call the Old Testament. Even if you prefer to begin with a text from what is called the New Testament, you should not overlook the "Old" Testament. Almost all texts in the gospels and the other New Testament books find a great deal of their explanation in the old adventures, stories, and prophecies of the Jewish people.

You can begin with the apostolic letters by Paul, Peter, John, and James. The difficulty then is that you find recommendations and lots of what we would call theology, but not stories. You might even start with the Book of Revelation, but that, too, is in part very difficult to understand.

Another possibility is to begin with texts from Acts, especially the first chapter of that book. That book is often underrated. You don't often hear a sermon on the readings from Acts, though our liturgy contains many readings from that book. The advantage is that Acts can tell you how different groups of believers applied in their own lives what they heard about Jesus. They were convinced that they were equipped with his spirit, and they tried to live it out.

Another interesting thing about the communities in Acts is that they did not always succeed; they often had to review their approach. It remained quite a struggle for them, just as it is for us.

Bible Group VIII
Letter and Spirit

"I bless you, Father, Lord of heaven and earth, for hiding these things from the learned and the clever and revealing them to little children."
Matthew 11:25-26

It is as if Jesus is here on a kind of anti-intellectual tour, something Paul seems to do, too, when he makes almost the same remarks about the foolishness of those wise in the eyes of the world and those wise in the eyes of God.

Does this mean that all scientific studies of the Bible are useless? No one who ever seriously tries to engage in a Bible group will ever think so. Scientific research and exegesis are a great help, and they are needed. It is definitely helpful for any Bible group or members of such a group to read a good commentary on a text one intends to use. It would be good to go—even as a group—to a Bible study session or update. As mentioned before, one might even confine oneself to such a study.

The main interest of the Bible groups we are discussing here is different; it is the Spirit. The study of the letter should lead us here to the practically expressed experience of the Spirit of God alive in our own lives. There is a written Bible, and there is the Bible of our lives. There are the Acts of the Apostles that continue in the acts of our own communities and lives. God's Spirit is hiding in, through, under, above, and beside all we do, and in all that happens around us, inspiring, cajoling, taunting, warning, and sometimes just opposing. Tracing all those reactions in ourselves is the intention of a Bible group (and of this book of Bible reflections).

Judas

*"[Judas] said this, not because he cared for the poor, but because he
was a thief; he was in charge of the common fund and used to help
himself to the contents."*   John 12:1-11

No one likes to be compared to Judas, the one who betrayed Jesus. No
one knows what went on his heart when he kissed Jesus in the garden.
Had he hoped that at the moment of his arrest Jesus would show his
power and start his kingdom? Was it his intention to force the hand of
Jesus, as has recently been suggested in some plays and musicals?
Had he hoped that Jesus would have convinced his judges, or that he
would have shown them his glory? Was that the reason that he went
back to the high priests with the thirty silver coins he had received for
his information when he heard how Jesus was going to be condemned?

John tells us that Judas was not only a traitor, but also a thief. Maybe that is how the tragedy began. "Judas was in charge of the common
fund, and used to help himself to the contributions" (John 12:6). He
kept what was destined for the poor for himself.

We live in a world where about three percent of the population is
consuming 60 percent of the wealth. Doesn't the world's approach re-
semble Judas's? Aren't the goods of this world destined for all, not
just those who are powerful and rich?

These are hard questions. The gospel and our church leaders are
asking them all the time. Pope John Paul II insists in most of his letters
that "the goods of creation are meant for all" (*Sollicitudo Rei Socialis*,
39).

All of us would be willing to meet Jesus with a kiss and a hug. Are
we willing to live his life?

Satan Means Opponent

"At that instant, after Judas had taken the bread, Satan entered him."
John 13:21-33, 36-38

"Satan" means "opponent." Satan had been around Jesus and his followers from the very beginning.

Satan was the influence that opposed him: the power at work in all those who had their doubts about the feasibility of the life Jesus introduced in this world, the doubt and opposition that grew into the hatred and violence that surrounded him during his last days.

It is a power that will be with us as long as we live and strive, just as it must have been with Judas from the moment he joined Jesus.

Even Judas must have resisted Satan. It was only at the last supper, at the very moment he took the piece of bread that Jesus gave him, that he allowed it to overcome him.

At that moment Satan entered his heart and his mind.

As soon as he had taken that piece of bread, Judas left the table and went outside. John very appropriately notes: "Night had fallen" (John 13:30).

We are involved in the struggle against Satan. We all find ourselves opposing the call of God's Spirit, the opening of our too egoistic individualistic, family, and tribal circles to the wideness of God's family and intentions. "[It] is essential to overcome day by day, the opposition, obstacles and ingrained privileges which are to be met in the advance towards a more humane society" (*Justice in the World*, 27).

No wonder that Jesus asks us to pray to be protected against that power: "and lead us not into temptation!"

All Saints

"After that I saw that there was a huge number, impossible for anyone to count, of people from every nation, race, tribe and language...dressed in white robes and with palms in their hands."

Revelation 7:2-4, 9-14

Today the Catholic tradition asks us to celebrate all the saints, not just those who are officially canonized, but especially all those others who did and do contribute to the building of God's reign here on earth. Saint Paul does not hesitate to call the faithful "saints" in the different churches he founded.

That title "saint" is not always welcome, however. It seems to indicate a piously bent head, a rather mild non-compromising approach to reality, a sweet face, and a halo.

Bob Dylan began a "comeback" at the beginning of the 1990s. A reporter from the *London Times* who interviewed him noted that Dylan had been the voice of everything that should happen to America in the seventies, but that when he became a Christian his creativity had dwindled and his songs had become practically irrelevant to the modern scene.

That is strange. It is amazing that someone who "plugs in" to the energy of Jesus Christ should become bored, boring, and dull.

Yet, in many cases a rebirth or conversion seems to have that effect. The converts know it all; they are often self-righteous in a way that upsets others, and they don't seem to see any problems at all any more.

They must have missed something. How could it happen that switching over to the energy and spirit of Jesus Christ, who lived the most dramatic human commitment ever, would desensitize your life?

Did it not bring an engagement in human reality to all those we commemorate today as never before?

All Souls

"For I was hungry and you gave me food, I was thirsty and you gave me drink, I was a stranger and you made me welcome...."
Matthew 25:31-46

All of us have been at funerals and memorial services. All of us have heard the words spoken on those occasions. Often there is something strange about them. It is not for nothing that they are called "eulogies," or "good and nice words."

A man is praised for his family-mindedness, though during his lifetime everyone said that he only had time for work. A woman whose only interest was money is praised for her open heart and open hand to all who asked her help.

It sounds almost like a conspiracy. And it is! We are quite willing to forgive each other, because we all know that we need to be forgiven, too!

The way Matthew sees it, when we all stand in front of Jesus at the end of time, we all will hope to be judged in that way. We all will be only too aware of the times that we didn't live up to the Christian ideal. We will also remember the times we did.

And even if we remember at that moment the times that others betrayed us and left us alone, we will be only too glad when Jesus doesn't remember, and forgets and forgives them. We definitely wouldn't remind him of it, hoping that we, too, will be treated in the same way.

It is the moment when "forgive us our trespasses as we forgive those who trespass against us" takes on new meaning.

That might be the reason that we don't want to hear anything but good about the dead!

Let us pray that the good we do will be remembered, and that the evil will be forgotten and forgiven. Let us live in a way that makes this final judgment possible.

Fallen Asleep in Love

"Blessed...those who have fallen asleep in love...."
Ecclesiasticus 48:1-4, 9-11

You don't hear this blessing very often. "Fallen asleep" is a euphemism for having died. You use it when you don't want to speak or hear about death and dying.

Our modern society has trouble dealing with death. We prefer not to think or speak about it. We hide it as well as we can.

Sometimes we tend to deny it even when celebrating the eucharist. Many priests will change the words before giving out Holy Communion. Instead of saying: "Happy are those who are called to his supper," as they are supposed to do, they change the word "supper" to "meal." They will tell you that they do it because they are celebrating Mass in the morning or in the afternoon. Sometimes the reason is that they don't want to remind themselves and the people who are with them of the heavenly banquet, our final everlasting supper with Jesus.

Often it seems as if only the very old ones among us are still hoping to be finally with him. Practically everything in our culture seems to be geared toward life here on earth, a life as long as possible, and even a bit longer than that—if possible!

There is nothing wrong with the desire to live here on earth as long and as well as we can. But that desire should not hide us from another one, the desire to be with him, to fall asleep, and to do that in love. Happy for the gift of our lives, happy for all the good we were able to do, happy about the ways in which we helped the Kingdom of God to grow in us and and in others, happy in the knowledge and experience of the divine love that made all this possible.

Creativity

"If the world hates you, you must realize that it hated me before it hated you."   John 15:18-21

The best way to see your own town, city, or region is to do it with a guest, someone who has never seen it before. The best way to find out how to reorganize your business or routine is to ask someone who is unaccustomed to your way of doing things to check it and to tell you what changes he would suggest.

The one you invite should not be a total stranger to the situation, but just enough of an outsider to see the difference.

It is difficult to be creative in an environment you are totally accustomed to.

To be at home and to feel at home is a great thing, but to be totally at home and to feel completely homely does not lead to great ideas or creativity.

Jesus is a case in point. He lives in this world, he feels at home up to a point, yet he has hardly any fixed abode. He is a traveler on his way. He is working with a double frame of reference all the time. Everything he says and does has a kind of doubleness. His home is here and with God. His life is here and it is there. He sees sickness, health, bread, oil, water, salt, the sky, a sunset, the sea, fish, and especially human beings in a kind of double way.

It all reminds him of something else. Christians should have something of this if they want to be like him, if they want to be as creative as he was in our world. We can't settle in the world as the world is. We have to set it off against something else, the Kingdom of God, the world to come.

We are in this world, but not of this world. We are children of our time, and at the same time we are not.

G.K. Chesterton said it well: "The Church is the one thing that saves a person from the degrading servitude of being a child of one's time."

Catholic

"Now there were devout people living in Jerusalem from every nation under the sun....They all assembled, and each one was bewildered to hear these men speaking his own language."　　　Acts 2:5-12

Being a Christian is something catholic, in the old sense of that word, something that is as wide as the world and that at the same time keeps us together.

It not only connects us to that amazing human being Jesus, it connects us to everyone. It is good to reflect on this from time to time, as the film star Alec Guinness did when he wrote: "A few years ago, on an Ash Wednesday, I was standing in line to be smudged on the forehead with ashes, as is the custom. A small boy of about seven was immediately in front of me. In front of him shambled a man probably in his eighties. Behind me stood a very pretty young woman. Each of us, as the ashes were imposed, would hear the words, 'Remember that you are dust and that to dust you will return.'"

The point he wanted to make was about being together with so many different people—old and young, rich and poor, black and white, Hispanic and Anglo-Saxon, African and Asian—in the same enormous movement. The same gathering, the same swell, the same reaching out, the same divine impulse.

And he adds: "The Holy Roman Catholic and Apostolic Church...has books to read aloud, pictures to show, consolations to offer, strength to give and some marvelous people, from all ages, to hold up for the world's admiration; not many in high places perhaps, but thousands in the market square, hospital ward, back pew, desert, and jungle." (*Blessings in Disguise*)

It must have been such a joy for Jesus to see people respond to his words and acts. It must have saddened him so much when they veered away from him.

Fortune

"We are well aware that God works with those who love him, those who have been called in accordance with his purpose, and turns every-thing to their good."   *Romans 8:26-30*

Many interpretations of this text from Paul's letter to the Romans have been given all through the centuries, interpretations that are not always helpful, and that sometimes are just wrong.

Sometimes the text is even turned around. We have all heard those preachers who say that if you want to get rich, you have only to pray to God, getting God on your side, and the millions will flow in. They would even go so far as to blame you for not getting rich.

You can't reason like that using Paul's words. Paul writes that if you live and work in accordance with God's purpose, God will be with you. He does not say that if you yourself set a purpose God will be with you.

The creator gave us the power to master our fortune. In other words, we can control things in such a way that things will work in our favor. We do that when we pray for something. But those prayers are conditioned by God's purpose. It is when we pray in accordance with God's Spirit that things will go well "because the prayers that the Spirit makes for God's holy people are always in accordance with the mind of God" (Romans 8:27).

Many saints used Paul's saying to find out or discern what they should do. If it is true that doing God's will is good for you, then what is good for you might be an indication that it is according to God's will. If you are sincerely interested in doing God's will and what you do constantly turns against you, perhaps you are going against what God wants you to do. Perhaps you are swimming against the divine flow.

New Age

"We are well aware that the whole creation, until this time, has been groaning in labor pains." Romans 8:18-24

A Catholic Development Agency had decided to take environmental problems as a theme for one of their educational programs, a wise decision because human underdevelopment is often due to an unwise use of resources, and because many human groups get into serious difficulties when their environment is destroyed. Consider people who have been living for ages in tropical forests and whose habitat is now suddenly destroyed around them.

The agency developed a program that asked for a greater respect for nature. The program suggested that we remember in the biblical creation story that every time God creates something, God calls it "good" (the Hebrew word *tof*). They argued that cutting down the tropical forest and doing violence to the world was comparable to the suffering of God in Jesus Christ.

Having declared this, they got a good deal of mail. Many saw their point and agreed, but several did not agree at all, calling it heretical "new age" spirituality. They did not agree with a theology that made us part of nature and its forces.

Yet, it is Paul who speaks about the whole of creation as created in Jesus (Colossians 1:15), and who suggests that without Christ all created things would be dispersed and fragmented. It is Paul, too, who says to the Council of the Areopagus in Athens that he preaches God "in whom we live, move and exist" (Acts 17:28), and who notes: "We are well aware that the whole creation until this time, has been groaning in labor pains" (Romans 8:22), "and that the whole creation is waiting with eagerness for the children of God to be revealed" (Romans 8:19).

Believing that we are created and belong together is no "new age" theology. It is the spirituality of the one who once said that we are the branches and he is the vine.

Crossing Yourself

"...in the name of the Father, and of the Son, and of the Holy Spirit."
Matthew 28:16-20

This text speaks about the life of God and the family God forms; it also is about us. That is what we tell ourselves when we make the sign of the cross.

In the name of the Father—and we touch our foreheads, indicating that we are speaking about ourselves.

In the name of the Son—and we touch our chest, making it clear once again that I am indicating "me, myself."

In the name of the Holy Spirit—saying that, we embrace ourselves from one shoulder to the other.

It is a sign that follows us from our baptism to our death. It is a sign you see popping up on the most varied occasions—swimmers before they dive into the deep; travelers when they sit down in a plane or car; whole families before they begin eating; students before they begin an exam; sportswomen and men before they start a match. Some start the day with it, when they get out of bed; others make it just before they fall asleep. You see parents teach it to their children when they enter church on a Sunday morning (and you see that those children have some difficulty with the coordination and logistics when making it). We begin and end our worship with it.

It is our most personal identity mark; we can only make it ourselves. At the same time, it is our most communal sign. All of us can and should make it. It is valid for the whole of humankind. It is an expression of our real value and dignity. It is God's registered trademark imprinted on us. It explains why Jesus gave his life for all of us. It is, as Pope John Paul II never ceases to remind us, the basis and foundation of our human rights. So let us make it "In the name of the Father, and the Son, and the Holy Spirit," and finish it so appropriately with, "Amen": "Let it be, O let it be!"

Rosary

"Yahweh our Lord, how majestic your name throughout the world."
Psalm 8:9

When Cardinal Charles Lavigerie—a Frenchman who was Archbishop of the North African city of Carthage—began the Society of Missionaries of Africa in the 1880s, he dedicated this new foundation in the church to Our Lady of Africa. That is one of the reasons that the members of that society hang a large rosary around their necks over the traditional Arab dress they wear as their religious habit.

There was another reason to do that. The Arabs among whom they started to live and work used something that resembled a rosary, a string of beads they use while reciting the names of God. Those prayer strings often count ninety-nine beads for the ninety-nine names of Allah in the Koran.

The rosary has many more beads. The number of the beads refers to the Bible. There are 150 Hail Mary beads, the number of the psalms.

That is not mere chance. It was the intention from the beginning. From ancient times monks and nuns and, later, deacons and priests used to recite the 150 psalms as one of their main tasks to praise and thank God. It was difficult for laypeople to do that, if only because in those days many could not read and write.

It was for them that the arrangement of 150 beads was made. Initially they used them to say 150 Our Fathers. It was only later that these were replaced by Hail Marys. Another way in which the rosary relates to Sacred Scripture is the custom of meditating on the fifteen main events in the life of Jesus—the joyful, sorrowful, and glorious mysteries.

Because it is such a simple and relaxing way to pray, the rosary has been loved by intellectuals and the untutored, contemplatives and apostles, rich and poor, people of all categories and social backgrounds.

Millions, including popes and my own mother, died holding the rosary in their hands.

Hail Mary

"Rejoice, you who enjoy God's favor!" Luke 1:28, 42

The first "Hail Mary, full of grace, the Lord is with thee" came from the mouth of the archangel Gabriel, according to Luke's gospel (Luke 1:28).

The second part of the first line, "blessed are thou among women and blessed is the fruit of thy womb" is Elizabeth's greeting when Mary visits her (Luke 1:42).

Putting those two greetings together in a prayer to Mary dates from the early African Christian communities in North Africa and Ethiopia.

The first time there is an official ruling about the prayer is in 1198, when Odo, Bishop of Paris, exhorted his clergy: "Let priests ceaselessly exhort the people to say the Lord's prayer, the 'I believe in God' and the salutation of the Blessed Virgin."

When we pray it we are repeating words that came from an archangel and from a saint, the mother of John the Baptist.

When we say it we remind Mary of words that changed her life. They are words that her son Jesus must have repeated so often when he returned home.

They are words that introduced a new dimension to her life and to the whole of the world. They are words that reveal to us the great dignity of the feminine in our world, bringing God's Spirit to life in the midst of creation.

This femininity is eternal and universal. "Hail Mary, full of grace, the Lord is with thee; blessed art thou among women and blessed is the fruit of thy womb, Jesus. Pray for us sinners, now and at the hour of our death. Amen!"

November 11

Daily News

"It was just about this time that some people arrived and told him about the Galileans whose blood Pilate had mingled with that of their sacrifices."   *Luke 13:1-33*

Jesus often reacts to the daily news. Mark gives us an example of this when he notes: "After John had been arrested, Jesus went into Galilee" (Mark 1:14). At certain news he goes into hiding, at better news he reemerges. His whole life was influenced by what happened around him. This started immediately after his birth, when angels came to warn his parents about political developments and decisions.

Jesus uses the daily news and gossip around him for his stories and parables. In their turn, people around him come to tell him the news and ask him his opinion. "It was just at this time that some people arrived and told him about the Galileans whose blood Pilate had mingled with that of their sacrifice" (Luke 13:1). On that same occasion he uses another news item of the day to explain himself, that of a tower at Siloam that fell over, killing eighteen people.

Jesus was not living in the air, far away from social and political things, unable to discuss them. If he lived among us now he would be interested in the daily news, too. He would listen to the radio or watch television news. He would not do just that, however. He would continue what he did in the Palestine of his time. He would have judged persons and events, just as he did when he called Herod a "fox" (Luke 13:32).

Among the hundreds of courses taught at the Washington Theological Consortium is one where people learn how to read the main news in the *New York Times* from a "Kingdom of God" point of view.

Jesus would be interested in such an approach, and he definitely would have his opinion!

Pessimists and Optimists

"And Yahweh said to Moses: 'How much longer will this people treat me with contempt? How much longer will they refuse to trust me...?'"   *Numbers 13:25–14:39*

Moses decided to send spies into the promised land to get some strategic information about it before entering it. One man from each tribe was chosen. They went out and stayed away for forty days. When they came back the group was divided on what to do. Ten of the spies said, "Yes, the country is flowing with milk and honey, but we will not be able to make it. The people there are of enormous size, and we felt like grasshoppers, and so we seemed to them."

Only two of the twelve, Caleb and Joshua, struck a more optimistic note. They reasoned, "Of course, we are able to make it. Yahweh brought us this far, and Yahweh is not going to betray us."

But the people believed the ten and not the two. The crisis was great until Yahweh intervened, angry at what was happening. Yahweh spoke in favor of the two, and against the ten, who were all struck dead. As for the people, Yahweh told them that none of them would ever see the promised land, that they would have to go back into the desert for forty years, and that none of them, except Caleb and Joshua, would be allowed to enter it.

A tough story, but one that keeps its significance even in our days. Many of us also waver when thinking about the final outcome and the fulfillment of God's promises. Many of us are inclined to be pessimists, not optimists.

God is with the optimists. God is faithful to the promises made to us.

Rainbow

"When the bow is in the clouds I shall see it and call to mind the eternal covenant between God and every living creature on earth, that is, all living things."
Genesis 9:1-17

A rainbow stretching from one side of the horizon to the other appears now and then. It is always quite a sight. Children will point it out to each other. Parents will draw their children's attention to it if they don't see it.

It is a sign, too, a sign appointed by God to remind us of a covenant God made with us. God promised that the world would never again be destroyed by the waters of a flood. And Noah and his descendants had to agree to their side of the agreement: that the blood of no human being would ever be shed. The reason for that prohibition is given, too: "For in the image of God the human person was created" (Genesis 9:6).

Pope John Paul II uses the same argument in all his letters on human rights and the social teaching of the church. Every human being, of whatever color, has the same basic and intrinsic value. Every human being is created in the image of God and, consequently, has an absolute and eternal value and dignity.

John Paul II is convinced that the wars and the violence, the Holocaust and concentration camps in this century can only be explained because this truth was overlooked. The same can even be said about the way we tolerate the famine and misery of millions and millions around us.

As a sign to help us to keep to the old covenant the rainbow will spread over us again and again, at the most unexpected moments, as a sign of humanity's covenant with God.

Sun-Robed Woman

*"Now a great sign appeared in heaven: a woman, robed with the sun,
standing on the moon, and on her head a crown of twelve stars."*
Revelation 12:1-3

Even when we don't know this text, most of us have seen that woman.
Many churches, Catholic schools, and families have a statue or picture
of the Blessed Virgin Mary, dressed in white and blue, standing on a
half moon with a crown of twelve stars around her head. And all of us
would recognize the image of Our Lady of Guadelupe, showing Mary
surrounded by the rays of the sun.

We give her all kinds of titles—Mother of God, Queen of the Earth,
and Queen of the Universe.

There is another sign that appeared in heaven not so very long ago.
Astronauts saw the earth from outer space in the light of the sun, sun-
robed, in the midst of the stars, as a whirl of white and blue.

Of course, the two are not the same. One should not be taken for
the other. Yet, there is a relationship. All the astronauts who saw the
earth from that far away saw her as one living organism. Whether
Russian, American, or whatever nationality, they all had the same
kind of mystical experience. They all returned as changed persons.

They had all seen that we belong together, that borders and conflicts make no sense, that it is one world or no world. In 1948, Sir Richard Hoyle, a famous British astronomer, said that if we were only able
to see the earth from outside, it would make all the difference.

We saw her, our Mother earth, like that, and it is going to make a
difference.

Long before that, however, we had seen Mary, robed in the sun, in
the midst of the stars, standing on the moon, as the mother of Jesus
Christ and all of us, Queen of the Universe.

Gut Language

"My soul proclaims the greatness of the Lord, and my spirit rejoices in God my Savior, because he has looked upon the humiliation of his servant."
Luke 1:46-56

Many parts of the Bible were written by people who were struck low. They often are what we call a *cri de coeur*, something that comes straight from the heart, or, better, from the "guts." They are "gut feelings."

This is the reason that poor people, or people in difficulties, understand those texts better than well-off people do.

This is a real problem to those of us who read the Bible who are not really poor. We need the help of the poor to understand them.

It is even a greater problem for the better-offs to read the prayers in the Bible. Those prayers, too, are often the prayers of the *anawin*, those "bent down." They often call on God's anger.

A Benedictine monk, Dom Thomas Cullinan, wrote, "It is indeed as unthinkable that the psalms could be written within the walls of a comfortable presbytery, monastery, or convent, as it is unthinkable that protest songs could be written by the polite guitar-playing groups which so often sing them" (*The Passion of Political Love*).

Even Mary in her Magnificat does not pray *for* the poor, she prays *with* the poor.

When you pray with her, or when you pray with the psalmist, you are committing yourself to something much deeper than some paternal or maternal charity for the poor and the sick.

Last Temptation

"Was it useless, then, to have kept my own heart clean, to have washed my hands in innocence?"   Psalm 73

It was a bitter cold night. Snow had covered the hills when Saint Francis of Assisi came out of his shelter. He had been tossing and turning on his straw mat. A thought, a temptation, had hit him. Standing in the snow, Francis thought about all he had given up, the riches of his father, the possibility of a nice marriage, the consolation of a family and children. He made a snow woman and some snow children out of the snow, and he prayed, "Lord, was it worth it? Was it worth it to do all this 'for the sake of the Kingdom?' Was it useless, then, to have kept my own heart clean, to have washed my hands in innocence" (Psalm 73:13).

This is not only Francis's question, or that of a religious brother or sister. It is an issue in the life of all of us, married or unmarried, who live our vocation as well as we can, honest and faithful, charitable and law-abiding.

All of us risk being struck by that same anguish from time to time. Was all we did really worth it, did we not deceive ourselves, are we not deceived? It is, you might say, the ultimate temptation, a temptation expressed in Psalm 73, where it reads: "Yet my feet came close to stumbling. I was filled with envy of the proud when I saw the wicked prosper" (Psalm 73:2-3).

In his book *The Last Temptation of Christ*, Nikos Kazantzakis imagines that it might even have been Jesus' temptation when he was sitting together with Mary, Martha, and Lazarus in their home.

"For those who choose the wicked path there are no pains, their bodies are sound and sleek. They have no share in human sorrows" (Psalm 73:3-4).

Saint Francis found his answer, and he went back to his shed. It was the same answer the psalmist found: "Who else is there for me in heaven? And, with you, I lack nothing on earth" (Psalm 73:25).

American Deuteronomy

"Do not become proud of heart!" Deuteronomy 8:12-20

There is a warning in Deuteronomy, Dom Thomas Cullinan suggests, that was paraphrased some thousands of years later by Abraham Lincoln.

The Bible text reads:

Remember when you have eaten all you want, when you have built fine houses to live in...your silver and gold abound and all your possessions grow great, not to become proud of heart...Beware of thinking to yourself, 'My own strength and the might of my own hand have given me the power to act like this. Remember the Lord your God. God was the one who gives you power...if you follow other gods, you will surely perish (Deuteronomy 8:12-20).

And Abraham Lincoln said, on March 30, 1863:

We have been the recipients of the choicest bounties of heaven; we have been preserved these many years in peace and prosperity; we have grown in numbers, wealth, and power as no other nation has ever grown. But we have forgotten God. We have forgotten the gracious hand which preserved us in peace and multiplied and enriched and strengtened us, and we have vainly imagined, in the deceitfulness of our hearts, that all these blessings were produced by some superior wisdom and virtue of our own. Intoxicated with unbroken success, we have become too self-sufficient to feel the necessity of redeeming and preserving grace, too proud to pray to the God that made us. It behooves us, then, to humble ourselves before the offended Power, to confess our national sins, and to pray for clemency and forgiveness.

Faith and Works

"In the same way faith: if good deeds do not go with it, it is quite dead."   James 2:14-17

It must have been a problem among Christians from the beginning, otherwise James would not have written about it in a letter that many consider to be the earliest writing of the Christian Scriptures.

It was one of the main points of division in the days of the Reformation, and it has remained a discussion point up to now.

How do faith and good works relate to each other? Are we saved by our faith alone, or do we save ourselves by our own good works?

James kept the two together when he wrote: "How does it help, my sisters and brothers, when someone who has never done a single good act claims to have faith? Will that faith bring salvation? If one of the brothers or one of the sisters is in need of clothes and has not enough food to live on, and one of you says to them, 'I wish you well, keep yourself warm and eat plenty,' without giving them these bare necessities of life, then what good is that? In the same way faith, if good deeds do not go with it, is quite dead" (James 2:14-17).

Our faith makes us see the whole of humanity, the whole of creation, as being created in Christ. That faith cannot but ask for an expression in deeds, in good works. Those deeds are only explicable if in one way or another we believe in our cohesion in Christ. That belief of faith is a gift that accompanies our very existence, life, and activity.

The two belong together. They can be separated in our discussions and, consequently, in our lives.

It remains a division that does not make sense, as James notes; therefore it is unwholesome and leads to death.

Baptismal Roots

"...at any rate, you have tasted that the Lord is good." 1 Peter 2:2-3

It is sometimes difficult to find the house in which you were born. So many of them disappear over the years, replaced by new developments. In general, churches are more permanent buildings. That is why it is often easier to find the place where you were baptized.

Did you ever make a pilgrimage to the baptismal font you were baptized at? Many modern churches have movable fonts, but you find permanent ones in the older churches. Praying there is such a nice way to remember all the gifts you received from God and your human family and community.

Maybe you even have some photographs of that occasion you can take with you on your pilgrimage to imagine how you were there as a small baby, carried by your parents and godparents, surrounded by other family members, some people from the parish, and the deacon or priest who baptized you.

It is there that you were officially and formally taken up in the life of the Blessed Trinity. It is there that you were initiated into the life of Jesus Christ, "priest, prophet, and king." It is good to remember at such a moment that you should remain like a newborn baby longing for what you tasted there, as Peter once wrote: "Like newborn babies all your longing should be for milk—the unadulterated spiritual milk—which will help you to grow up to salvation, as you tasted that the Lord is good" (1 Peter 2:2-3)

Chastity

"We must be self-restrained and live upright and religious lives in the present world...."   Titus 2:11-15

Saint Paul often uses the word "chaste," a word that seems to have become almost an embarrassment. Chastity seems an old-fashioned, almost taboo word. When you mention it in certain circles a silence follows it, a shrug of the shoulder, or a grimace.

Paul always uses the word in context, a context we often lose in our talks and sermons and exhortations on chastity. It is not exaggerated to say that the impression was sometimes given that chastity only applied to sexuality, and that sex was the main message of the church.

Chastity has everything to do with our bodies, but our bodies belong to a larger context. We are more than our bodies; that is point one. We belong to Christ; that is point two. When Paul exhorts us to be chaste, he is asking us to draw the consequences of those two points. We should not be the slaves of our bodies, and we should see ourselves—body, spirit, and soul (those are the terms Paul uses for us)—as taken up in the work of bringing forth Jesus Christ and God's Kingdom in this world.

Everything, all of us, all our potentialities—including our sexuality—all possibilities, powers, and relationships should be lovingly directed toward that realization.

As he writes to Titus: "[God's grace] has taught us that we should give up everything contrary to true religion and all our worldly passions; we must be self-restrained and live upright and religious lives in the present world, waiting in hope for the blessings which will come with the appearance of the glory of our great God and savior Christ Jesus" (Titus 2:11-13).

That is the chastity Paul is speaking about. Paul also uses another word for it, "purity." We should be pure, living the love of God and God's Kingdom without additives or adulterations. He even adds in the same letter to Titus: "To those who are pure themselves, everything is pure" (Titus 1:15).

Breach Mender

"You will be called 'Breach-mender,' 'Restorer of streets.'"

Isaiah 58:12

Recently I visited a retreat center bookshop. There were the usual audiotapes and videotapes, cards, plenty of books and pamphlets. Practically all of them were on the same topic. And if you have ever been in such a shop, you might guess what that topic is: healing. One of the reasons people come to those retreat houses is obviously to be healed. All through his public life here on earth women and men came to Jesus to be healed. He said himself that he came to heal us.

But he did not come only to heal the individual. We are sick because we do not relate well to ourselves, to others, to things, and to the earth. Those relations have to be restored, they have to be strengthened. Isaiah wrote that we have to be "breach menders," "restorers of streets," and "rebuilders." We cannot restrict ourselves to healing ourselves. Society has to be mended. The world has to be healed. Personal healing is just the beginning.

This is the reason that the American bishops recently wrote pastoral letters on issues like war, peace, and economic justice. In *Economic Justice for All* the bishops put it well: "We have to move from our devotion to independence, through an understanding of interdependence, to a commitment of human solidarity. That challenge must find its realization in the community we build among us" (365). Such a move will help to heal all of us.

Taking Yourself Seriously

"On this mountain, for all peoples, Yahweh Sabaoth will prepare a
banquet of rich food, a banquet of fine wines....The Lord will wipe
away the tears from every cheek...."   Isaiah 25:6-10

Some students laughed when Isaiah's text was read during a school
meeting recently. Asked why they did so, they said they did not believe those prophecies would ever be fulfilled. It was so naïve, they
thought, that it seemed almost ridiculous.

Yet, some of those same students had organized themselves at
news of a disaster in Bangladesh to get some help for the people in
need. They did not seem to understand that they were actually fulfilling Isaiah's prophecy by "removing the mourning evil" from Bangladesh. It happens so often that we aren't even aware of the role we play
and the influence we have in our world. The stories we prefer to tell
about each other are often grim and depressing.

The times we were badly treated are told with greater eagerness
than the occasions when people we met were kind, friendly, and helpful.

We underrate what we do ourselves, and what others do. We say
things like: "We are only human." We overlook, like those teenagers,
the Spirit that is with us.

They were not going to solve all problems; they were not going to
wipe away all tears. They did, however, wipe some tears away. They
made a beginning.

They loved humanity as Jesus does. They were witnesses, missionaries to the message he left us.

Don't Be Afraid

"Be strong. Do not be afraid. Here is your God...." Isaiah 35:1-10

Pope John Paul II wrote: "If we look at today's world, we are struck by many negative factors that can lead to pessimism" (*Missio Redemptoris*, 86).

That is putting it mildly.

Confronted with the disastrous situation in so many parts of the world, and even in our own country, we might wonder whether there is any hope at all.

The pope tells us something we should know for ourselves, that we can't betray our confidence in God, and that we should not give up on our own daily prayers, "Thy Kingdom come. Thy will be done on earth, as it is in heaven!"

The pope gives a whole series of reasons to believe that we are, in fact, "drawing closer to Gospel ideals and values, a development the church seeks to encourage." And he explains why he thinks so: "Today, in fact, there is a new consensus among peoples about these values: the rejection of violence and war; respect for the human person and for human rights; the desire for freedom, justice, and brother/sisterhood; the surmounting of different forms of racism and nationalism; the affirmation of the dignity and role of women" (*Missio Redemptoris*, 86).

In other words, he believes that the words of the prophet Isaiah: "Strengthen all weary hands, steady all trembling knees, and say to all faint hearts, 'Courage! Do not be afraid. Look, your Lord is coming'" (Isaiah 35:3-4), are not only going to be fulfilled, but that this fulfillment is gradually taking shape among us.

He hopes this is a reason for us to engage in the mission of the church to bring all this to its completion.

Being With God

"I shall open rivers on barren heights, and waterholes down in the valleys...."   Isaiah 41:13-20

It was somewhere in the parched fields of Ethiopia, a country devastated by drought and a lengthy civil war exploited by outside forces. Hunger, thirst, devastation, cholera, sickness everywhere! Finally, some totally unexpected help came from a mission organization.

That evening there was food, real food, not something scraped together, for women and men, parents and children.

An older woman embraced the young volunteers who had accompanied the food. It was a solemn moment. She thanked them as if they were angels direct from God.

The volunteers felt embarassed by the gesture. Of course, they were not angels, neither did they come directly from God. Or did they?

In a way they did, because the food distributed that day came from an aid organization that had asked its supporters to donate money in the name of Jesus Christ. The people responded to that call. It is God who is drawing us together. "The poor and needy ask for water, and there is none, their tongue is parched with thirst. I, the Lord, will answer them, I, the God of Israel, will not abandon them" (Isaiah 41:13-20).

That is what the woman in Ethiopia understood. It is what we should understand, too, when we feel moved to help others. That "being moved" is something precious, it is God's work in us, it is the way God fulfills God's promises.

This truth does not pertain only to those extraordinary situations in other continents; it is a principle that counts in our everyday life, the way we meet people, greet them, relate to them, do not exploit them, and serve them.

Depressed

"What comparison can I find for this generation? It is like children shouting to each other in the marketplace: 'We played the pipes for you and you wouldn't dance; we sang dirges, and you wouldn't be mourners.'"   Mattthew 11:16-19

I have heard mothers say something similar when their children said they were bored and didn't know what to do. Mothers aren't the only ones. It is something you hear over and over again: "I did everything I could, what more could I do? You never seem to be satisfied! Whatever I do is wrong."

It is good to know that even Jesus was struck by this mood so familiar to parents, educators, pastors, and managers.

Jesus adds another remark we all know and have often used: Whatever you do is wrong. When you eat and drink they say of you, "Look at that drunkard and glutton," and when you don't eat and drink, they say, "Look at that miser."

You can't win. Pope John Paul II suffered this kind of blues when he recently complained: "...activity is waning...difficulties both internal and external have weakened the missionary thrust...a fact which must arouse concern... a lessening that [always is seen] as a sign of a crisis of faith" (*Missio Redemptoris*, 2).

Many a priest and many a parish member might suffer this kind of inner turmoil when they think about their parish community, or even about their own personal life.

How did Jesus blow these blues away? How should we get rid of them? By putting things back in real perspective. By opening ourselves up to the larger mission and to the larger picture. All those smaller tensions fall away when we realize the task that is waiting to be done.

Song of Songs

"Come to me, my love, my lovely one, come." Song of Songs

He showed me the Bible. It was in a college library. First it was difficult to see what made it so special. Then he showed me how in one part all the pages had been glued together. "Not by a user," he said, "but by the librarian."

The book was the Song of Songs, sometimes also called the Canticle of Canticles. It is a love song, a beautiful one:

I hear my beloved,
See how he comes
leaping on the mountains,
bounding over the hills...
My Beloved lifts up his voice,
he says to me,
"Come to me, my love,
my lovely one, come."
(Song of Songs 2:8-14)

Nowadays we would hardly call this "explicit language." Someone must once have judged that it was. Maybe the language was not the real difficulty, but the underlying idea that God loves us as a groom loves his bride, and that we should love God as a loving woman does her lover.

It is often said that the best hidden secret in the church is her social teaching. Something even better hidden is this love.

It is great to apply the Song to yourself and to your relations with God and Jesus Christ, as you may and should. You should not forget that God and Jesus Christ are also in the same kind of relationship to your neighbor.

Accepting this fact is where the real difficulty starts. We need to be aware of it in our mutual relations. If we can be, it could change the world—from the pope, to you, me, and everyone else.

Belonging Together

"…it is never the will of your Father in heaven that one of these little ones should be lost." Matthew 18:12-14

"Tell me. Suppose a man has a hundred sheep and one of them strays; will he not leave the ninety-nine on the hillside and go in search of the stray?…It is never the will of your Father in heaven that one of these little ones should be lost" (Matthew 18:12-14).

They were celebrating their golden jubilee. Their marriage had been blessed with ten children and many more grandchildren and great-grandchildren. The day was beautifully organized, with a eucharist in the morning, a choir of their grandchildren playing and singing, a well-attended reception, and a grand dinner for all their own sons and daughters and their in-laws in the evening.

During the entire Mass the couple had been checking to see whether they were all there. One of their sons was missing. He had had a row with another one, and they had been afraid that he would not come.

All during the reception as they shook hands, they checked the end of the line to see whether he had turned up. He did not come.

At dinner one place remained empty at the table. They pushed the places together so that the gap would not be noticed, but they knew it was there.

When at the end of the day one of their guests said to them, "A beautiful day, wasn't it?" they answered in unison, "No, it wasn't; not everyone was here! It was a hopeless day!"

This is the story of the lost sheep. It is the story of the prodigal son. It is the story of humankind. It is the story of Jesus' mission in this world, and it explains his presence among us.

We all are asked to be marked by the charity of Christ, "who came 'to gather into one the children of God who are scattered abroad'" (John 11:52), of the Good Shepherd who knows his sheep, who searches them out and offers his life for them.

Sower and Seed

"This is what the Kingdom of God is like. A man scatters seed on land." Mark 4:26

"A sower went out to sow his seed." How often have we heard those words? Too often, maybe. Jesus was that sower. The seed is the word of God.

Jesus sowed that seed. He believed in the power and vitality of the seed. You don't sit next to the field to watch the seeds you have sowed, either. You, too, trust that what you sowed has so much power that it will come up without difficulty.

That seed has to grow in us. It will, it should grow all through our hearts until we have the feelings of Jesus.

It should master us so that we make the decisions Jesus made.

It should be the spark in our fingers so that we act, heal, comfort, and nurture as Jesus did. It should even get into our feet and toes so that we walk Jesus' path.

There is another thing to be said.

No one would sow only one seed. You can't plant one palm tree, you can't plant one banana plant, you can't grow one stalk of corn or one blade of grass.

One plant would never profit from the shadow of others when the sun shines. One plant would never stand up against the storm and the rain.

It is only when plants stand together and grow together that they help each other with their shadow and break the power of the sun; that they break the force of the wind together, and overcome the beating of the rain.

And so it is with you and with me.

Intimacy

"Jesus, knowing that his hour had come...loved them to the end."

John 13, 1-16

The life of everyone is colored and directed (you might even say consecrated) by some private moments—the moment your mother really spoke to you, heart to heart, the moment your father kept a promise, or your friend gave you a piece of advice.

It was the same with Jesus' apostles that evening. He was with them in that upper room, alone, very privately, very intimately. He had invited them, he had called them over, they had eaten, they had drunk, they had broken bread, they had shared wine, just as we do. For them, however, that evening had been much more private, much more personal, especially when he had taken that jug of water and that towel and had washed their feet.

Having your feet washed is something very private, very personal, and very powerful.

I don't know whether you have ever had the experience. Have your feet ever been washed by someone who loved you after a tiring trip?

If they were you know what I am talking about. Did you ever wash and massage the feet of someone you loved? Do it once, and you, too, will know what I am talking about.

He had washed their feet, he had dried them—in a way he had consecrated them—and it was at that moment that he had said to them: "I am sending you, you have to go, if you want to be faithful to me." And though they were very ambitious, very shallow, very consumer-minded, very competitive, and very contentious, they never forgot that moment.

Moments like that kept them together with him and with each other. It is those private moments with someone we love and respect that keep us together, that keep us faithful at unexpected moments in our lives.

Don't you remember a happening, an event, a private moment that determined and still determines your life's direction?

Personally

"I have given you an example so that you may copy what I have done to you." John 13:16-20

Let me give you another example to make my point clear.

His name is Hussein. He was a student long ago. I was in charge of the dormitory where he lived.

One evening he came home very drunk. Being a Muslim, he had never drunk before. Now he had. He was drunk and sick.

He got in a quarrel with another student. Being out of his mind he pulled a knife and threatened everybody around; he broke a window; he made a mess. Then I came in. I was able to calm him down. I gave him stomach tablets, and he went to bed.

Next morning I called him over and told him what had happened the night before. He did not remember anything. I took him through the dormitory. I showed him where I had put his knife the night before, I showed him the broken window, and back in my office I told him: "Hussein, now you know what happens when you get drunk. Some get funny when drunk, they start telling jokes; some get very pious, they start to pray or sing hymns; you get nasty and murderous. Now you know. Never drink again."

He never did. I got a letter from him some weeks ago. He wrote that he was doing fine, and he added: "I never forgot what you told me that day in the privacy of your office; that is why I am who I am. Thanks again."

Something like that must have happened to the disciples. Every time they got discouraged, lost their hope, or got depressed, they thought of that evening when he washed their feet and said: "I have given you an example."

He not only said that to them, he said it to us, privately, too. Did he never have such a moment with you? Aren't we sent as they were?

Advent

"I am with you, always, till the end of the age." Matthew 28:20

Pope John Paul II used the word "advent" in the introduction to his encyclical *On Social Concern*. He wrote that in our time, practically on the eve of a new millennium, everyone is to some extent touched by a feeling of expectancy, rather like a new "advent."

The pope added that he senses that time is passing ever more quickly, that things are changing, and that they have been changing notably in the course of the last twenty years. Rather solemnly he warns that the "configuration of the world" presents some totally new aspects (4).

It is not difficult to agree with the pope on this. Our world has changed considerably over the last twenty years, whether we like it or not.

The pope neither condemns nor commends those changes, but he is definitely of the opinion that a new spirituality is needed. He writes that all those responsible for ensuring a "more human life" should be aware of "the urgent need to change the spiritual attitudes which define each individual's relationship with self, with neighbor, with even the remotest human communities, and with nature itself, and all of this in view of higher values such as the common good or the full development of the whole individual and of all people" (38).

It is in this spirit that we begin the reflections of the last month of the year. It is a sad month, because things are ending; it a is a happy month because the new is hanging in the air.

It is a month when we should be aware of what Jesus tells us: "And I am with you always, till the end of the age" (Matthew 28:20). It is that promise that keeps us alive and together!

Christmas Preparation

"Let us go to Bethlehem and see this event which the Lord has made known to us."   Luke 2:15-20

We are going to celebrate the cosmic event of almost 2000 years ago when the sky opened, a star appeared, angels sang, and Life was born again. It all came as a surprise, though it had been dreamed and foretold for thousands of years.

The oldest hope had never died in Mary, Joseph, shepherds, wise women and men. The whole of nature, not just humanity, had been waiting.

There is an old legend, sometimes called "the golden legend." It tells how at the moment of Jesus' birth all of nature sprang into new life. The whole of creation—from the minerals to the angels—was aware of what happened. Stars started to move that night. The water of a Roman spring changed into the finest oil. Vines in Spain suddenly flowered and bore the sweetest grapes. Oxen, donkeys, camels, and sheep surrounded the manger. Angels appeared and, in the light of the singing heavenly host, cocks started to crow in the middle of the night to herald this new dawn.

We often celebrate Christmas as if it remained a dream, amid shining tinsel, flickering lights, and a setting often as sweet as the icing on our Christmas cake. We forget that for those involved it meant long journeys, homelessness and God-with-us, poverty and presents, sweat and blood, songs and tears, deep sorrow and endless joy.

Let us try to reflect on what happened when the dream became reality in a woman's womb and in our own midst, how Mary and Joseph, kith and kin, shepherds and kings, children and elders, soldiers and officials reacted on the Birthday of Life, the dawn of a new day.

We do this not only because we are interested in the past; we need the light of that newness to shine in our own lives, in the lives of those dear to us, in our society and in our environment.

December 3

Forever and Ever

"Look! the virgin is with child and will give birth to a son whom they will call Emmanuel."   Matthew 1:18-24

The four who wrote the gospels—Mark, Matthew, Luke, and John—all have their own intentions. They agreed with each other on Jesus, but they did not always agree with each other's way of telling the story. That is why they all developed their own approach, and saw Jesus from different points of view.

One thing that intrigued Matthew was the name that was to be given to Jesus: *Emmanuel.* He thought it so important that he quoted it from the prophet Isaiah, who used it first.

He uses that name in the beginning of his gospel when the angel announces Jesus' conception to Joseph. He also uses it at the end of his gospel. The very last words Jesus speaks in Matthew's gospel are: "And I am with you always, to the end of the age" (Matthew 28:20), that is, I will be *Emmanuel,* God-with-you, always.

Christmas is only the beginning. Jesus will be with God's human family and the whole of creation forever and ever!

"Father, you have given all peoples one common origin, and your will is to gather them all in one family in yourself. Fill the hearts of all with the fire of your love and the desire to ensure justice for all brothers and sisters. By sharing the good things you give us may we secure justice and equality for every human being, an end to all division, and a human society built on love and peace" (*On Social Concern,* 49)

Forerunner

"I tell you, of all the children born to women, there is no one greater than John, yet the least in the kingdom of God is greater than he."
                                                                Luke 7:28

All of us know stories about parents who sacrifice their whole life to ensure a better life for their children. Maybe it is your own story. There have been periods in human history when a whole generation did that. Isn't it the really heroic story of so many immigrant families? People dedicated their lives to a future they wouldn't even see, the tale of an old grandmother or grandfather planting a tree for their grandchildren when they don't expect to eat from that tree themselves.

John was that type of prophet. He was there to announce something he was not really part of. He was a forerunner. Once he had seen Jesus he knew that he should get smaller and smaller to give place to the new future in Jesus.

Jesus admired him for that. He said: "There is no greater one than John," but he added, "yet the least in the kingdom of God is greater than he is." John was willing to put his whole life at the service of a newness that he himself would not live to see. That was John's greatness. He remains an example for us who struggle for a peaceful and a just society in the future.

"Let us have the courage to believe in the bright future and in God who wills it for us—not a perfect world, but a better one. The perfect world, we Christians believe, is beyond the horizon, in an endless eternity where God will be all in all. But a better world is here for human hands and hearts and minds to make (*The Challenge of Peace*, 337)."

Anticipation

*"A feeling of expectancy had grown among the people, who were be-
ginning to wonder whether John might be the Christ."*   Luke 3:15

Luke describes the mood of the hundreds and thousands of people
who came to listen to John the Baptizer at the river Jordan.

This should be the mood of Advent. It is a time of anticipation, only
a few weeks from Christmas. Children are getting more impatient every day—how many nights till Christmas?!—they are hoping that their
wishes are going to be fulfilled. They can hardly wait.

The people around John the Baptizer were full of anticipation. They
were hoping for other, more serious things. They hoped so much that
the world would change, that the future of their children would be assured, that their own sins would be forgiven, justice would be done,
oppression would end, and peace would be restored.

John the Baptizer saw their eagerness. He felt their urgency. He
could sympathize with them. He had had the same feelings from the
beginning of his existence. He had leaped for joy when Mary announced to Elizabeth that she was pregnant with Jesus.

Those around John thought that he would be the one. They made a
double mistake. He was not the one, and Jesus would not liberate
them in the way they expected.

John was the forerunner, Jesus was the fulfillment, but people
themselves would have to change the world by being changed themselves. John could only baptize with water; Jesus would baptize us
with Holy Spirit and fire.

Humility

"This man John wore a garment made of camel-hair with a leather loin-cloth round his waist, and his food was locusts and wild honey."   *Matthew 3:1-6*

From the way John the Baptizer is described in the gospel you can gather that many had difficulties with this prophet clothed in animal skin and eating grasshoppers. Many found him much too earthy.

Meister Eckhart, a medieval mystic, taught that "humility" comes from *humus*, or earth, the stuff of our very own planet, the stuff we ourselves are made of. When we admit this—"You are earth and to earth you will return"—we are not humiliating ourselves. We are speaking the truth. By denying our earthiness we deny the facts. It is one of the reasons we lack respect for our environment. Holiness embraces humility and respects earthiness.

Jesus had no hesitations about matter and earth. He was faithful to the Jewish tradition where matter and spirit are not divided against each other.

Jesus spoke constantly and lovingly of lilies and fig trees, sparrows and foxes, vines and mustard seeds, furrows and wheat, salt and oil, water and fishes.

He loved life, he loved the earth, he loved the people around him.

It is with that same love that we should celebrate this season singing and praying, with straw and holly, mistletoe and candles, stars and tinsel, currants and raisins, turkey and plum pudding, smiles and laughter, song and dance, lovemaking and presents. To appreciate earth's gifts is a step toward humility, toward the manger, toward a healthier world, and toward God.

Rest

"Come to me...and I will give you rest." Matthew 11:28

Finding our way through life is tiring. All kinds of things happen at the most unexpected times. You thought you were settled; something happens and everything changes.

Mary and Joseph knew about this better than most. Angels kept flying in and out. What those angels said was not even always consistent. Take the case of their return from Egypt. First an angel came to tell them that they could leave Egypt, that the danger was over. So they packed, walked, got tired, and finally came to the last bit of the journey to Bethlehem.

Then, during one of the last nights before they arrived there, the angel returned. They were not supposed to go to Bethlehem. The danger was not over. They had to go to Nazareth—enough to make anyone impatient, to say the least!

Joseph and Mary had a way out of all these problems. Their lives revolved around Jesus. They were willing to change at every new signal from heaven because of their child.

Jesus was their center. This is something we often find in the lives of mothers and fathers around us. A mother works almost day and night to earn college tuition for her son; a father takes on a double job to help his daughter finish an internship. Their children are the center and even the explanation of their lives.

We find it in the lives of many others as well. A friend helps a friend through the greatest difficulty of all, that of facing death after a lingering and devastating disease like AIDS. The lives of millions turn around the lives of others in life and death.

Jesus said that if we take anyone as the center of our lives in such a way, we center around him. He promised that he will never forget it. Just as we will be with him, he will be with us, and our weariness will be taken away. He will give us rest!

Immaculate

"Mary said: '...Let it happen to me as you have said.' And the angel left her."   Luke 1:38

Paul was the first to mention Mary in the Christian Scriptures. He did so probably around the year 57 in his letter to the Galatians, when she might still have been alive.

He wrote that Jesus was "made of woman." That woman was Mary who gave herself, body and all, to the fulfillment of a desire as old as humanity itself.

It is amazing that our daily and weekly newspapers, television and radio programs, books, libraries, universities, research institutes, and learned papers are full of ideas about what should happen to this world. There is no lack of ideas, but there is a great lack of will—we fail to desire sufficiently.

Do we really want to celebrate God's advent in this world? Do we really take our hope seriously?

Mary, whose feast we celebrate today, did accept it. That is why she became an example for all of us. It is the reason we call her our mother. She is the mother of all fulfilled humanity. She became our mother when she said: "Let what you have said be done to me!" No more and no less! What a mother she is! She was "perfect" in that word's original sense, "whole." Mary was an ordinary young girl—she spent hours fetching water, grinding wheat, fanning the fire, and dancing in the evening. And, giving birth to a child in the warmth of ox breath, ass, and straw, and welcoming the poorest and the richest, shepherd and king, she lived the wholeness and oneness of the human family.

One Family

"There are others I shall gather besides those already gathered."

Isaiah 56:6-8

The gospel readings are full of descriptions of the justice and integrity, togetherness and blessing that Anna and Simeon, Elizabeth, Zechariah, and John the Baptizer, were daily praying for. They all lived in occupied zones with freedom fighters in the hills. People were divided into oppressors and oppressed. They yearned for a more beautiful and just tomorrow. It is against that background that Jesus says that he came to do something, referring to "the works my Father has given me to carry out" (John 5:36).

Isaiah explains that assignment in terms Jesus would make his own: "It is the Lord who speaks, who gathers the outcasts of Israel; there are others I will gather besides those already gathered. My house will be called a house of prayer for all peoples" (Isaiah 56:6-8).

God recognizes no outcasts, foreigners, aliens, or "others." Neither should we. In the human family, in God's family, all are welcome. We belong together. It is only together that we form humanity, that we reach our full potential. When the wise men from the East came to visit Jesus and his mother, that prophecy began to be fulfilled.

The final day will be a glorious day. All nations and religions will have their own gift to offer. Not only myrrh, frankincense, and gold, but Africans their hospitality, Quakers their tolerance, Buddhists their compassion, Native Americans their love for the earth, Hindus their vision of God everywhere, Christians their God incarnated, and Muslims their belief in God's transcendency. We are a rainbow of color, in one human family, the one started in the starlight of Bethlehem.

His Days

*"And Jacob fathered Joseph the husband of Mary; of her was born Je-
sus who is called Christ."*   *Matthew 1:1-17*

"In his days justice shall flourish and peace till the moon fails" (Psalm
72:7), the responsorial psalm reads, just before Jesus' genealogy is tri-
umphantly announced in Matthew's gospel.

This is the world and time Mary and Joseph, Simeon and Anna,
and so many others dreamed of, a world of human dignity where everyone is a shepherd of creation.

An earth where all children play, run, dance, shout, and sing, not
die of malnutrition, where young people look forward to a life everyone shares and no one is marginalized, where old people see visions
and young people dream dreams, where all people are cherished and
no one is abandoned, where swords are hammered into ploughshares,
the lion lies with the lamb, and a little child leads them—and there is
no preparation for war.

Is this merely a naïve dream? Isn't it Jesus' dream? It is God's
dream, God dreaming the world and we dreaming with God!

Stephen Naidoo, the Catholic Archbishop of Capetown in South Africa, arrested on an anti-apartheid mission, said: "You can kill the
dreamer but you cannot kill the dream! The dream is freedom and the
dream is alive—and no amount of force is going to change that."

December 11

Extraordinary Ordinary

"Elizabeth gave a loud cry and said, 'Look, the moment your greeting reached my ears, the child in my womb leapt for joy.'"   Luke 1:44

Mary must have been a delightful person. Just think of her hurrying through the hills and the valleys of her country to Elizabeth. And think of Elizabeth, that older woman, the day she saw her cousin Mary, young and bouncy, come around the corner of her house. Suddenly her worries were over: "The moment your greeting sounded in my ears, the baby stirred in my womb for joy!"

The water jugs Elizabeth had to fill at the well had seemed heavier and heavier each day. She had trouble getting her things washed on the rocks in the river, and sometimes she had those terrible pains in her back, because her old frame had trouble accommodating that young, jumpy, prophetic new life in her.

She was full of joy seeing Mary, because she recognized in Mary the mother of her Savior, but also because she knew that Mary—full of grace—would be a grace to her in her difficult days.

Mary, knowing herself to be the mother of Jesus, translated her extraordinary mission into such ordinary action!

Isn't the ordinary the test of the reality and relevance of the extraordinary? Isn't it the ordinary from which we live? Isn't that what her Son came to save? Does peace not start at home?

It is the ordinary things that form the warp and the woof of our lives—a cup of coffee well made, a car carefully serviced, a greeting not forgotten, a smile from a stranger, a flower to a loved one, a letter to one far away, a glass of water at the right time, a chair left free—the thousands of things that surround us day in, day out.

Silencing Zechariah

"Look, since you do not believe my words, which will come true at their appointed time, you will be silenced...." Luke 1:20

Mary, young, full of hope and expectation, believed when the angel appeared to her. Zechariah, uncertain and experienced in life, did not. Mary immediately burst out in song, touched as she was by God's Life. Zechariah was stunned into silence when the angel came to announce to him that Elizabeth would be with child.

Often, those among us who are full of hope and vision are silenced by those who say that they are more experienced in life, those who say that they have seen it all and have turned sarcastic and bitter. They believe only what they see selectively around them; they only notice failure and disappointment.

It is not that Mary was an optimist and Zechariah a pessimist. Optimism and pessimism are no help to anyone. In a way, they are both unrealistic points of view. Optimism and pessimism are each a bias, a prejudice. You see things as you want to see them.

Mary and Zechariah were invited by the angel to be realists, to believe in a world and in a humanity as God sees them, a world and a humanity with endless possibilities, as Jesus, God's unique offspring, would reveal.

Mary accepted the proposition joyfully. Zechariah could not immediately accept the same invitation; he did it only later when he saw with his own eyes the new life born. He was silenced till that moment, not allowed to broadcast his unrealistic doubts. The angel told him: "Since you have not believed my words, which will come true at their appointed time, you will be silenced and have no power of speech until this has happened" (Luke 1:20).

Do you believe in the promise of a new world, in a reborn humanity, in one great human-divine family relating healthily to the whole rest of creation? This is what this season of Advent, this season of expectation, is all about.

Peace Challenge

"'Elijah...will set everything right again....he has come already and they did not recognize him....' Then the disciples understood that he was speaking of John the Baptist."   Matthew 17:10-13

When I was a child, my country was at war. We considered the occupying troops our enemies. As boys we would pester them all the time. We would walk behind them as near as we could, trip them, and run away as fast as possible. We would deflate the tires of their cars and consider ourselves to be great heroes.

We would never dream of being friendly to them. When they asked directions, we would send them the wrong way. We would never take candy from them, though they sometimes offered us sweets. We would steal all we could from them. We would never think of eating with them. We thought we were obliged to hate them with all our hearts. Things between them and us were not as they should be.

There was one exception that I remember well. One Christmas night the military commander of the town lifted the curfew so that we all could go to the midnight Mass. We did. It had snowed that night; we could see our footsteps in the fallen snow.

At the beginning of Mass there was some noise in the back of the church, a noise we knew only too well, the sound of the heavy hob-nailed boots of the occupying troops. The soldiers remained in the back of the church with their guns. They came up for communion. They knelt next to us, and at that moment we were for some moments as we should be.

"The Mass in particular is a unique means of seeking God's help to create the conditions essential for true peace in ourselves and in the world....Nowhere is the Church's urgent plea for peace more evident in the liturgy than in the Communion Rite....Therefore we encourage every Catholic to make the sign of peace at Mass an authentic sign of our reconciliation with God and with one another" (*The Challenge of Peace*, 295).

What Authority?

"The chief priests and elders of the people asked him, 'What authority have you for acting like this? And who gave you this authority?'"
Matthew 21:23-27

I once heard that question when I was regularly helping out in a church on Sundays. It was a nice church with a very kind community. Every Sunday we had the usual prayers for the faithful after the homily and the creed. Those prayers were well made, they covered a lot of human needs, and every week there was a prayer for peace.

One day a letter came to the priest in charge. The letter protested that those prayers were too political. "On what authority were those prayers said? All prayers for peace should stop, otherwise..." The letter was not signed. At the end it read: "Some worried Christians."

This is not the only story of its kind. There are many like it. When they wrote their pastoral letter on war and peace the bishops in this country felt from the very beginning that they had to defend themselves against that sort of objection. They did not write for a political reason. They wrote with the authority given to them as church leaders by Jesus Christ himself. They stated:

"Peacemaking is not an optional commitment. It is a requirement of our faith. We are called to be peacemakers, not by some movement of the moment, but by our Lord Jesus. The content and context of our peacemaking is not set by some political agenda or ideological program, but by the teaching of his Church" (*The Challenge of Peace*, Summary).

Prostitutes

"...prostitutes are making their way into the kingdom of God before you."
                                          Matthew 21:28-32

He was a parish priest of good standing. All his life he had been interested in social work. Lately he had been struck by the plight of the homeless. He decided to find out what it meant to be like that. One day he put on some shabby clothing and a knapsack. After some days he had a shaggy stubble of a beard and nobody recognized him any more.

He told me his story afterwards. He could hardly ever reach those better off to get some help. Their homes were unapproachable; he was chased away from their lawns by dogs. He went to the presbytery of one of his friends. He was not recognized. His friend's housekeeper let him in the kitchen. She had pity on him. While he was sitting there, in a place he knew very well, his priest colleague and friend came in. He was told to leave immediately. He did.

He began to notice that the only ones who helped him were those not too well off. It was the kind of experience Mary and Joseph had when they looked for a place for Mary to give birth to Jesus. The innkeepers had no place for them. But someone must have shown them the shed where Mary brought Jesus into this world. And if the shepherds did not show or lend that shed to them, they definitely did not chase them away from it. Those shepherds—in that region and time ranked with prostitutes and sinners—allowed them to use their stable, and welcomed him. They respected their plight and human dignity. Wouldn't he say afterwards: "I tell you solemnly, tax collectors and prostitutes are making their way into the kingdom of God before you" (Matthew 21:31). A hard saying, but as my friend experienced, very true!

Patience

"...the blind see again, the lame walk, lepers are cleansed, and the deaf hear, the dead are raised to new life, the good news is proclaimed to the poor...."   Luke 7:19-23

John the Baptizer was in prison. He had been arrested because Herod did not like what John had said about his behavior. John had announced a total change. He had said: "The axe is at the root of the tree. God is going to intervene with power and might. All will be different."

John had been enthusiastic when he saw Jesus coming from Nazareth. With his own eyes he had seen Jesus, the one who was going to bring the change he had announced. Now he was in this horrible dungeon, and Jesus was walking about. Why did not he do something? What about the change?

We know the answer: "Go back and tell John what you have seen and heard: the blind see again, the lame walk, lepers are cleansed, and the deaf hear, the dead are raised to new life, the good news is proclaimed to the poor and happy is the person who does not lose faith in me" (Luke 7:22-23).

Jesus spoke about the people around him, who in his presence were healed. He was not speaking about himself healing and changing. He was speaking about them being changed and healed, and walking around as they had never done before.

The change was greater than even John had guessed, and different from what he expected. No brimstone and fire, but a gradual healing process that slowly but surely would heal us in our everyday activities.

This change would ask for a great patience from John, and from all of us. This patience will bring forth its fruit, because in the end we will be able to say, together with Jesus Christ, "we" did it. We got through to the Kingdom that will last forever and ever. The signs of its coming are visible all around us, for the blind see again, the deaf hear....Patience!

Democracy

"...blessed is anyone who does not find me a cause for falling."
                                                    Matthew 11:11-15

We sing that God holds the whole world in God's hands. Yet, many of us frequently complain that God does not seem to take care of God's world. We forget that the hands of God in this world are ours. Those hands can build and destroy, they can assist and boycott. They can be used meaningfully or in vain. They can also remain limp and lame, when they are not used at all.

According to a recent survey, 20 to 25 percent of the citizens of the Western world know that racism, poverty, sexism, missile madness, and the fierce competitive nature of their society must come to an end. To know what should be done is not sufficient. Words alone do not help, deeds are needed. One finds the doers among those who are socially and politically active: community organizers, environmentalists, feminists, and those working for racial equality and against nuclear madness. There is a large group of others who sympathize with these issues, but who continue to live non-active private lives. In a democracy, however, one needs a majority. How are others to come to a more active engagement? Where is the energy to come from to carry through a fundamental change in values?

Why did people follow Jesus? They definitely worked with him for the happiness of others. But let us not forget that, in choosing his Way, they also restored meaning to their own lives in a world that could no longer provide that meaning. The energy that should help us, therefore, is twofold: the other and ourselves. It is an energy that comes from God, drawing us toward each other while drawing all of us to God's self.

Ten Commandments

"...up to this present time the kingdom of Heaven has been subjected to violence, and the violent are taking it up by storm."
Leviticus 26:1-12

He was an older man, simple in the sense that he had never gone for modern things. He hardly had the opportunity in his African village. Now he had come to town to visit his children and also to see his first movie. His children had picked it with great care. He was going to see *The Ten Commandments*. They went with him.

He came home overwhelmed. He had always been a believer, but now he had seen with his own eyes, he thought, how the Jews walked through the Red Sea, and especially how God burned the ten commandments into the two stone tablets he gave to Moses.

He had seen the fire, he had seen the stones, he had seen the writing. His children told me that he had been so thrilled that he almost broke his seat by clamping his strong hands over the armrests.

Late in the evening we could hear him telling his friends what he saw.

I saw him again the next day. If everyone would see that film, he told me, the world would change. Everyone would understand the foundations of human life cut out in those rocks.

He was wrong, mixing up the special effects in that film with historic facts. But he was right in his belief that the world would change if all would accept those two stone tablets as their foundation in life.

Dreaming Dreams

"If you live according to my laws...I shall give peace in the land."
Matthew 9:27-31

Two blind men come to Jesus to be healed. He does heal them, then he adds something: "I heal you because of your faith." The healing is an almost mutual thing. If they had not been able to believe in him, he would not have been able to heal them. They would not even have come to ask him!

Do you really believe that the Christmas message of justice and peace can be realized? If you don't, would you seriously ask for it or be able to work for it? Our belief and hope are essential. Faith in each other works wonders.

The most prestigious literary prize in the United Kingdom was presented in 1988 to Christy Nolan, who, with cerebral palsy, is unable to move and speak. Everyone except his mother thought him a hopeless case. She saw the locked-up potential in his eyes and believed in him. She attached a kind of "unicorn" stick to his forehead and, by holding his head, enabled her son to use a typewriter with that stick. Christy wrote his book, and won his prize.

Looking around in our paralyzed world, Jesus knew about our potential for holiness and wholeness, for righteousness, justice, and peace. If only we would believe as the two blind men did.

We depend on our visions and our dreams. Psychologists and educators today lament that our youth is so often listless. Maybe it is because parents and teachers no longer see visions and dream dreams. Are we examples of hope?

How often must have Mary cradled Jesus' head. Weren't her visions and dreams, her encouragement and hope, the substance of his life?

Newborn Child

"'Do you believe I can do this?' They said, 'Lord, we do.'"
                                          Matthew 15:29-37

I had been giving a homily on today's reading. I had mentioned hunger in the world. I am always a bit embarrassed mentioning something like that—it isn't good news to hear that others in this world are so badly off, that they have nothing to eat, and sometimes not even enough water to drink.

After Mass a boy of about seven came to me. He took three quarters, a cookie, and two candies from his pocket. He said: "Can you send this to the hungry children you talked about?" I said I could, and took all he had. I got tears in my eyes, because I suddenly thought of that boy who put up his hand when Jesus asked: "Is there here no one with some food?" and said: "Yes, Sir, here, Sir!" He was the only one in that enormous crowd. I thought of him while the boy disappeared among all the adults, who shook my hand and said what a nice sermon it had been.

In fairy tale and Scripture, it takes a child to see the nakedness of the emperor and the world as it could be. Yet, this should not just make us feel guilty. Guilt feelings are no help at all. We should develop more realistic expectations about where we are and where we would like to be.

The American bishops put it succinctly: "Christians are called to live the tension between the vision of the reign of God and its concrete realization in history. The tension is often described in terms of 'already but not yet': that is, we already live in the grace of the kingdom, but it is not yet the completed kingdom. Hence, we are a pilgrim people in a world marked by conflict and injustice" (*The Challenge of Peace*, 58).

Mary's Haste

"I feel sorry for all these people:....I do not want to send them off hungry, or they might collapse on the way."　　　　　　Luke 1:39-45

Unnoticed, Mary hurried through towns and villages, along roads and over rivers.

In her all newness was developing, out of her all newness was going to be born. Everything went on around her in the usual, old-fashioned way. It was as if everything was happening; it was as if nothing was happening at all. She was alone with her pregnancy and the promise.

When the Roman security forces stopped her she thought: "If only you knew." When she went to buy some food she thought: "If only you guessed." But nobody knew and nobody guessed. She knew and believed. Joseph knew and believed. Who else besides them? No one, until the moment that she met Elizabeth with John in her womb.

She must have been so glad that Elizabeth understood, that Elizabeth confirmed her in her hope and belief. It is after that affirmation that she really bursts out in song. So does Elizabeth. They had greatly needed each other's support, which explains Mary's haste to go to her.

We, too, need that kind of affirmation in our belief that this world is pregnant with newness, with God's life. Is it not strange that we so rarely speak about an issue like this? Isn't it strange that life seems to go on almost heedless of our most fundamental human hope? Isn't it strange how we relegate it to a sermon, a prayer on Sunday, or an almost private devotion?

Leaving our faith dimension unspoken affirms it neither in ourselves nor in others. Isn't that affirmation the thing we need most, in a time when being a believer is sometimes so difficult, and doubts creep into the hearts of the best among us?

Mary's Song

"Mary set out at that time and went as quickly as she could...."
Luke 1:46-56

Mary's song expresses her feelings. She does not mince words; she makes it clear what she expects her son to do. She must have sung that song to him often when he was a baby, and even when he was older, explaining to him why she had agreed to accept him as her child.

It is not a violent song. It is a song about peaceful change. We are not incited to take up arms or anything like that. The song describes how God will take care of all those who cannot come into their rights, how God will work the original plan of creation when all were considered to be good without preference or discrimination.

Mary had suffered much discrimination as a Jewish woman, living in an occupied country, taxed and administered by strangers.

Her son was going to restore the old *shalom*. That is what he did when he broke bread with everybody. Mary was his earliest inspiration when she gave him bread and wine at home.

Children hear the gospel message first from the lips of their parents who consciously introduce them to the issues of justice and peace, who introduce them into the practice of love, and who help their children to solve their conflicts in nonviolent ways, enabling them to grow up as peacemakers.

Christmas Hope

"My soul proclaims the greatness of the Lord, and my spirit rejoices in God my Savior....He has pulled down princes from their thrones and raised high the lowly."
Luke 1:57-66

Once John the Baptizer started his mission he had bad news and good news to announce. He started with the bad news. John told them that they had to convert. They had to change. They had to become aware of themselves and the world around them. That would enlighten their understanding of their sinful and disorderly situation.

They already knew that, in a way. That insight brought them to John. They came because they were confused; they felt sinful and guilty. But those negative feelings about themselves and their world were not all. That would not have been sufficient to bring them to the water of the river Jordan.

There was something else. They were convinced they were wrong, but they were also certain that there was hope, hope that they would be able to change and grow, and that the whole world would take on a new form and a new shine with them. They had hope that their relations with God and, consequently, their relations with each other would improve.

We express that newness in our Christmas decorations. Trees suddenly light up with thousands of lights, candles in windows welcome guests, towns and cities decorate streets and malls, and carol singing is heard in places where for the rest of the year no one ever sings.

Tender Mercy

"And you, little child, you will go before the Lord, because of the faithful love of our God in which the rising Sun from on high has come to visit us...."   Luke 1:67-79

Zechariah was standing with his little son in his large hands. He was a priest; his hands had carried many offerings to the altar of God. He understood what his son's role would be. He must have foreseen his son's martyrdom, his unavoidable end in this world.

Yet, he speaks about God's tenderness and love. That little baby in his hands makes him speak of God's mercy and goodness. So often you hear that someone changes when he holds a baby in his hands.

We have been preparing for Christmas. There are many ways we can do that. Jesus came to bring the peoples of the earth together. He came to undo sins. He came to die for us. He came to restore God's peace, a peace that implies a right relationship with God, bringing with it forgiveness, reconciliation, and union.

Yet, we should not forget that many theologians and saints thought that God would have been born among us as a human being even if we had not sinned and weren't in need of redemption.

God would have done that in God's love. God would have come to us because, as our Mother and Father, God wants to be with us.

So don't be afraid. God visits us out of love. God would have come to be with us anyway. Doesn't that say something about God? In one translation of Luke's gospels it is put so nicely: "By the tender mercy of our God, who from on high will bring the Rising Sun to visit us" (Luke 1:79).

Christmas

That night
God's angels did not go to the high priests,
not to the king,
not to the military commanders,
not to the professors at the university,
not to those who write big books,
not to the corporate executives in town,
but to the shepherds,
people like you and me,
and
the glory of God shone round them.

> They got the message,
> they hurried away,
> they found the child,
> as they had been told,
> they praised and glorified
> the Lord,
> while all the rest of the official world
> was silent,
> asleep,
> and absent.

He started humankind
anew
with the shepherds
in that open field,
and from them
his glory will shine
around you
and around me,
and finally
around all of us,
women, men,
plants, animals,
minerals,
and our common mother:
Earth. Amen. A Happy Christmas.

Child Jesus

"...revealing them to little children. Yes, Father, for that is what it has pleased you to do." Luke 10:21-24

There is something touching about a newborn child. Children have their own way of relating to the world around them. They were so one with the womb of their mother; they are so one with her breast. They relate to the world around them with that sense of oneness. It is as if the whole world is their friend.

You can see it sometimes in the way they play, step through puddles, and seem to trust humans and animals alike. You have to be careful when you visit a zoo with small children. Without hesitation they would walk up to a lion to pat its shoulder. Of course, that would be impossible in a zoo since fences and moats give sufficient protection. When a child meets a dog in the street, however, the danger is more real. The dog might not be as friendly as expected, and it might give a sharp growl. But children are fearless. They really embrace all life around them. They sit down in the most dangerous places. They eat mud, and try to catch the sun and the moon. They trust everyone they meet.

Jesus must have noticed this attitude. It touched him. For him, it was a picture of the ideal world, a world without danger and fear. He said that we should relate to each other as children. He knew from bitter experience that this was often impossible, but he asked us to strive after it.

This is why he invited us to be like small children in order to be ready for him and God's reign among us.

At Christmas he presents himself as a child. Soon, as a young man, he will explain what he comes to do among us, what his intentions are. He wants to introduce a new world, a period of grace, the paradise children carry with them in their eyes, hearts, heads, and dreams.

Peace Be to You

"Glory to God in the highest heaven, and on earth peace for those he favors."   Luke 2:1-14

Everyone knows the angel's message at Christmas was: "Peace, peace to all people of good will!" That is not always a welcome message.

One of my friends who lives in a modest residential area put a peace sticker on her car—not an aggressive one, a very kind one. It read: "Arms are for hugging." After a few days some of her neighbors came as a group to ask her to remove it. When she asked them why, they answered: "The sticker lowers the image of the neighborhood. It seems so unpatriotic!"

I met a parish priest who had published a short Lenten reflection in his parish bulletin; it is a shame, he said, that so much money is spent on armaments while so many human needs are overlooked. He got a very angry letter from one of his parishioners, stating that it was a shame that he let the parish be infiltrated by "pacifists."

The director of a retreat center phoned me. He had planned a retreat called "Peace and Justice in the Gospels." He informed me that the retreat would not be given. When I asked him why, he answered that only a few had registered. When I told him that I was surprised at that, he answered, "All retreat centers seem to have the same difficulty. Peace and justice are not attracting people. I should have thought of another title."

People are divided over peace. It is what Jesus foretold when he said, "I came to bring peace," and when he added that this would cause a good deal of consternation in many circles. It would, so he said, even divide families! Yet, peace was the Christmas message, and Jesus asked us to proclaim this message all through our world.

Annual Stock-Taking

"Let every valley be filled in, every mountain and hill be leveled...."
Luke 3:4-12

He had offended her badly. She was hurt. He knew it. He could see it in her face. He would have liked to tell her how much he loved her, but he could not. Every time he tried it was as if something choked him. She couldn't speak, either. The whole thing had paralyzed them both.

They had been doing all kinds of things together before. They had both been working as volunteers in social work, bringing alienated husbands and wives together, rescuing families so that children had a home again. Their enthusiasm for that work had stopped, too. It seemed almost silly to do something like that while they were at war with each other.

Then one of the couples they had helped came to thank them for helping them learn to forgive each other. They said they were very grateful. It had changed their lives. When the visitors left the man and the woman looked at each other. They fell into each other's arms. Being at peace with themselves and each other, they were able to get out of their paralysis. They got up and started to move again.

It is no great help to yourself when you can make peace in the world and live at war yourself.

As the bishops wrote: "To have peace in our world, we must first have peace within ourselves. As Pope John Paul II reminded us in his 1982 World Day of Peace message, world peace will always elude us until peace becomes a reality for each of us personally....Interior peace becomes possible only when we have a conversion of spirit. We cannot have peace with hate in our hearts (*The Challenge of Peace*, 284).

It is almost the end of the year. Time to take stock, time to come together, time to forgive! Leave behind what happened in the year that is ending, and peace be with you! Let us get up and walk!

Joseph's Plight

"...suddenly the angel of the Lord appeared to Joseph in a dream and said: 'Get up, take the child and his mother with you, and escape into Egypt, and stay there till I tell you....'"   *Matthew 18: 12-14*

We might pray for all kinds of spiritual and material graces, or pray for peace. But prayer can be deceptive. We might be tempted to leave it all to God. For example, do you ever catch yourself asking God to do things for you because you are too lazy to do them yourself? Do you ever complain about a situation you could easily solve by yourself?

Joseph might teach us a lesson here. He was sure his Father in heaven would protect Mary, the unborn child, and himself. God did. Every time a danger threatened, God sent an angel to warn them. But that was all the angel did. When they had to flee into Egypt, *Joseph* had to wake up Mary, *Mary* had to wake up the child. *They* had to pack their luggage. *They* had to dress the child against the cold of the night. *They* had to walk all the way, while the angel flew off.

Were they not just left alone, like lost sheep in the night? We might think so, but we would be mistaken. We are never left alone.

Mary and Joseph did not consider themselves lost sheep. They had all they needed to do the things they were asked to do. They were not lost. They had their common sense, their hands, and their feet, just as we do.

In His Presence

"...he saw two brothers, and he said to them: 'Come after me....'"
                                                    Matthew 4:18-22

There is a story about a little bird lying on its back in a field, its legs stretched up to the sky. Another bird saw this and landed next to it. "Little brother," he said, "what are you doing?" "Hush," the bird on its back said, "Don't disturb me. It might be fatal for all of us!" "What are you doing?" "Don't you understand," the bird answered, "I am carrying the sky. If I turn around, it will crash all over us." At that moment a gust of wind blew through a nearby tree. A branch fell off with a big crack and landed just behind the bird on its back. The frightened bird turned around and flew off. The sky remained in its place!

Some people act as if they are carrying the whole world on their shoulders. They don't, and you shouldn't. It will wear you out in no time.

Jesus did not want to be left all by himself when he started his mission among us. One of the first things he did was to find some company. He needed comfort and support. He had company around him up to the last moment of his earthly life.

In the garden of Gethsemane he pleaded with the disciples to remain with him and not to fall asleep. From the cross, he was comforted by the compassion of the murderer on his side and by the presence of his mother and John.

He advised us not to remain alone on our way. He tells us to come to him to ease our burden.

If we all go to him, we also come together to carry the weight of our task in this world side by side. Only in that way will we be able to walk in the direction of the realization of God's vision for us, a peaceful and just world, the reign of God.

"I shall be with you all days." It is in Jesus' continuing presence that we find the courage to follow him.

Epilogue

"You are to follow me." John 21:1-19

Another day was ending. His disciples were living in that on-and-off period between his absence and his appearance, between resurrection and ascension. They did not know exactly what to think or what to do. No wonder Peter said, "I am going fishing." The others replied "We'll come with you." The fishing did not help. They caught nothing.

When they returned to the shore, he was waiting for them. At first they did not recognize him. He asked them for some fish, and when they said they hadn't caught anything, he told them to throw out the net once more. They did and caught 153 fish.

Then they saw that it was Jesus. He invited them for breakfast. He had made some bread and there was some fish on the fire. They sat down and had their breakfast with him. As far as we know, this was their first meal with him since the last supper.

We always talk about the last supper together, but we hardly ever hear about this first breakfast! And yet, before it was over, they had heard questions like: "Peter do you love me?" And they had heard answers: "You know, Lord, I do!" Consequences had been drawn: "If you love me feed my sheep." It was a busy breakfast. They stood up from it at the beginning of a new day, the start of a new era.

Today is the last day of the year. There will be many last dinners to celebrate the end of the year, and as many first breakfasts to start the new one. Let us join him letting go of the old and engaging in the new. A blessed New Year!

Scripture Index

(The books of the Bible are listed in alphabetical order.)